MOHAMMED

AND

MOHAMMEDANISM

UXORI MEÆ,

NULLIUS NON LABORIS PARTICIPI,

HUJUSCE PRÆSERTIM OPUSCULI INSTIGATRICI ET ADMINISTRÆ,

STUDIORUM COMMUNITATIS

HAS, QUALESCUNQUE SUNT, PRIMITIAS

DEDICO.

PREFACE

THE SECOND EDITION.

———◦◦◦———

WHILE preparing a Second Edition of these Lectures for the press, I have had the advantage of reading many notices of the First, the great majority of them incisive yet kind, just yet scrupulously appreciative. This has been a great advantage, but it involves a corresponding responsibility. Next to the responsibility and pleasure of writing what it is hoped may serve, in however humble a measure, the cause of truth, charity, and justice, there is no greater pleasure or responsibility than that of reading a keen yet sympathetic criticism on it by one who is evidently a master of his subject, and who is aiming at the same goal, even though his standpoint be different, or he be travelling by a different road. The knowledge of the critic, as in more than one instance has been notably the case, may be deeper, his experience wider, his judgment more profound ; he may find out with unerring certainty all the weak points in one's armour, but none the less is he eager to discover 'generosity in the motives,' and conscientiousness in the work done, to recognise the identity of the end in view, and such advance as may have been made towards it. In a Preface to a new edition I may, indeed I must, refer to such criticisms, because on the one hand I am bound to express my gratitude for the service they have done me, and to indicate how far they have modified my views; and, on the other, because I am quite conscious that I owe them far more to the intrinsic interest and importance of the subject than to any merits of my own.

It is unnecessary to reply here to objections in detail, but there is one general criticism which perhaps had better be noticed fully now rather than referred to repeatedly by way of controversy in the book itself. It has been said by more than one critic, who is entitled at once to my respectful consideration and my gratitude, that my account of Islam and its founder, though true on the whole, is somewhat too favourable. The objection is natural, and, from more than one point of view, is just. But it seems to me that some at least of those who have dwelt on this point, have not taken sufficiently into account my purpose in venturing to approach the subject, nor yet its vastness and complexity. So many Christian writers, as it seemed to me, had approached Islam only to vilify and misrepresent it, that it appeared desirable that one who was at least profoundly impressed with the dignity and importance of the subject, should, in default of better qualified persons, make an attempt to treat it, not merely with a cold and distant impartiality, but even with something akin to sympathy and friendliness. The defects of Islam are well known; its merits are almost ignored, at all events by the great majority of Englishmen. It is not likely that a Christian and a European will err on the side of over-appreciation of another, and that an Eastern creed : the balance therefore, if perchance it has been held for a moment unconsciously to myself, with uneven hand, will soon right itself.

Again, Islam in its various ramifications is a subject so vast and so complex, and is so full of apparent contradictions, that independent enquirers may honestly arrive at the most opposite results. It ought, for this reason, to be approached from as many and as different points of view as possible ; and assuredly the precise point of view from which I have approached it, whether it be the best *per se* or not, is the one from which hitherto there has been hardly any attempt to approach it at all. This, then, is the *raison d'être* of my book ; to this, in the main, is doubtless due such favourable reception as it has met with at the hands of both Musalmans and Christians ; and it is to a want of perception of what this involves that I think I can trace many criticisms on it. In the treatment of a religious revolution which from its mere extent, from what it has achieved, as well as from what it has failed to achieve, must afford an ample field alike for exaggerated panegyric and depreciation, he who endeavours to avoid both extremes must expect to find fewer thorough-going partisans, and must be willing or even anxious to be criticised by both sides alike.

To say that subsequent study, or that the remarks of my critics, have only confirmed me in all my views, would of course be equivalent to saying with Pontius Pilate, that 'what I have written I have written;' a comfortable but a sorry conclusion to come to, for one who is bound to begin by asking himself with Pontius Pilate, 'What is truth?' and, unlike him, must feel himself bound by the most sacred of obligations to keep his ears always open for the reception of such fragments of the answer as he may be able from time to time to catch. Some of my views on matters of detail have been modified; but apart from errors of detail, apart from errors of commission and omission, apart from short-comings incidental to ignorance at first hand of Oriental languages and of Musalman countries, I more and more cherish the earnest hope that the spirit and the purpose with which I have, at least, tried to approach my subject is the right spirit, and the right purpose with which to approach the study of a creed different from one's own.

To dwell on what is good rather than on what is evil; to search for points of resemblance rather than of difference; to use a relative and an historical judgment in all things; to point out what is the out-come of mere human weakness as distinguished from the flaws in the primal documents of the religion, or in the life of its founder; to discriminate between the accidental and the essential, the transitory and the eternal; above all, constantly to turn the mirror in upon oneself, and to try to make sure that one is complying with that great principle of Christianity of judging and of treating others as we should wish ourselves to be judged and treated; this, I am convinced, is the only way in which the better spirits of rival creeds can ever be brought to understand one another, or to sink all their differences in the consciousness of a likeness which is more fundamental than any difference, and which, if it is not felt before, will at least be felt hereafter, in

> That one far off Divine event
> To which the whole creation moves.

These are the aims I have kept and will continue to keep steadily in view, however imperfectly I have been able or may yet be able to carry them out.

If the alterations or additions, therefore, I have made to the text of my Lectures seem less than those high authorities who have done me the honour of criticising my book have a right to expect, I would assure them that it is not from any want of respect to their judgment, or because I have not carefully weighed their criticisms. The dropping of an epithet, the addition of a word here or there, the omission of a note, or the turn of a sentence, will often indicate the silent homage that I have paid, wherever I could do so, to their superior right to speak upon the subject. There may be little to show for it, otherwise than by way of expansion and addition, in the general aspect and arrangement of the book; but there is more than appears at first sight ; and, assuredly, the amount of apparent change bears no proportion at all to the time and care I have taken in making it.

And if I have forborne to enlarge my work by dwelling at length, as I have been asked by some critics to do, upon the darker side of the picture, the reason is not because I am ignorant of that darker side, still less because I am indifferent to it, but because it would be wholly inconsistent with the end I have in view. To denounce fundamental conditions of Oriental society; to ignore the law of dissolution to which Eastern no less than Western dynasties are subject; to confuse the decadence of a race with that of a creed; to be blind to the distinction between progressive and unprogressive, between civilised and uncivilised peoples; to judge of a religion mainly or exclusively by the lives of its professors, often of its most unworthy professors; to forget what of good there has been in the past, and to refuse to hope for something better in the future, in despair or in indignation for what is—all this may occasionally be excusable, or possibly even necessary; but it cannot be done by me so long as I think it neither excusable nor necessary.

The object of these Lectures, therefore, in their revised as well as in their original shape, is not so much to dwell upon the degradation of the female sex, for instance, in most Musalman countries—for that is admitted on all hands—as to show what

Mohammed did, even in his time, to raise the position of women, and to point out how his consistent and more enlightened followers may best follow him now ; not so much to dwell upon the horrors of the Slave Trade—for these too are universally recognised—as to show those Musalmans who still indulge in it that it forms no part of their creed, that it is opposed alike to the practice and precept of their Prophet, and that, therefore, if they are less to blame, they are only less to blame than those Christians who, in spite of a higher civilisation, and an infinitely higher example, indulged in it till so late a period. My object is not so much to dilate on the evils of the appeal to the sword, still less to excuse it, as to point out that there were moments, and those late in the life of the warrior Prophet, when even he could say, 'Unto every one have we given a law and a way;' and again, 'Let there be no violence in religion.' My object is, lastly, not so much to dwell on the fables, and the discrepancies, and the repetitions, and the anachronisms which form the husk of the Koran, as to show how they sink into

a

insignificance before the *vis viva* which is its
soul—not so much to define or to limit inspiration as to indicate by my use of the word that
it cannot, as I think, be limited or defined at all;
to imply, in fact, that inspiration, in the broadest
sense of the word, is to be found in all the
greatest thoughts of man ; for the workings of
God are everywhere, and the spirits of men and
nations are moulded by Him to bring about His
purposes of love, and to give them, in a sense that
shall be sufficient for them, a knowledge of Himself.   In a word, my object is—with all reverence
be it said—not to localise God exclusively in this
or that creed, but to trace Him everywhere in
measure; not merely to trust Him for what
shall be, but to find Him in what is.

HARROW : *August,* 1875.

Among the books which, in accordance with the
plan pursued in the First Edition of my work, I would
wish to mention here as having, apart from the special
acknowledgments which I have made in the notes,
afforded me assistance in the preparation of the Second
Edition, are the following :—

' Sirat-er-Raçoul' of Ibn Hisham: German translation, by G. Weil, Stuttgart, 1864; the earliest and most authentic history of the Prophet, and founded on a still earlier one, that of Ibn Ishak.

' Mishkat-ul-Masabih ' = ' niche for lamps :' a collection of the most authentic traditions regarding the actions and sayings of Mohammed, translated by Captain A. N. Mathews, Calcutta, 1809. This valuable book is extremely scarce ; but there is a prospect, if a sufficient number of subscribers can be obtained, of a new edition being brought out by Messrs. Allen and Co., under the editorship of the Rev. T. P. Hughes, Missionary at Peshawur.

' History of Mohammedan Dynasties,' by Major Price, London, 1812 : a voluminous and somewhat dreary account of the wars and crimes of Musalman princes, but throwing very little light on the social and religious life of their subjects.

' Histoire des Musalmans d'Espagne jusqu'à la Conquête de l'Andalousie par les Almoravides, A.D. 711-1110,' by R. Dozy, Leyden, 1861; a work of first-rate historical importance. The author is equally at home in the Arabic literature relating to Spain, and the Spanish literature relating to the Arabs, and he has corrected many of the mistakes of Condé.

' Ueber das Verhältniss des Islam zum Evangelium,' by Dr. J. A. Mohler (1830), Author of ' The Symbolik,' a most suggestive and thoughtful essay. I am happy to find that it has anticipated some of the conclusions, with regard to both the Prophet and the Faith, which I had set forth in my First Edition, in entire independence of it.

' Mohammed's Religion nach ihrer inneren Entwickelung, und ihrem Einflüsse, eine historische Betrachtung,' by Dr. Döllinger, Ratisbon, 1838. The distinguished author has brought together the statements of a large number of travellers, &c., and has weighed them with much ability, and with every wish to be impartial or even generous towards Islam. He seems, however, at the time when he wrote, to have been more unable than he would probably be now, to divest himself of his ecclesiastical prepossessions, and condemns, for instance, Islam for the absence of visible symbols, sacraments, a priesthood, and even a Pope ; forgetting that these things, however essential to his own creed, may have been, not sources of strength, but of weakness, to another.

'Essays on the Life of Mohammed and Subjects subsidiary thereto,' by Syed Ahmed Khan Bahador, 1870.

'A Critical Examination of the Life and Teachings of Mohammed,' by Syed Ameer Ali Moulla (1873). It is satisfactory to find that the hope I ventured to express in the Preface to my First Edition, as to the sympathy of views and the conciliatory spirit of these two learned Musalman reformers, has been amply justified by a study of their works ; and it is difficult not to believe that books like these point, at however remote a period, to a better understanding between the best followers of the two creeds.

' L'Islamisme d'après le Coran, l'Enseignement doctrinal et la Pratique,' by M. Garçin de Tassy, Paris. Third Edition, 1874 ; the work of a most accomplished Orientalist ; the most instructive and original part of the whole being, perhaps, the essay on the modifications which Islam has undergone in India.

' La Langue et la Littérature Hindustanies,' by M. Garçin de Tassy, a collection of Lectures delivered between the years 1850 –1875; each Lecture being the commencement of a course upon Hindustani Literature, and containing a very valuable Review of the Events that have taken place in India in the preceding year, with Notices of the Literary and Religious Life of the Natives which are not to be found elsewhere.

' L'Islam et son Fondateur, Étude Morale,' by Jules Charles Scholl, Neuchatel, 1874 ; an able and candid enquiry, which, though written from a different point of view to mine, often arrives at somewhat similar conclusions.

' Necessary Reforms of Mussalman States,' by General Khérédine, Prime Minister and Minister of Foreign Affairs at Tunis ; Athens, 1874 ; interesting in itself, and doubly interesting owing to the quarter from which it comes, as showing that India is not the only Musalman country where the ' Mohammedan social and political reformer ' is at work.

'Notes on Mohammedanism,' by the Rev. T. P. Hughes, Missionary at Peshawur, 1875. A valuable compendium of facts. The author has studied Islam both theoretically and practically ; and though he uses the stock phrases ' imposture,' ' would-be

Prophet,' &c., with ominous frequency, he does more justice than most of those, whose duty it is to argue with Mohammedans, to the character of the Prophet.

In Periodical Literature :

' Mahometanism,' an able, thoughtful, and generous article in the ' Christian Remembrancer ' for January 1855, which has been reprinted in a separate form by its author, Dr. Cazenove.

Among books of Travel, Essays, &c., throwing light on different periods or different parts of the Mohammedan world :

' Travels of Marco Polo,' translated and edited by Col Yule, with copious illustrations, Second Edition, 1871.

' Travels of Ibn Batuta,' translated by Rev. S. Lee, 1829.

' Travels in the Interior Districts of Africa,' by Mungo Park, 1810.

' Turkey, Greece, and Malta,' by Adolphus Slade, R.N., 1837.

' The Spirit of the East,' by D. Urquhart, 1838.

' Christianity in Ceylon,' by Sir J. Emerson Tennent, 1850.

' Nestorians and their Rituals,' by Rev. G. P. Badger, 1852.

' Nineveh and Babylon,' by A. H. Layard, 1853

' The Ansayrii, or Assassins,' by Hon. F. Walpole, 1854.

' Mémoires de l'Histoire Orientale,' by M. C. Defrémery, 1854.

' Nouvelles Recherches sur les Ismaeliens de Syrie,' by M. C. Defrémery, 1855.

' Travels in Central Asia,' by Arminius Vambéry, 1861.

' Monasteries of the Levant,' by Hon. R. Curzon, Fifth Edition, 1865.

' East and West, Essays by different hands,' 1865.

' History of India,' by John Clark Marshman, 1867.

' Sketches of Central Asia,' by Arminius Vambéry, 1868.

' The People of Africa—Essays,' New York, 1871.

'Journey to the Source of the Oxus,' by Lieutenant Wood, New Edition, 1872.
    'African Sketch-book,' by Winwood Reade, 1873.
    'History of India,' by J. Talboys Wheeler, Vol. III., 1874
    'Women of the Arabs,' by Rev. H. Jessup, 1874.
    'Literary Remains of Emanuel Deutsch,' 1874.

NOTE.—In the absence, as yet, of any thorough consensus among Oriental scholars as to the details of transliteration, I have thought it desirable to retain the ordinary spelling in such words as Mohammed, Koran, Sura, Mecca, Medina, rather than adopt the more accurate Muhammad, Kuran, Surah, Makkah, Madyna. With words less universally known, such as Koreishites, Hegira, Mussulman, Sheeah, Sonna, &c., though I have not thought it necessary to use accents, I have adopted the more correct forms of Kuraish, Hijrah, Musalman, Shiah, Sunni, &c.

PREFACE

THE FIRST EDITION.

————

THE substance of these Lectures was written early in 1872 : they were originally intended only for a select audience of friends at Harrow, but, on the suggestion of some of those who heard them, they were afterwards considerably enlarged, and were delivered before the Royal Institution of Great Britain in the months of February and March 1874.

They are an attempt, however imperfect, within a narrow compass, but, it is hoped, from a somewhat comprehensive and independent point of view, to render justice to what was great in Mohammed's character, and to what has been good in Mohammed's influence on the world. To original Oriental research they lay

no claim, nor indeed to much originality at all ;
perhaps the subject hardly now admits of it :
but, thanks to the numerous translations of the
Koran into European languages, and to the
great works of Oriental scholars, such as
Caussin de Perceval, Sprenger, Muir, and
Deutsch, the materials for forming an impartial
judgment of the Prophet of Arabia are within
the reach of any earnest student of the Science
of Religion, and of all who care, as those who
have ever studied Mohammed's character must
care, for the deeper problems of the human
soul.

The value of the estimate formed of the
influence of Mohammedanism on the world at
large must, of course, depend upon such a
modicum of general historical knowledge, and
such Catholic sympathies, as the writer has been
able, amidst other pressing duties, to bring to
his work. The only qualification he would
venture to claim for himself in the matter is
that of a sympathetic interest in his subject, and
of a conscientious desire first to divest himself
of all preconceived ideas, and then by a careful
study of the Koran itself, and afterwards of its

best expounders, to arrive as nearly as may be
at the truth. How vast is the interval between
his wishes and his performance the author knows
full well, and any one who has ever been
fairly fascinated with a great subject will know
also; for he will have felt that to have the will
is not always to have the power, and that the
framing of an ideal implies the consciousness
of failure to attain to it.

A Christian who retains that paramount
allegiance to Christianity which is his birthright,
and yet attempts, without favour and without
prejudice, to portray another religion, is inevitably exposed to misconstruction. In the study
of his subject he will have been struck sometimes by the extraordinary resemblance between
his own creed and another, sometimes by the
sharpness of the contrast; and, in order to avoid
those misrepresentations, which are, unfortunately, never so common as where they ought
to be unknown, in the discussion of religious
questions,—he will be tempted, in filling in the
portrait, to project his own personal predilec-
tions on the canvas, and to bring the differences
into full relief, while he leaves the resemblances

in shadow. And yet a comparison between
two systems, if it is to have any fruitful results,
if its object is to unite rather than divide, if, in
short, it is to be of the spirit of the Founder of
Christianity, must, in matters of religion above
all, be based on what is common to both. There
is, in the human race, in spite of their manifold
diversities, a good deal of human nature; enough,
at all events, to entitle us to assume that the
Founders of any two religious systems which
have had a great and continued hold upon a
large part of mankind must have had many
points of contact. Accordingly, in comparing,
as he has done to some extent, the founder of
Islam with the Founder of Christianity—a
comparison which, if it were not expressed,
would always be implied—the author of these
Lectures has thought it right mainly to dwell
on that aspect of the character of Christ, which,
being admitted by Musalmans as well as Christians, by foes as well as friends, may possibly
serve as a basis, if not for an ultimate agreement,
at all events for an agreement to differ from one
another upon terms of greater sympathy and
forbearance, of understanding and of respect.

That Islam will ever give way to Christianity
in the East, however much we may desire it,
and whatever good would result to the world,
it is difficult to believe; but it is certain that
Mohammedans may learn much from Christians and yet remain Mohammedans, and that
Christians have something at least to learn
from Mohammedans, which will make them
not less but more Christian than they were
before. If we would conquer Nature, we must
first obey her; and the Fourth Lecture is an
attempt to show, from a full recognition of the
facts of Nature underlying both religions—of
the points of difference as well as of resemblance
—that Mohammedanism, if it can never become
actually one with Christianity, may yet, by a
process of mutual approximation and mutual
understanding, prove its best ally. In other
words, the author believes that there is a unity
above and beyond that unity of Christendom
which, properly understood, all earnest Christians so much desire; a unity which rests upon
the belief that 'the children of one Father may
worship Him under different names;' that they
may be influenced by one spirit, even though

they know it not; that they may all have one
hope, even if they have not one faith.

HARROW: *April* 15, 1873.

I have to return my best thanks to my friend
Mr. ARTHUR WATSON, for a careful revision of
my manuscript, and for several valuable suggestions.

It may be serviceable to English readers to mention the more accessible works upon the subject,
to the writers of which I desire here to express my
general obligations, over and above the acknowledg-
ment, in the text, wherever I am conscious of them,
of special debts. I am the more anxious to do this
fully here, as, while I am quite aware that I could not
have written on this subject at all without making
their labours the basis of mine, I have yet in the
exercise of my own judgment been often obliged to
criticise their reasonings and their conclusions. I can
only hope that even where I have ventured to express
a somewhat vehement dissent from my authorities,
they will kindly credit me with something at least of the
verecunde dissentio, which becomes a learner, and of
the zeal for truth, or for his idea of it, which becomes
a writer, however diffident of himself, on a great
subject.

'The Koran,' translated by Sale, with an elaborate Introduction and full Notes drawn from the Arabic Commentators (1734).

'The Koran,' translated by Savary (1782), also with instructive explanatory Notes.

'The Koran,' translated by Rodwell (1861): the Suras arranged, as far as possible, chronologically, with an excellent Introduction and concise Notes.

Gagnier's 'Vie de Mahomet' (1732); drawn chiefly from Abul Feda and the Sonna.

Gibbon's 'Decline and Fall of the Roman Empire;' Chapters L., LI., LII. (1788). A most masterly and complete picture.

Weil's 'Mohamed der Prophet' (1845). Able and to the point.

Caussin de Perceval's 'Essai sur l'Histoire des Arabes,' &c. (1847) gives particularly full information upon the obscure subject of early Arabian history and literature, and is written from an absolutely neutral point of view.

Sprenger's 'Life of Mohammed,' Allahabad, 1851; and his greater work, 'Das Leben und die Lehre des Mohamad' (1851–1861), the most exhaustive, original, and learned of all, but by no means the most impartial; he is often, as I shall point out, on one or two occasions, in the notes, flagrantly unfair to Mohammed.

Sir William Muir's 'Life of Mahomet' (1858–1861). Learned and comprehensive, able and fair; though its scientific value is somewhat impaired by theological assumptions as to the nature of inspiration, and by the introduction of a personal Ahriman, which, while it is self-contradictory in its supposed operation, seems to me only to create new difficulties, instead of solving old ones.

'The Talmud,' an article in the 'Quarterly Review' (October, 1867); 'Islam,' an article in the 'Quarterly Review' (October, 1869); two most brilliant essays. Had the lamented author lived to finish the work he shadowed forth in the last of these, he would probably have drawn a more vivid picture of Islam as a whole than has ever yet been given to the world.

For less elaborate works :—

Ockley's 'History of the Saracens from 632-705.' Picturesque ; dealing largely in romance (1708-1718).

Hallam's 'Middle Ages,' Chapter VI. (1818) ; Milman's 'Latin Christianity,' Book IV., Chapters I. and II. (1857); both good samples of the high merits of each as an historian.

Carlyle's 'Hero as Prophet' (1846). Most stimulating.

Washington Irving's 'Life of Mahomet' (1849). The work of a novelist, but strangely divested of all romance.

Lecture by Dean Stanley in his 'Eastern Church' (1862). Has the peculiar charm of all the author's writings. Catholic in its sympathies, and suggestive, as well from his treatment of the subject as from the place the author assigns to it on the borders of, if not within, the Eastern Church itself.

Barthélemy St.-Hilaire's 'Mahomet et le Koran' (1865), a comprehensive and very useful review of most of what has been written on the subject.

On the general subject of Comparative Religion :—

'Religions of the World,' by F. D. Maurice (1846). Perhaps of all his writings the one which best shows us the character and mind of the man.

'Études d'Histoire Religieuse,' by Renan (1858). Ingenious and fascinating, but not always, nor indeed often, convincing.

'Les Religions et les Philosophies dans l'Asie Centrale,' by Gobineau (1866), gives the best account extant of Bâbyism in Persia.

'Chips from a German Workshop' (1868), and 'Introduction to the Science of Religion' (1873), by Max Müller. Unfortunately the author says very little about Mohammedanism, but from him I have derived some very valuable suggestions as to the general treatment of the subject.   Perhaps it is well that the learning and genius of Professor Max Müller should be given mainly to subjects which are less within the reach of ordinary European students than is Islam, but it is impossible not to wish that he may some day give the world a ' Chip ' or two on the Religion of Mohammed.

For books which throw light on the specialities of Mohammedanism in different countries:—

Al-Makkari's ' History of the Mohammedan Dynasties in Spain' (Eng. Trans.).

Sir John Malcolm's ' History of Persia,' 1815.

Condé's ' History of the Dominion of the Arabs in Spain ' (1820-21).

Crawfurd's ' Indian Archipelago ' (1820).

Colonel Briggs's ' Rise of the Mohammedan Power in India,' translated from the Persian of Ferishta (1829).

Sir Stamford Raffles' ' History of Java ' (2nd edition), (1830).

Burckhardt's ' Travels in Arabia ' (1829).

Caillé's ' Travels through Central Africa to Timbuctoo,' (1830.)

Burckhardt's ' Notes on the Bedouins and Wah-Habees' (1831).

Lane's ' Modern Egyptians ' (1836).

Burton's ' Pilgrimage to Mecca and Medina ' (1856).

Barth's ' Travels in Central Africa ' (1857).

Waitz's ' Anthropologie der Naturvölker ' (Leipsig, 186c).

Lane's ' Notes to his Translation of the Thousand and One Nights' (new edition, edited by E. S. Poole, 1865).

Elphinstone's ' History of India ' (3rd edition), (1866).

Palgrave's ' Arabia ' (1867).

Hunter's ' Indian Mussulmans,' (1871).

Shaw's ' High Tartary, Yarkand, and Kashgar' (1871).

Burton's ' Zanzibar ' (1872).

Palgrave's ' Essays on Eastern Subjects ' (1872).

' Report of the General Missionary Conference at Allahabad' (1873).

Three Articles in Periodical Literature, besides ' Islam ' mentioned above, are of very high merit, and have furnished me, in enlarging my work, with some matter for reflection or criticism :—

' Mahomet,' ' National Review ' (July 1858).
' The Great Arabian,' ' National Review ' (October 1861).
' Mahomet,' ' British Quarterly Review ' (January 1872).

Among other works which I regret I have not been able to consult may be mentioned:—

Gerock's ' Versuch einer Darstellung der Christologie des Koran ' (Homburg, 1839).
Freeman's ' Lectures on the History and Conquests of the Saracens ' (1856).
Geiger's ' Was hat Mohammed aus dem Judenthume aufgenommen ? '
Nöldeke's ' Geschichte des Qorans.'
' Essays on the Life of Mohammed and subjects subsidiary thereto,' by Syed Ahmed Khan Bahador, 1870.
' A Critical Examination of the Life and Teachings of Mohammed,' by Syed Ameer Ali Moulla (1873).

The last two books I had not heard of when I wrote the substance of these Lectures ; and in enlarging my work, I have purposely abstained from consulting them, as I have been given to understand that from a Mohammedan point of view they advocate something of the spirit, and arrive at some of the results, which it had been my object to urge from the Christian stand-point. I would not, of course, venture to compare my own imperfect work, derived as it is in the main from the study of books in the

European languages, and from reflection upon the materials they supply, with works drawn, as I presume, directly from the fountain-head. But if the starting-points be different, and the routes entirely independent of each other, and yet there turns out to be a similarity in the results arrived at, possibly each may feel greater confidence that there is something of value in his conclusions.

CONTENTS.

———◆◇◆———

LECTURE II.

MOHAMMED.

LECTURE III.

MOHAMMEDANISM.

LECTURE IV.

MOHAMMEDANISM AND CHRISTIANITY.

The Future Life of Mohammedanism—of other Religions.—Use Mohammed made of Heaven and Hell—their legitimate use.—Does Mohammedanism encourage self-indulgence ?—Morality of Mohammedanism.—Mohammed's attitude towards existing institutions compared with that of other Founders—Solon—Moses—Christ.—How Islam dealt with Polygamy—Divorce—Women generally—Slavery—Caste, as illustrated by Arabia, India—Africa.—How it dealt with Orphans—the poor – the insane—origin of lunatic asylums — the lower animals—moral offences, drunkenness and

gambling.—How then ought Christianity to regard Mohammedanism ?—How does it ?—Three Monotheistic creeds—Heroes common
to all—Spirituality of each.—Mohammed and Moses compared.—
Iconoclasm.—Absence of priestcraft and ritual, yet great success
in proselytising—reverence for Christ, and sympathy for Christians
—three reasons suggested for Mohammed's rejection of Christianity.
—Mohammed's views of Christ—of the Virgin Mary—of the
Trinity—of the Crucifixion—of God.—Lessons to be learnt from
them.—Has Mohammedanism kept back the East by hindering the
spread of Christianity ?—Is it a curse or blessing to the world at
large ?—Limits of Mohammedanism and of Christianity.—Aspects
of Mohammedanism in different countries—Africa—Spain—Sicily—
Turkey—Persia—India—Contrast between Christianity and Mohammedanism and their founders.—Is the East progressive or not ?
—Corruptions of Mohammedanism—Evils more or less rife in
Musalman countries, e.g. Religious feuds, Fatalism, disregard of
human life, and of humanity in punishments—degradation of
women.—Judicial corruption—misgovernment and consequent
stagnation or decay—unbridled despotism—conquests of Christian
Powers—do these evils imply that the religion is dead ?—Illustrations from history of Christendom—the other side of the question
—inhabitants of Asia Minor—Wonderful power of Islam—Necessity of Revival in all religions—Wahhabis in Arabia and India—
revival in Eastern Anatolia—Maintenance of Ottoman supremacy
in Europe not necessary to Islam—Russian conquests in Asia not
fatal to it—Russian conquests do not spread a living Christianity—
Eastern Christians, their strength and weakness—Limits to the
influence of the West on the East—Despotism—Polygamy—
slavery—the slave-trade—condemned by Islam and by all religions
—mistakes of travellers and missionaries on this head—Is Mohammedanism reconcilable with Civilisation ?—With Christianity ?—
Modifications possible or necessary.—Mohammed's place in His-

LECTURES

DELIVERED AT THE

ROYAL INSTITUTION OF GREAT BRITAIN

IN

FEBRUARY AND MARCH 1874

LECTURE I.

DELIVERED AT THE ROYAL INSTITUTION,
FEBRUARY 14, 1874.

INTRODUCTORY.

Sua cuique genti religio est, nostra nobis.—CICERO.

'Αλλ' ἐν παντὶ ἔθνει ὁ φοβούμενος αὐτὸν, καὶ ἐργαζόμενος δικαιοσύνην, δεκτὸς αὐτῷ ἐστι.—ST. PETER.

THE Science of Comparative Religion is still in its infancy; and if there is one danger more than another against which it should be on its guard, it is that of hasty and ill-considered generalisation. Hasty generalisation is the besetting temptation of all young Sciences; may I not say of Science in general? They are in too great a hurry to justify their existence by arriving at results which may be generally intelligible instead of waiting patiently till the result shapes itself from the premises; as if, in the pursuit of truth, the chase was not always worth more than

B

the game and the process itself more than the result !
Theory has, it is true, its advantages, even in a young
Science, in the way of suggesting a definite line which
enquiry may take. A brilliant hypothesis formed,
not by random guess work, but by the trained imagination of the man of Science, or by the true
divination of genius, enlarges the horizon of the
student whom the limits of the human faculties themselves drive to be a specialist, but who is apt to
become too much so. It throws a flood of light upon
a field of knowledge which was before, perhaps, half
in shadow, bringing out each object in its relative
place, and in its true proportions ; finally, it gathers
scattered facts into one focus, and explaining them
provisionally by a single law, it makes an appeal to
the fancy, which must react on the other mental
powers, and be a most powerful stimulus to further
research. In truth, much that is now demonstrated
fact was once hypothesis, and would never have been
demonstrated unless it had been first assumed. But
since there are few Keplers in the world—men ready
to sacrifice, without hesitation, a hypothesis that had
seemed to explain the universe, and become, as it
were, a part of themselves, the moment that the facts
seem to require it—great circumspection will always
be needed lest the facts may be made to bend to the
theory, instead of its being modified to meet them.

Bearing this caution in mind, we may, perhaps, think that the Science of Comparative Religion, young as it is, has yet been in existence long enough to enable us to lay it down, at all events provisionally, as a general law, that all the great religions of the world, the commencement of which has not been immemorial, coeval that is with the human mind itself, have been in the first instance moral rather than theological; they have been called into existence to meet social and national needs; they have raised man gradually towards God, rather than brought down God at once to man.

Judaism, for instance, sprang into existence at the moment when the Israelites passed, and because they passed, from the Patriarchal to the Political life, when from slavery they emerged into freedom, when they ceased to be a family, and became a nation. 'I am the Lord thy God, which brought thee out of the land of Egypt, and out of the house of bondage.' The Moral Law which followed, the Theocracy itself, was the outcome of this fundamental fact. The nation that God has chosen, nay, that He has called into existence, is to keep His laws and to be His people. Consequently, all law to the ancient Hebrew was alike Divine, whether written, as he believed, by the finger of God on two tables, or whether applied by the civil magistrate to the special cases brought before him. Moral and political offences are thus offences against God, and the ideas of crime and sin are identical alike in fact and in thought.

Again, take a glance at the religion of Buddha. We speak of Buddhism, and are apt to think of it chiefly as a body of doctrine, drawn up over two thousand years ago, and at this day professed by four hundred and fifty millions of human beings ; and we wonder, as well we may, how a *summum bonum* of mere painlessness in this world, and practically, and to the ordinary mind, of total extinction when this world is over, can have satisfied the spiritual cravings of Buddha's contemporaries ; and, in its various forms, can now be the life guidance of a third of the human race.[1] But we forget that, in its origin at least, Buddhism was more of a social than of a religious reformation. It was an attack upon that web of priestcraft which Brahmanism had woven round the

---

[1] To Buddha himself and to his immediate disciples, it is now nearly certain that Nirvâna meant, not the cessation of being, but its perfection. Many of his followers in all ages have, no doubt, developed one side of his teachings only on this subject ; but there are not a few who know, as a friendly critic, the Rev. John Hoare, on the high authority of Mr. Beal, has pointed out to me, that on the last night which their master spent on earth he is said to have held high converse with his disciples, much after the manner of Socrates in the Phædo, on the future life ; and that a Sûtra still remains in which the four characteristics of Nirvâna are said to be personality, purity, happiness, and eternity.

whole frame-work of Indian society.[1] It was the levelling of caste distinctions, the sight of a 'man born to be a king' throwing off his royal dignity, sweeping away the sacerdotal mummeries which he had himself tested, and found unfruitful, preferring poverty to riches, and Sûdras to Brahmans. It was Buddha's overpowering sense of the miseries of sin, his dim yearnings after a better life, his moral system of which the sum is Love, which wrought upon the hearts of his hearers.[2] 'He founded, it is true, a new religion, but he began by attacking an old.' He reconstructed society first, and it was his social reform that led to his religion, rather than his religion which involved his social reconstruction. The half we may, perhaps, think would have been more than the whole—

'Quæsivit cœlo lucem ingemuitque repertâ.'

Nor is it much otherwise with Christianity itself. Christ was before all things the Founder of a new

[1] See Max Müller's 'Chips from a German Workshop,' vol. I., 210-226, especially p. 220 ; and Spence Hardy's 'Legends and Theories of the Buddhists,' Introduction, p. 13-20. Cf. also Beal's 'Buddhist Pilgrims,' Introduction, p. 49, seq.

[2] See in 'Travels of Marco Polo,' translated by Colonel Yule (II. 300, seq.), the remarkable story of the devotion of Sakya Muni to an ascetic life, as a preliminary to all that followed. 'Had he been a Christian,' says the good Venetian, 'he would have been a great saint of our Lord Jesus Christ, so good and pure was the life he led.' See also Colonel Yule's notes *in loc.*, and Mr. Talboys Wheeler's 'History of India,' vol. III. chap. iii.

Society ; not, it is true, of a political Society : had it been so, more of His countrymen would have seen in His person the Messiah that was to come, and in His kingdom the golden age of their own poets and prophets. The political frame-work, indeed, of the world Christ came neither to destroy, nor to recon-struct, except indirectly and remotely. He recognised the logic of facts ; above all, the tremendous logic of the Roman Empire. Tribute was to be paid to Cæsar, even though that Cæsar was a Tiberius. The new Society was potentially a world-wide one, a vast democracy in which Jew and Roman, slave and free-man, rich and poor were on a footing of absolute equality. Enthusiastic love to Christ Himself, evi-denced by purity of heart, by forgetfulness of self, and by enthusiastic love to all mankind, was the one condition and the one test of membership. He who would serve God should first serve his fellow-creatures, and he who with singleness of mind should serve them best should be the least unworthy member of the new brotherhood.

It is true, that to this new Creation of His, Christ gives a name, which we are accustomed to look upon as conveying mainly theological ideas ; He calls it 'the Kingdom of Heaven,' but how does He explain the term Himself? His great precursor, John the Baptist, had predicted its immediate advent. Christ

says, It is here already, it is *within* you. At the
very opening of His work, He speaks of it as already
existing; the outline was there, even if the details
were not filled in. Now if the Kingdom of Heaven
existed before it had dawned, even upon the most
favoured of His followers, that He was more than
'that Prophet,' it would seem to follow that the
essence of His Kingdom was, not the doctrine which
they did not and could not as yet accept, but the
higher life they saw Christ leading, the life of the
soul; and which, seeing, they reverenced, and reve-
rencing, as far as might be, wished to imitate. The
Sermon on the Mount, so far as that which is indescribable can be described at all, and that which is
the fountain head of goodness in infinitely varied
types can be judged by one or two of the rills which
issue from it, is little else than Christ's own life translated into words; and those who, least imperfectly,
re-translated His words back into their own lives,
were the very 'salt of the earth.' They were members
of the Kingdom of Heaven, even though they did not
believe, as some did not even to the end, that He who
'spake as never man spake' was something more
than man.

If we go back to the *ipsissima verba*, so far as we
can now get at them, of Christ Himself, how much
of the doctrine that we are apt to attribute to Christ, we

shall find to be Pauline—how much more Patristic, Scholastic, Puritan! How little dogma, and how much morality, there is in the Founder of our religion ; how few words, and how many works; how little about consequences, how much about motives; in a word, how little theology, and how much religion ! I do not of course mean to deny that Moses, Buddha, Christ Himself were founders of a theology as well as of a life; I only say that the life came first, since it was that which was most called for by the time, and it was their new views of life which prepared their followers to receive and develope their new views of God. 'If any man will *do* His will, he shall know of the doctrine whether it be of God.' 'He that loveth not his brother whom he hath seen, how can he love God whom he hath not seen ?' 'Blessed are the pure in *heart*, for they shall see God.'

I am aware that distinguished German philosophers, Professor Max Müller among them,[1] have laid it down that men cannot form themselves into a people till they have come to an agreement about their religion, and that community of faith is a bond of union more fundamental than any other bond at all. But I do not think that if the distinction which I have drawn between the primeval and the historical Religions of

---

[1] 'Introduction to the Science of Religion,' Lecture III., 144-153.

the world be kept in sight, there is much necessary antagonism between their view and mine ; that a new religion is, in order of time, the outcome and not the cause of a general movement towards a higher life, whether moral or national. Religion is, no doubt, practically all that they say it is, a tie so strong that it can give an ideal unity, as it did in Greece, to tribes differing from one another in degrees of civilisation, in interests and in dialect ; but it does not follow that it was historically ever the original moving power in the aggregation of scattered tribes, or that a new religion was at first a revelation of God rather than a revelation of morality. There must have been a previous community of race and language for the religion to work upon ; there must also have been a strong, though very possibly an ill-directed and a desultory upheaval of society. The fragments still existing of the primeval creed are no doubt a factor in that upheaval, and feel its force ; but the new religion is the result and not the cause of the general movement. It is not till later that it pays the debt it owes to what gave it birth, by lending a higher sanction to each institution of the new society, and so does in truth become, what philosophers say it is, the most important bond in a national life. First the aspirations, then that which satisfies them! First a new conception of the relation of men to one another, then that conception sanctioned, vivified, lit up by the newly perceived relation of all alike to God!

I would also remark that Greece itself, though Professor Max Müller appeals to it in favour of his own conclusions, seems to supply an argument in favour of my view. For even in the Persian wars the common danger and the common hatred of the 'Barbarian' failed to bring about more than a very transitory coalition between two or three of the leading states. The ideal unity of the Greek races was only an ideal, and Panhellenism never went so far as to unite the different states into a homogeneous people. If there had been a real and spontaneous movement among the autonomous cities of Greece towards centralisation, a great reformer might have taken advantage of it, and working upon the 'dim recollection of the common allegiance they owed from time immemorial to the great Father of Gods and men, the old Zeus of Dodona, the Panhellenic Zeus,'[1] have welded the fragments into a nation. The One would not merely have been dimly discerned behind the Many by the highest minds, but the perception would have been converted into a practical reality. The intellectual mission of Socrates might have taken something of the shape, and realised something of the results of the mission of Mohammed.

[1] 'Science of Religion,' p. 148.

But there was no such national movement in Greece, and therefore no opportunity either for the birth of a new religion, or a revival of the old one. In Greek Polytheism we see historically nothing but decay. Mythology thus early had overgrown Religion, and the gross stories of Homer and of Hesiod which so scandalised Socrates and Plato, had, even in their time, concealed from all but the highest minds the vague primitive belief, common probably to the whole Indo-Germanic race, in one Father who is in Heaven.

To what extent the principle I have laid down as to the origin of the three great historical religions, is also true of that of Mohammed, will develope itself gradually in the sequel.

It has been remarked, indeed, by writer after writer, that Islam is less interesting than other religions, inasmuch as it is less original. And this is one of the favourite charges brought against it by Christian apologists. In the first place, I am inclined to think that the charge of want of originality, though it cannot be denied, has been overdone by recent writers; most conspicuously so by M. Renan, who, ingenious and beautiful as his Essay is, seems disposed to explain the whole fabric of Islam by the ideas that existed before Mohammed; and the political direction given to it by his successors, most notably by Omar;

in fact, it seems to me that the only element left out, or not accounted for, in his analysis of Mohammedanism, is Mohammed himself. His Mohammedanism resembles a Hamlet with not only the Prince of Denmark, but with Shakespeare himself cut out. The disjointed members and some few elements of the fabric remain; about as much as we should have of the Hamlet of Shakespeare in the Amlettus of Saxo-Grammaticus; but the informing, animating, inspiring soul is wanting.

It is undeniable that a vague and hearsay acquaintance with the Old Testament, the Talmud, and the New Testament, and the undefined religious cravings of a few of his immediate predecessors, or contemporaries, influenced Mohammed much, and traces of them at second hand may be found in every other page of the Koran; but then, in the second place, it may be asked whether want of originality is any reproach to a religion; for what is religion?

It is that something, which, whether it is a collection of shadows projected by the mind itself upon the mirror of the external world, explaining the Macrocosm by the Microcosm, and invested with a reality which belongs only to the mind that casts them, if indeed even to that, or whether it is indeed an insight of the soul into realities which exist independently of it, and which underlie alike the world of sense and the world of reason; it is something, at all events, which satisfies the spiritual wants of man. Man's spiritual wants, whatever their origin, are his truest wants; and the something which satisfies those wants is the most real of all realities to him.

The founder, therefore, of a religion which is to last must read the spiritual needs of a nation correctly, or, at all events, must be capable of seeing the direc- tion in which they lead, and the development they will one day take. If he read them correctly, he need not care about any originality beyond that which such insight implies; he will rather do well to avoid it. The religious world was startled a few years ago by the revelations of an Oriental scholar that much sup- posed to be exclusively the doctrine of the New Tes- tament is to be found in the Talmud, as though some reflection was thereby cast upon the Founder of our religion! Positivists, again, have laid great stress on the fact that some of the moral precepts supposed to be exclusively Christian are to be found in the sacred writings of Confucius and the Buddhists. But what then? Is a religion less true because it recognises it- self in other garbs, because it incorporates in itself all that is best in the system which it expands or sup- plants? What if we found the whole Sermon on the Mount dispersed about the writings of the Jewish Rabbis, as we unquestionably find some part of it?

Christ Himself was always the first to assert that He came, not to destroy, but to fulfil. But it is strange that the avowed relation of Christianity to Judaism has not protected Islam from the assaults of Christian apologists, grounded on its no less explicitly avowed relation to the two together !

But what of interest, I am ready to admit, the religion of Mohammed loses on the score of originality, it gains in the greater fulness of our knowledge of its origin. It is the latest and most historical of the great religions of the world.

Renan has remarked that the origin of nearly all the leading phenomena of life and history is obscure. What, for instance, can Max Müller tell us of the origin of language? What well-authenticated facts can political philosophers like Hobbes or Locke, or even scientific antiquaries like Sir Charles Lyell or Sir John Lubbock, tell us of the origin of society? What can Darwin tell us of the origin of life? Trace the genealogy of all existing languages into the three great groups of Aryan, Semitic, and Turanian ; find, if you can, the parent language from which even these three families have originally diverged ; are we any nearer an explanation of what language really is? Our hopes, indeed, are aroused by hints dropped throughout Professor Max Müller's fascinating book that he has a secret to divulge to those who have gone through an adequate process of initiation. But to our disappointment we find that the explanation of 'Phonetic Types' is only a roundabout way of saying what, no doubt, is true, that language is instinctive, and that we know nothing whatever of its origin. That sound expresses thought we knew before; but how does it express it? That is the question. Trace elaborately through·Geological Periods, if you can, the steps by which the Monad has been developed into Man, and show that there is no link wanting, and that Nature, so far as we can trace, never makes a leap. Perhaps not; but there is a leap somewhere, and who can say how vast the leap before the Protoplasm can have received the something that is not Protoplasm but Life, and which has all the dignity of life, even though it be a Monad's?

So, too, if the Science of Religion lasts long enough, we may one day be able to trace a continuity of growth from the very dawn of man's belief till, as in history so in religion,

'We doubt not through the ages one increasing purpose runs
And the thoughts of men are widened with the process of the suns.'

We shall find, however, that, even in the dimmest dawn of history, the essence of religion was already there, not forming, but already formed ; a feeling of mystery which, as it is the beginning of philosophy, so, perhaps, it is the very first beginning of religion ; the distinction between right and wrong ; the idea of a Power which is neither Man's nor external Nature's, though it is evidenced by them both ; the sense that there is something in this world amiss ; and the fear, or, possibly, the hope, that it may be unriddled by-and-bye.[1] Where did those ideas come from ? And do we know anything more of the origin of religion itself by having traced it to some of its elements ?

And, what is true of religion generally, is also true, unfortunately, of those three religions which I have called, for want of a better name, historical— and of their founders. We know all too little of the first and earliest labourers ; too much, perhaps, of those who have entered into their labours. We know less of Zoroaster and Confucius than we do of Solon and Socrates ; less of Moses and of Buddha than we do of Ambrose and Augustine. We know indeed some fragments of a fragment of Christ's life ; but who can lift the veil of the thirty years that prepared the way for the three ? What we do know indeed

---

[1] I do not mean to touch here upon the disputed question whether there are races without any definite religious ideas at all. Sir John Lubbock ('Origin of Civilisation,' cap. iv.) has brought together the testimony of many missionaries and travellers as to a great variety of tribes, which seem to be, at all events, without anything beyond the elements I have named ; but I much doubt whether these elements, or some of them, do not exist in all tribes, even in the lowest. It is certain that a longer acquaintance and minuter observation among savage tribes, especially the African, have often led to the reversal of an opinion naturally but hastily formed in the first instance. See Waitz, 'Anthropologie der Naturvölker,' ii. 4.

has renovated a third of the world, and may yet renovate much more; an ideal of life at once remote and near; possible and impossible; but how much we do not know! What do we know of His mother, of His home life, of His early friends, and His relation to them, of the gradual dawning, or, it may be, the sudden revelation, of His divine mission? How many questions about Him occur to each of us that must always remain questions!

But in Mohammedanism everything is different; here instead of the shadowy and the mysterious we have history.[1] We know as much of Mohammed as we do even of Luther and Milton. The mythical, the legendary, the supernatural is almost wanting in the original Arab authorities, or at all events can easily be distinguished from what is historical.[2] Nobody here is the dupe of himself or of others; there

---

[1] Cf. Renan, 'Études d'Histoire Religieuse,' pp. 220 and 230.

[2] The belief in Djinn, beings created of smokeless fire 2,000 years before Adam, as a part of the original Arab mythology, was not discarded by Mohammed (Koran, Sura i. 7-8; xlvi. 28, 29; lvii. 17-18, lxxii. 1, &c.), but, in other respects, the miraculous and mythological element in Mohammedanism comes almost exclusively from Persian sources. Persia has revenged the destruction of her national faith by corrupting in many particulars the simplicity of the creed of her conquerors. For an exhaustive account of Arab ideas on the Djinn, their creation, their influence on human affairs, and their abode, see Note 21 to the Introduction of Mr. Lane's edition of 'The Thousand and One Nights.' The legends illustrating the power of Solomon over the Genii are well known. The notes to Mr. Lane's edition of the 'Arabian Nights' form a storehouse of accurate information upon Arab manners and customs.

C

is the full light of day upon all that that light can
ever reach at all. 'The abysmal depths of personality' indeed are, and must always remain, beyond
the reach of any line and plummet of ours. But we
know everything of the external history of Mohammed—his youth, his appearance, his relations, his
habits; the first idea and the gradual growth, inter-
mittent though it was, of his great revelation ; while
for his internal history, after his mission had been
proclaimed, we have a book absolutely unique in its
origin, in its preservation, and in the chaos of its
contents, but on the substantial authenticity of which
no one has ever been able to cast a serious doubt.
There, if in any book, we have a mirror of one of the
master-spirits of the world ; often inartistic, incoherent, self-contradictory, dull, but impregnated with
a few grand ideas which stand out from the whole ;
a mind seething with the inspiration pent within it,
'intoxicated with God,' but full of human weaknesses,
from which he never pretended—and it is his lasting
glory that he never pretended—to be free.[1]

Upon the striking resemblances between the
Koran and the Bible—the book with which it is most
naturally compared—and the still more striking differences, I need not now dwell at length, especially

[1] It was a proverbial saying in very early times among Musalmans
that 'Mohammed's character was the Koran.'

as the latter have been admirably drawn out by Dean Stanley.[1]

To compress, as best I may, into a few sentences what he has said so well, making only a few amendments or additions where, from my point of view, they seem to be called for.—The Koran lays claim to a verbal, literal, and mechanical inspiration in every part alike, and is regarded as such by almost all Mohammedans. The Bible makes no such claim, except possibly in one or two controverted passages; and there are few Christians who do not now admit at least a human element in every part of it. The text of the Koran is stereotyped; in the Bible there is an immense variety of readings. The Koran has hitherto proved to be incapable of harmonious translation into other languages, and good Musalmans have always on that account consistently discouraged the attempt; the Bible loses little or nothing in the process, and those Christians who value it most have been most anxious to translate it into all the known languages of the world. The Bible is the work of a large number of poets, prophets, statesmen, and lawgivers, extending over a vast period of time, and incorporates with itself other and earlier, and often conflicting documents; the Koran comes straight from the brain, sometimes from the ravings, of an unlettered enthusiast,

[1] 'Lectures on the Eastern Church,' viii. p. 266-273.

who yet in this proved himself to be poet and prophet, statesman and lawgiver in one.   Finally, the
strength of the Koran lies in its uniformity, in its
intolerance, in its narrowness ; the strength of the
Bible in its variety, its toleration, its universality.   In
all these points, as in the more important one of the
morality of its highest revelations, the supremacy of
our sacred books over the one sacred book of the
Mohammedans is indisputable.

Dean Stanley asks somewhat triumphantly, but
on the whole rightly enough, whether there is a
single passage in the Koran that can be named, as a
proof of inspiration, with St. Paul's description of
Charity.   But it is worth remarking that sayings of
Mohammed's have been preserved, which, though
they are in no way equal to this, the sublimest passage of the greatest of the Apostles, yet show a real
insight into the nature and comprehensiveness of this
Christian grace ; and may at all events serve as a
comment on 1 Corinthians xiii.   They are in the
form of an Apologue : ' When God made the earth, it
shook to and fro till He put mountains on it to keep
it firm.'—Then the angels asked, ' O God, is there
anything in thy creation stronger than these mountains ? '—And God replied, ' Iron is stronger than the
mountains, for it breaks them.'—' And is there anything in thy creation stronger than iron ? '—' Yes, fire

is stronger than iron, for it melts it.'—'Is there anything stronger than fire?'—'Yes, water, for it
quenches fire.'—'Is there anything stronger than
water?'—'Yes, wind, for it puts water in motion.'—
'O our Sustainer! is there anything in thy creation
stronger than wind?'—'Yes, a good man giving
alms; if he give with his right hand and conceal it
from his left, he overcomes all things.' But Mohammed did not end here, or restrict his notion of charity
to the somewhat narrow sense which, in common
language, it bears now, that of liberal and unostenta-
tious almsgiving; he went on to give almost as wide
a definition of Charity as St. Paul himself. 'Every
good act is charity; your smiling in your brother's
face; your putting a wanderer in the right road;
your giving water to the thirsty is charity; exhorta-
tions to another to do right are charity. A man's
true wealth hereafter is the good he has done in this
world to his fellow-man. When he dies, people will
ask, what property has he left behind him? But the
angels will ask, what good deeds has he sent before
him?'[1]

---

[1] See 'Mishkat-ul-Masabih,' translated by Captain Matthews, I. vi.
445, 447, 450, &c. The authorities are Abu Hurairah, Abu Dhar and
Anas. A friendly American critic in 'The Nation' (New York), May 20,
1875, points out that much of this view of charity is to be found in the
Talmud, Baba Bathra, fol. x. a; another proof that traditional Judaism
is an important component part of Islam. Mohammed did not claim originality for this, or for any other part of his teaching.

But from one point of view the Koran has to the comparative mythologist, and therefore to the student of human nature, an interest quite unique, and not the less absorbing that it springs out of the very defects that I have pointed out. By studying the Koran, together with the history of Mohammedanism, we see with our own eyes, what we can only infer or imagine in other cases, the precise steps by which a religion naturally and necessarily developes into a mythology.

In the Koran we have, beyond all reasonable doubt, the exact words of Mohammed without subtraction and without addition. We see with our own eyes the birth and adolescence of a religion. In the history of Mohammedanism we descry the parasitical growth that fastens on it, even in its founder's lifetime. We see the way in which a man who denied that he could work miracles, is believed to work them even by his contemporaries, and how in the next generation the extravagant vision of the nocturnal flight to the seventh heaven, with all its gorgeous imagery, and the revolutions of the moon round the Kaaba, is taken for sober fact, and is propagated with all the elaboration of details, which, if they came from anybody, could have come only from Mohammed himself; and yet all of it with the most perfect good faith. We see how a man, who, though he had once in an outburst of anger uttered a prophecy which turned out true, always denied that he could predict the future, and was yet, in spite of himself, credited with all the supernatural insight of a seer. Lastly, we mark how the formalities and the sacrifices and the idolatries which he spent his life in overthrowing, revived in another shape out of the frequency of prayers and fasts that he enjoined, and of the pilgrimages he permitted. The holy places themselves became more holy, as having been the scene of his preaching and of his death, and so, in time, received more than human honours. We know from history what the outgrowth and superstructure have been, and we read in the Koran how narrow the foundation was.

But from the Bible, by its very nature, and owing to those peculiarities which constitute its special strength, we fail to know, in the same sense, the exact limits of the foundation of the Christendom that has overspread the world. In the outward shape in which it has come down to us, and in the questions connected with the authorship of its different parts and the variety of its contents, the Bible resembles not so much the Koran as the Sunnah, which, in its authorised form of the 'six correct books,' is, of course, rejected by the Shiah half of the Mohammedan races.[1]　Even in the Gospels as we have them, comment and inference and the individuality of the writer are mixed with verbal accuracy and exact observation.　We can detect conflicting currents of feeling and of thought which it taxes the ingenuity and honesty, even of harmonists to harmonise.　The New Testament is not less, but more valuable because of these discrepancies.　Its undesigned discrepancies have been as valuable in widening the base of our Christianity as its undesigned coincidences are in assuring it.　Whether we may legitimately apply the inferences to be drawn from our full knowledge of the growth of Mohammedanism to our imperfect knowledge of the growth of other religions is, of course, open to argument, but the interest and importance of the enquiry can hardly be overestimated.

And over and above the interest attaching to the one religion of the world which is strictly historical in its origin, and which therefore may, rightly or wrongly, be used to explain the origin of those of which we know less, there is the fascination that must always attach to those mixed characters of whom we know so much, and yet so little ; who

---

[1] The Shiahs, however, have four books of their own which they are said to look upon as only inferior in authority to the Koran itself. (See Hughes's Notes, p. 35–39.)

have made the world what it is, and yet whom the
world cannot read.

> ' Hero, impostor, fanatic, priest, or sage :'

which element predominates in the man as a whole
we may perhaps discover, and most certainly we can
say now it was not the impostor ; but taking him at
different times and under different circumstances, the
more one reads the more one distrusts one's own conclusions, and, as Dean Milman remarks, answers with
the Arab ' Allah only knows.' [1]

Nor does Mohammedanism lack other claims on
our attention. . Glance for one moment at its marvellous history. Think how one great truth working in
the brain of a shepherd of Mecca gradually produced
conviction in a select band of personal adherents ;
how, when the Prophet was exiled to Medina, the
faith gathered there fresh strength, brought him back
in triumph to his native place, and secured to him for
his lifetime the submission of all Arabia ; how, when
the master-mind was withdrawn, the whole structure
he had reared seemed, for the moment, to vanish away
like the baseless fabric of a vision, or like the mirage
of the desert whence it had taken its rise ; how the
faith of Abu Bakr and the sword of Omar recalled it
once more to life and crushed the false prophets that
always follow in the wake of a true one, as the jackals

[1] Latin Christianity, I. 555.

do the trail of a lion ; how it crumpled up the Roman Empire on one side, and the Persian on the other, driving Christianity before it on the west and north, and Fire-Worship on the east and south ; how it spread over two continents, and how it settled in a third, and how, the tide of invasion carrying it headlong onward through Spain into France, it at one time almost overwhelmed the whole, till Charles the Hammer turned it back upon itself in his five-days' victory at Tours ; how throughout these vast conquests, after a short time, to intolerance succeeded toleration, to ignorance knowledge, to barbarism civilisation ; how the indivisible empire, the representative on earth of the Theocracy in heaven, became many empires, with rival Khalifs at Damascus and Bagdad, at Cairo, Cairoan, and Cordova ; how horde after horde of barbarians of the great Turkish or Tartar stock were precipitated on the dominions of the faithful, only to be conquered by the faith of those whose arms they overthrew, and were compelled henceforward, by its inherent force, to destroy what they had worshipped, to worship what they had destroyed ; how, when the news came that the very birth-place of the Christian faith had fallen into their hands, ' a nerve was touched,' as Gibbon says, ' of exquisite feeling, and the sensation vibrated to the heart of Europe ; ' how Christendom itself thus became for two hundred years half Mohammedanised, and tried to meet fanaticism by counter-fanaticism—the sword, the Bible, and the Cross, against the scymitar, the Koran, and the Crescent ; how, lastly, when the tide of aggression had been checked, it once more burst its barriers, and seating itself on the throne of the Cæsars of the East, threatened more than once the very centre of Christendom, till at length,

> 'The Moslem faith, though flickering like a torch
>   In a night struggle on the shores of Spain,
>   Glared, a broad column of advancing flame,
>   Along the Danube and the Illyrian shore
>   Far into Italy, where eager monks
>   Who watch in dreams, and dream the while they watch,
>   Saw Christ grow paler in the baleful light,
>   Crying again the cry of the forsaken.'

—all this is matter of history, at which I can only glance.

And what is the position of Islam now ?

It numbers at this day more than one hundred millions, probably one hundred and fifty millions, of believers as sincere, as devout, as true to their creed as are the believers in any creed whatever. It still has its grip on two continents, and a foothold, even if a precarious foothold, in a third. It extends from Morocco to the Malay peninsula, from Zanzibar to the Kirghis horde. It embraces within its ample circumference two extensive empires, one Sunni, the other Shiah, the first of which, though it has often been pronounced sick unto death or even dead, is not dead yet, and is even showing some signs of reviving vitality.   It still claims the allegiance of those widely scattered countries from which in the dimmest antiquity sprang the worship of Stars and of Fire, the worship of Baal and of Moloch, of Al Lat and of Al Uzza, of Ormuzd and of Ahriman, of Isis and of Osiris.   It still grasps Mount Sinai, the cradle of the Jewish, and Bethlehem, the cradle of the Christian Faith.   It is to be found beneath the shadow even of those giant mountains of Nepal which gave birth to Buddha.   To the votaries, therefore, of Islam belong the spots which, from their antiquity or their associations, are most dear to the great religions of the world ; and the countries which are the birthplace of them all. Theirs is the Cave of Machpelah, theirs the Church of the Nativity, theirs the Holy Sepulchre, theirs Mount Elburz.   To Islam belong El Azhar at Cairo, the Taj at Agra, Saint Sophia at Constantinople, the Dome of the Rock at Jerusalem, and the Kaaba at Mecca. Africa, which had yielded so early to Christianity, nay, which had given birth to Latin Christianity itself, the Africa of Cyprian and Tertullian, of Antony and of Augustine, yielded still more readily to Mohammed ; and from the Straits of Gibraltar to the Isthmus of Suez may still be heard the cry which with them is no vain repetition of ' Allahu-Akbar,

Allahu-Akbar,'—' God is most great, there is no God but God, and Mohammed is the prophet of God.' [1]

And if it be said, as it often is, that Mohammedanism has gained no territorial extension since the first flame of religious enthusiasm, fanned, as it then often was, by the lust of conquest, has died out, I answer that this is far from the truth.

In the extreme East, Mohammedanism has since then won and maintained for centuries a moral supremacy in the important Chinese province of Yunnan, and has thus actually succeeded in thrusting a wedge between the two great Buddhist empires of Burmah and of China. [2] Within our own memory,

[1] In the Adhan, or morning call to Prayer, which at once by its musical cadences, and its associations, produces so deep an impression on all Eastern travellers, the words Allahu-Akbar are repeated four times at the beginning, and twice at the end. The translation of the call is as follows:—' God is most great. I testify there is no God but God. I testify that Mohammed is the messenger of God. Come to prayer. Come to salvation. Prayer is better than sleep. God is most great. There is no God but God.' See Curzon's ' Monasteries of the Levant,' p. 56, &c. Walpole's ' Ansayrii,' p. 55-59. Lane's ' Modern Egyptians,' I. 91.

[2] Marco Polo (II. 52 *seq.*) found Musalmans as well as Nestorian Christians in the province of Carajan, *i.e.* Yun-nan, in the thirteenth century ; and Colonel Yule in a note *ad loc.* cites a statement of Bashid-uddin, the Persian historian of the Mongols, that ' *all* the inhabitants of Yachi, its capital town, were in his time Mohammedans ;' an over-statement no doubt, but still substantially true. Ibn Batuta in the following century (Ibn Batuta's ' Travels,' translated by Rev. S. Lee), says (p. 208) that ' in every Chinese province there was a town for the Mohammedans, with cells, villages, and mosques, and that they were made much of by the Emperor of China ;' ' in each town too there was a Sheikh el Islam who administered justice.'

indeed, after a fifteen years' war, and under the leadership of Ta Wên Siu, one of those half-military, half-religious geniuses, which Islam seems always capable of producing, it succeeded in wresting from the Celestial Empire a territorial supremacy in the western half of this province. A few years ago an embassy of intelligent and, it is worth adding, of progressive and of tolerant Musalmans from Yun-nan, headed by Prince Hassan, son of the chieftain who had now become the Sultan Soliman, appeared in our own country, and the future of the Panthays,[1] as they are called, began at length to attract attention, not so much, I fear, from the extraordinary interest attaching to their religious history—that interests few Englishmen—as from the possible opening to our Eastern trade, the only Gospel which most Englishmen care now to preach, and one which we did consistently for many years propagate by our commercial wars in China and Japan, at the expense of every principle of religion and humanity. Unfortunately the interests of our trade were not sufficiently bound up with the existence of the Panthays to call for any representations on the part of a nation which, in spite of its higher instincts and aspirations, is still above all commercial,

---

[1] A name given to them by their Burmese neighbours, from whom the word has passed into the Western World. It is said to be a corruption of the Burmese 'Putthee,' *i.e.*, Mohammedan.

and Prince Hassan was compelled to return to Asia
without any prospect of moral support from us or from
the Sultan of Turkey. On arriving at Rangoon he
was met by the news that the Musalmans had at
length been overpowered by the fearful odds arrayed
against them ; that Tali-Fu, the capital, had fallen,
and men, women, and children to the number of some
thirty thousand had been massacred by the victors.
The fate of Momien, the other stronghold, was of
course only a question of time ; but though the short-
lived Mohammedan sovereignty has been destroyed,
and what was won by the sword has since perished
by the sword, Mohammedanism itself has not been
extinguished in the Celestial Empire. Within the
last eight years that vast tract of country called
Western Chinese Tartary, or Eastern Turkestan, has
thrown off the yoke of China, and has added another
to the list of Musalman kingdoms.[1] Khoten and
Yarkand and Kashgar are united under the vigorous
rule of the Atalik Ghazee,[2] Yakub Beg. Whatever

---

[1] By so doing, it has only returned to the faith professed by it in
the time of Marco Polo. 'The people of Khoten,' says he, I. 196, 'are
subject to the Great Khan, and are all worshippers [sic] of Mohammed.'
Ibn Batuta says (p. 86) of the inhabitants of Khavarism = Khiva, that
he 'never saw better bred or more liberal people, or those who were
more friendly to strangers.' He especially approved of the whip hung up
in every mosque to chastise those who absented themselves from prayers.

[2] The title was given him by the Amir of Bokhara. It means
'Guardian of the Champions of Religion.' For the abolition of the
slave trade see the best authority on the subject, Shaw's 'High Tartary,'

may be his private character, the abolition of the slave
trade throughout his dominions, his rigid administration of justice, his readiness to establish commercial
relations with India, and the respect shown even by
the Meccan pilgrims among his subjects for Christianity are some indication of what Mohammedanism
may yet have in store for it in Central Asia under the
influence of a master mind, and with the modifications
that are possible or necessary to it.   Throughout the
Chinese Empire, at Karachar for instance, there
are scattered Musalman communities who have higher
hopes than Buddhism or Confucianism, and a purer
morality than Taoism can supply.   The Panthays
themselves, it is believed, still number a million and
a half, and the unity of God and the mission of God's
prophet are attested day by day by a continuous
line of worshippers from the Atlantic to the Pacific
Ocean.

Nay, even beyond, in the East Indian Archipelago,
beyond the Straits of Malacca, if I may venture just
now so to call them, in Java and Sumatra, in Borneo
and Celebes, Islam has raised many of the natives
above their former selves, and has long been the
dominant faith.   It established itself in the Malay

p. 347 ; and for the view of Christians taken by some pilgrims to Mecca
from Central Asia, p. 65.   The letters received from Mr. Forsyth's
Mission (see *Times*, of March 17, 1874) seem quite to bear out the view
I had formed of Yakub Beg's position.

Peninsula and Sumatra in the thirteenth and four-teenth, and in Java and Celebes in the fifteenth century ; and it is interesting to note, as is remarked by Crawfurd, that about the time it was being gradu-ally expelled from Western Europe, it made up for its expulsion by extending itself to the East of Asia. The Arab missionaries were just in time, for they anticipated by only a few years the first advent of grasping Portuguese and ambitious Spaniards. It cannot, of course, be supposed that among races so low in the scale of humanity as are most of the Indian islanders, Mohammedanism would be able to do what it did originally for the Arabs or for the Turkish hordes; but it has done something even for them. It expelled Hinduism from some islands, and a very corrupt Buddhism from others. It was propagated by missionaries who cared very much for the souls they could win, and nothing for the plunder they could carry off. They conciliated the natives, learned their languages, and intermarried with them ; and in the larger islands their success was rapid, and, so far as nature would allow, complete.[1] The Philippines

---

[1] Crawfurd's ' Indian Archipelago,' II. 275 and 315.

Marco Polo (chap. IX.) says of Ferlec, a kingdom in what he calls Java the Less ▬ Sumatra : ' This kingdom is so much frequented by the Saracen merchants that they have converted the natives to the law of Mohammed.' In the following century, the Moorish traveller, Ibn Batuta, visited the island, and describes the king, Malik-al-Zhahir, as being ' one of the most eminent and generous of princes ; ' the learned

and the Moluccas, which were conquered by Spain and Portugal respectively, did not become Mohammedan, for they had to surrender at once their liberty and their religion.   It is no wonder that the religion known to the natives chiefly through the unblushing rapacity of the Portuguese, and the terrible cruelties of the Dutch, has not extended itself beyond the reach of their swords.   Here, as elsewhere in the East, the most fatal hindrance to the spread of Christianity has been the lives of Christians.[1]   I will only add further that the Musalmans of the East Indian Islands are very lax in their obedience to many of the precepts of their law, that they are tolerant of other religions, and that the women enjoy a liberty, a position, and

were admitted to his society and had free converse with him, while he proposed questions for their discussion.   So humble withal was he that he used to walk to the mosque divested of his royal robes, and wearing those of a doctor of divinity.   With the exception of the Sultan of Fez, Ibn Batuta thought him ' the most learned of all the Musalman Sultans ; ' and he had seen them all from Tangiers to China (p. 226) ; he found that the inhabitants of Sumatra had adopted Islam to a distance of twenty-one days' journey onward from the capital, Samathrah.

[1] For the cruelties of the Portuguese, see Crawfurd, II. 403, and for the Dutch, see especially II. 425 seq. and 441.   The Portuguese in the fifteenth century carried on a piratical crusade against every Musalman ship they could find.   Meeting with a vessel containing two hundred and sixty pilgrims bound for Mecca, of whom fifty were women and children, they saved and baptised twenty of the children ; the remainder were thrust down into the hold, and the ship scuttled and set on fire. For some startling facts as to the comparative morality of some native and Christian communities in India, see a paper by the Rev. J. N. Thoburn, in the Report of the Allahabad Missionary Conference, held in 1872 73, p. 467–470.

an influence which contrasts favourably with that allowed to them in any other Asiatic country.[1]

The New World, even, is not without some representatives of the Musalman faith. Islam has crossed the Pacific with the Coolies, and the Atlantic with the Negroes, and counts its adherents by thousands in some of the West India Islands, in Trinidad, and in Dutch Guiana.

In Africa, again, Mohammedanism is spreading itself by giant strides almost year by year. Everyone knows that, within half a century from the Prophet's death, the richest states of Africa, and those most accessible to Christianity and to European civilisation, were torn away from both, by the armies of the faithful, with hardly a struggle or a regret; but few except those who have studied the subject, are aware that, ever since then, Mohammedanism has

---

[1] Crawfurd, II. 260 and 269–271 ; and Sir Stamford Raffles' 'Java,' I. p. 261 and II. 2–5. During the latter half of the seventeenth century four Queens, all called 'Sultans,' reigned in succession over Achin. The Achinese Mohammedans are admitted to be more enterprising and sagacious than any of the Pagan tribes in Sumatra, and they have given conspicuous proof of their valour in their recent contest with the Dutch. I am informed that two works recently published by Professor Veth of Leiden, the one on Achin and its relation to the Netherlands, and the other on Java, contain most interesting particulars concerning the spread and influence of Islam in that part of the world, and are written in the most impartial spirit. It is to be hoped that they may be translated from the Dutch into more familiar European languages, as has been the case with the admirable work by Professor Dozy of Leiden, on the 'History of the Musalmans of Spain.'

been gradually spreading over the northern half of the Continent.

Let me now trace its progress through these vast regions, as clearly and as briefly as I can.

When the conqueror Akbah had overrun the States of Barbary from end to end, and, after passing through wildernesses in which he himself or his successors were one day to found the literary and commercial capitals of Fez, Cairoan, and Morocco, had reached the point where the Atlantic and the Great Desert meet, it was his 'career only, and not his zeal,' which was checked by the prospect of the ocean. Spurring, so it is said, his horse into its waves, and raising his eyes to heaven, he exclaimed, 'Oh Allah! if my course were not stopped by this sea, I would still go on to the unknown kingdoms of the West, preaching the unity of Thy holy name, and putting to the sword the rebellious nations who worship other gods than Thee!' Before many years had passed, the wish of this 'Mohammedan Alexander who sighed for more worlds to conquer'[1] was gratified in a direction and to an extent which he little expected. Muza crossed the Straits of Gibraltar to carry Islam northward into Spain, while Musalman missionaries, starting in the other direction, braved even the terrors of the Sahara to carry their message to the unknown kingdoms of the south. Leaping

---

[1] Gibbon, cap. 51, 464–466.

from Oasis to Oasis of the Great Desert with almost
the speed of its nomad horsemen, and subduing to its
message, as it passed, even some of the wild and wandering Touariks, we know that before the year 1000 it
had reached Timbuctoo, that mysterious city, a sea-
port, as it has been well described, in the heart of Africa,
situated on the remotest shore of the dry ocean, or
the sandy sea of the Sahara. It thence travelled to the
Jolofs between the Senegal and the Gambia, thence
to the wide-spread Mandingoes on the Niger,[1] thence
again to the Foulahs, and then, turning eastward
towards the land of its birth, it reached, by the thirteenth century, Lake Tchad, and the kingdoms beyond, where, finally, these Musalman missionaries of
the West were met by other Musalmans from the

---

[1] See the 'Travels' of Ibn Batuta, who, about the year 1357, found
Islam in full possession of some of the countries on the Niger, or, as he
calls it, the Nile (p. 237). At Zaga (Sego ?), the 'first city in these
parts to embrace Islam,' he found that the inhabitants were 'religious
and fond of learning.' At Mali there was an avaricious and worthless
Sultan, but 'the people paid great regard to justice.' 'A traveller may
proceed alone among them without the least fear of a thief or a robber ;'
'they are so regular in their attendance at the mosque, that unless one
makes haste he will find no place left to say his prayers' (p. 246). Every.
one knew the Koran by heart : a father would keep his son under restraint
till he could say the whole perfectly ! Negro Musalmans who had been
the Pilgrimage to Mecca were to be met with everywhere (p. 239, 241).
The women were not veiled, and accompanied their husbands to prayers
(p. 234). Among their bad customs, that which seems to have offended
Ibn Batuta most was their want of clothing, and 'the contempt in which
they held the white people' (p. 234), of whom, doubtless, in comparison
with the ebony Negroes, he considered himself to be one.

East in the very centre of the Soudan.[1] Of course enormous tracts of heathenism were left, and are still left, in various parts of this vast area, and it is mainly among these that, at this day, Mohammedan missionaries are meeting everywhere with a marked success which is denied to our own. We hear of whole tribes laying aside their devil-worship, or immemorial Fetish, and springing at a bound, as it were, from the very lowest to one of the highest forms of religious belief. Christian travellers, with every wish to think otherwise, have remarked that the Negro who accepts Mohammedanism acquires at once a sense of the dignity of human nature not commonly found even among those who have been brought to accept Christianity.

It is also pertinent to observe here, that such progress as any large part of the Negro race has hitherto made is in exact proportion to the time that has elapsed since their conversion, or to the degree of fervour with which they originally embraced, or have since clung to Islam. The Mandingoes and the Foulahs are salient instances of this ; their unquestionable superiority to other Negro tribes is as unquestionably owing to the early hold that Islam got upon them, and to the comparative civilisation and culture that it has always encouraged.

Nor can it be said that it is only among those

---

[1] 'Anthropologie der Naturvölker,' by Dr. Theodor Waitz, p. 248.

Negroes who have never heard anything of a purer
faith that Mohammedanism is making such rapid progress. The Government Blue Book of the year 1873
on our West African settlements, and the reports of
missionary societies themselves, are quite at one on
this head. The Governor of our West African colonies, Mr. Pope Hennessy, remarks that the liberated
Africans are always handed over to Christian missionaries for instruction, and that their children are baptised and brought up at the public expense in Christian schools, and are, therefore, in a sense, ready-made
converts. Missionary societies are not likely to err
on the side of defect in enumerating their converts;
yet the total number of professing Christians in all
our African settlements put together, as computed
by the missionary societies themselves[1]—very few
even of these, as the Governor says, and as we can
unfortunately well believe from our experience in
countries that are not African, being practical Christians—falls far short of the original number of Africans
liberated at Sierra Leone alone, and their descendants.[2] On the other hand, the Rev. James Johnson,
a native clergyman, and a man of remarkable energy
and intelligence as well as of very Catholic spirit,

---

[1] For further illustrations of this see Appendix to Lecture I. p. 351.
[2] Papers relating to Her Majesty's Colonial Possessions. Part II.,
1873, 2nd division, p. 14.

deplores the fact that, of the total number of Mohammedans to be found in Sierra Leone and its neighbourhood, three-fourths were not born Mohammedans,
but have become so by conversion, whether from a
nominal Christianity or from Paganism.[1]

And, what is still more to our purpose to remark
here, Mohammedanism, as it spreads now, is not
attended by some of the drawbacks which accompanied its first introduction into the country. It is
spread, not by the sword, but by earnest and simple-
minded Arab missionaries. It has also lost, except
in certain well-defined districts, much of its in-

---

[1] Papers relating to Her Majesty's Colonial Possessions. Part II.,
1873, 2nd division, p. 15. As Mr. Pope Hennessy's Report has been
much criticised, chiefly on the ground that he is a Roman Catholic (see a
letter to the *Times*, of Oct. 21, 1873, signed ' Audi alteram partem '), and
as I have based some statements upon it, it may be worth while to mention
that I have had a conversation with Mr. Johnson, who is a strong Protestant himself, and that he bore testimony to the *bona fides* of the Report,
and to its accuracy even on some points which have been most questioned. He told me that Mohammedanism was introduced into Sierra
Leone, not many years ago, by three zealous missionaries who came from
a great distance. It seems now not only to be rapidly spreading in the
colony itself, but in the countries to the North of it to be gaining the
ascendency, in spite of all the European influences at work. It may
perhaps be questioned, since he does not dwell much upon it, whether
Mr. Pope Hennessy, in his remarks on the diminished number of
Christians in Sierra Leone, made allowance for the return of a certain
number of true Christians, such as Bishop Crowther, to their own
countries. The object of Mr. Johnson in dwelling on the spread of
Islam in Africa was no doubt, as he has stated since, rather to stimulate
the zeal of Christian missionaries than to celebrate that of Musalmans ;
but, whatever his object, he spoke the simple truth, and the facts remain,
and are all the more striking, from the unexceptionable medium through
which they have come to us.

tolerant and exclusive character. The two leading doctrines of Mohammedanism, and the general moral precepts of the Koran, are, of course, inculcated everywhere. But, in other respects, the Musalman missionaries exhibit a forbearance, a sympathy, and a respect for native customs and prejudices, and even for their more harmless beliefs, which is no doubt one reason of their success, and which our own missionaries and schoolmasters would do well to imitate.

We are assured, on all hands, that the Musalman population has an almost passionate desire for education, and those in the neighbourhood of our colonies would throng our schools, first if the practical education given was more worth having, and, secondly, if the teachers would refrain from needlessly attacking their cherished and often harmless customs. Wherever Mohammedans are numerous, they establish schools themselves; and there are not a few who travel extraordinary distances to secure the best possible education. Mr. Pope Hennessy mentions the case of one young Mohammedan Negro who is in the habit of purchasing costly books from Trübner in London, and who went to Futah, two hundred and fifty miles away, to obtain an education better than he could find in Sierra Leone itself.[1] Nor is it an

---

[1] Papers relating to Her Majesty's Colonial Possessions. Part II., 1873, 2nd division, p. 10.

uncommon thing for newly-converted Musalmans to make their way right across the Desert from Bornu, or from Lake Tchad, or down the Nile from Darfur or Wadai, a journey of over one thousand miles, that they may carry on their studies in El-Azhar, the great collegiate Mosque at Cairo, and may thence bring back the results of their training to their native country, and form so many centres of Mohammedan teaching and example.[1]

Nor as to the effects of Islam when first embraced by a Negro tribe, can there, when viewed as a whole, be any reasonable doubt. Polytheism disappears almost instantaneously; sorcery, with its attendant evils, gradually dies away; human sacrifice becomes a thing of the past. The general moral elevation is most marked; the natives begin for the first time in their history to dress, and that neatly. Squalid filth is replaced by some approach to personal cleanliness; hospitality becomes a religious duty; drunkenness, instead of the rule, becomes a comparatively rare exception. Though polygamy is allowed by the Koran, it is not common in practice, and, beyond the limits laid down by the Prophet, incontinence is rare; chastity is looked upon as one of the highest, and

---

[1] Waitz, p. 251. He calculates the number of students returning each year to be about fifty. To his book, and to the authorities to whom he refers, I owe many of the facts mentioned in the text illustrative of the influence of Islam on the native mind and character.

becomes, in fact, one of the commoner virtues. It is idleness henceforward that degrades, and industry that elevates, instead of the reverse. Offences are henceforward measured by a written code instead of the arbitrary caprice of a chieftain—a step, as every-one will admit, of vast importance in the progress of a tribe. The Mosque gives an idea of architecture at all events higher than any the Negro has yet had. A thirst for literature is created, and that for works of science and philosophy as well as for commentaries on the Koran.[1] There are whole tribes, such as the Jolofs on the river Gambia, and the Hausas, whose manly qualities we have had occasion to test in Ashantee, which have become to a man Mohamme-dans, and have raised themselves infinitely in the process; and the very name of Salt-water Mohamme-dans given to those tribes along the coast who, from admixture with European settlers, have relaxed the severity of the Prophet's laws, is a striking proof of the extent to which the stricter form of the faith prevails in the far interior.

But lest any one should think that in giving so

---

[1] Waitz, p. 252-254. Aristotle and Plato are known to not a few Mohammedans in the interior—Barth, in his 'Travels in Central Africa,' Vol. V. p. 63, mentions that Sidi Mohammed, of Timbuctoo, main-tained that they were both Musalmans, that is to say, worshippers of the true God. Cf. III., 373, for the case of a Pullo at Massera, who had read Plato and Aristotle in Arabic, was well acquainted with the history of Spain, and sympathised with the Wahhabis.

favourable an account of Islam in Africa, I am drawing on my own imagination, or depending on the
testimony of untrustworthy travellers, I will select
from a large number of those whose works I have
read, and whose testimony all tends in the same
direction, the explicit statements of two or three, as
bearing on the points at issue.

Browne, an Englishman, who undertook extensive
travels in Central Africa in the years 1799 and 1806,[1]
remarks that, among the idolaters of Sheibôn and of
other places, the only persons whom he saw wearing
decent clothes, or indeed clothing at all, were Mohammedans ; that it was to the introduction of Islam
a century and a half before his time that Darfur
owed its settled government and the cultivation of
its soil ; and that the people of Bergoo were remarkable for their zealous attachment to their religion,
and read the Koran daily.   Here then we find the
use of decent clothing, and the arts of reading and
agriculture, attributed to Islam.

But Browne, perhaps, is not well known to those
who have not made a speciality of African travel.
Let us hear then what was the experience of a
traveller who is known to all the world, and who was
the first to explore a large district of the Western
Soudan.

[1] See Pinkerton's ‘Voyages,’ Vols. XV. and XVI.

Mungo Park, educated as he was for the Scotch church, and cruelly persecuted as he was throughout his travels by Moorish banditti, would not be likely to be a friend to Islam, and many of his remarks show a strong bias against it : his testimony therefore is all the more valuable. His travels lay almost exclusively among Mohammedan or semi-Mohammedan tribes, and he found that the Negroes were everywhere summoned to prayer by blasts blown through elephants' tusks. On reaching the Niger, the main object of his wanderings, he found, to his surprise, that Sego, the capital of Bambarra, was a walled town, containing some 30,000 inhabitants, that the houses were square and very often white-washed, and that there were Moorish mosques in every quarter. 'The view of this extensive city,' he writes, 'the numerous canoes upon the river, the crowded population, and the cultivated state of the surrounding country, formed altogether a prospect of civilisation and magnificence which I little expected to find in the bosom of Africa.'[1]

The Mandingoes, a Mohammedan tribe through whose territories he returned, he describes as being, unlike the Moors, a very gentle race, cheerful in their dispositions, hospitable, inquisitive, and credulous.

[1] See Mungo Park's 'Travels,' Cap. I. ad fin.

The propensity to pilfer, so common amongst barbarians, though he suffered himself by it, he thought
to be not greater than could be found among many
European nations.   His impression of the women
was most favourable.   'I do not recollect,' he says,
'a single instance of hard-heartedness towards me
among the women.   In all my wanderings and
wretchedness I found them uniformly kind and compassionate.'   One of the first lessons in which the
Mandingo women instructed their children was the
practice of truth.   In the case of an unhappy mother
whose son had been murdered by the Moors, her
only consolation was, that in the whole of his blame-
less life he had never told a lie.   On another point,
he remarks that the Negroes, whether Mohammedan
or Pagan, allowed a plurality of wives; but that the
Mohammedans alone were by their religion confined
to four.   Though in a position of inferiority compared with more civilised nations, their wives were
not as a rule ill-treated, each wife taking her turn in
ruling the household.   In a third and all-important
matter, that of sobriety, the advantage was entirely
on the side of the Mohammedans.   'The beverages,'
he says, 'of the pagan Negroes are beer and mead, of
which they frequently drink to excess.[1]   The Mohammedan converts drink nothing but water.'

[1] Cap. VII.

As to education, Mungo Park found schools and active teachers everywhere ; not, of course, advanced schools nor highly educated teachers, but institutions which, humble though they be, should not be scorned as they often are by the representatives of Christian missions, but treated with the respect and the sympathy with which the Founder of Christian missions, nay, of Christianity itself, would undoubtedly have treated them. The master of one of these schools in Kamalia, to whose care Mungo Park was himself for some time committed, adhered strictly to the religion of Mohammed, but was by no means intolerant towards those who differed from him.[1] His school consisted of seventeen boys, most of whom were sons of ' Kafirs,' i.e. unbelievers. He possessed the Koran, some commentaries on it, and a considerable number of Arabic manuscripts. Mungo Park witnessed the examination held in presence of the assembled ' Bushreens ' for the purpose of conferring the like degree on a young student. No one was admitted to the degree unless he had read through the Koran, and could answer questions intelligently upon it. Many of the Negroes were in possession of Arabic versions of the Pentateuch, the Psalms of David, and the Prophecies of Isaiah, and a considerable knowledge of the facts of Old Testament History was

[1] Cap. XI.

diffused amongst them. As to the thirst for knowledge and the desire to get books, an Arabic copy of
the Pentateuch was often sold for the value of a
prime slave, while a Negro offered Park himself an ass
and sixteen bars of goods for an Arabic grammar !

It is strange to read these accounts of the spread
and influence of Islam in Africa, and to discover on
a searching inquiry that—if allowance be made for
bias, or ignorance, or unreasoning indignation on
the part of a few travellers who have attributed to
Islam in Africa every crime it has not been able
to prevent, or which has been perpetrated by the
most unworthy of its professors—every one of Mungo
Park's statements may be strengthened and supported
by a continuous succession of dispassionate and philanthropic travellers ever since, and then to find it
gravely stated by the editor of a quasi official missionary periodical that ‘more Mohammedanism
means more slavery, more brutality, more polygamy,
and, we do not scruple to add’ (as if such a writer
would feel scrupulous in making any statement upon
any subject !), ‘more drunkenness for Africa,’ and
‘that in the waiting-room of Euston Square Station
all the Mohammedan Negroes in Africa who have
read the Koran, even once, could be most comfortably
accommodated.’ [1]

[1] Church Missionary Intelligencer, August 1874, p. 247, and March
1875, p. 75.

But lest it should be said as a last resource by such opponents that, whatever was the case at the time of Browne and Mungo Park, and other travellers, such as Caillié, and Laing, and Winterbottom, and Richardson, and Galton, and Winwood Reade, whose evidence, had I the time and space, I might quote, that Islam has now suddenly become a curse to Africa, I will adduce here the testimony of two other very recent travellers, each of whom is the eye-witness of what he records. The first is that of Dr. Barth, whose travels in Northern and Central Africa are probably more extensive than those of any other European traveller, and whose bias is certainly not in favour of Islam. The second is that of the Rev. Edward Blyden, which has reached me only since the first publication of these Lectures, and which is therefore the most recent evidence that I can obtain.

As to the rapid spread of Islam, Dr. Barth says that 'a great part of the Berbers of the Desert were once Christians, and that they afterwards changed their religion and adopted Islam ;' and he describes 'that continual struggle which, always extending further and further, seems destined to overpower the nations at the very Equator if Christianity does not presently step in to dispute the ground with it.' He remarks in another place, that Mohammedans alone seem able to maintain any sort of government in

E

Africa ; and, what is more important, that there 'is a vital principle in Islam which has only to be brought out by a reformer to accomplish great things.'[1]

On the other hand, the Rev. Edward Blyden, a native African of the purest Negro blood, a Christian missionary who has given the energies of his life to extending education and founding schools in the interior of Liberia, and who has learned by experience to deal with Mohammedan prejudices against Christianity, writes to me as follows. It may be worth while to add that he is now Principal of the Presbyterian High School in Monrovia, West Africa, that he was quite unknown to me before, and is known to me now only by his writings and his reputation.

'It is curious,' he says, 'how at a distance from the scene and only from "the study of books in the European languages, and from reflection upon the materials they supply," you have arrived at precisely the same conclusions with regard to the character

[1] Barth's 'Travels,' I. 164, 197, 310; II. 196, &c.   Mr. T. W. Higginson, to whom I am indebted for some of these references, and for several interesting publications on the subject of Comparative Religion, in a suggestive address delivered by him at Boston in America, on the 'Sympathy of Religions,' adduces the testimony to be found in favour of the effects of Islam in Africa in the following works, which I have been unable to consult :—Wilson's 'Western Africa ;' Johnstone's 'Abyssinia ;' Allen's 'Niger Expedition ;' Du Chaillu's 'Ashango Land ;' Reade's 'Savage Africa ;' but the authorities I have myself read and have quoted or referred to in the text seem to me to be ample to convince all who are open to conviction, that Islam is, on the whole, a great forward movement for the Negroes.

and influence of Mohammedanism in Africa which I
have reached after years of travel among, and intercourse with, the people. Your remarks as to the
superiority of the Mohammedan Negro are quite in
accordance with my own observation and experience.
If those Christians who are so unmeasured in their
denunciations of Mohammedanism could travel, as I
have travelled, through those countries in the interior
of West Africa, and witness, as I have witnessed, the
vast contrast between the Pagan and Mohammedan
communities—the habitual listlessness and continued
deterioration of the one, and the activity and growth,
physical and mental, of the other ; the capricious and
unsettled administration of law, or rather absence of
law, in the one, and the tendency to order and regu-
larity in the other ; the increasing prevalence of ardent
spirits in the one, and the rigid sobriety and con-
servative abstemiousness of the other—they would
cease to regard the Musalman system as an unmitigated evil in the interior of Africa.'

It is melancholy to contrast with the wide-spread
beneficial influences of Mohammedanism, on which I
have insisted, the little that has been done for Africa,
till very lately, by the Christian nations that have
settled in it, and the still narrower limits within
which it has been confined. Till a few years ago
the good effects produced beyond the immediate

territories occupied by them were absolutely nothing. The achievement of Vasco da Gama, for which Te Deums were sung in Europe, proved for centuries to be nothing but the direst curse to Africa. If the Oceanic slave trade has been, to the eternal credit of England in particular, at last abolished by Christian nations, it cannot be forgotten that Africa owes also to them its origin, and on the West Coast, at all events, its long continuance. The message that European traders have carried for centuries to Africa has been one of rapacity, of cruelty, of selfishness, and of bad faith. It is a remark of Dr. Livingstone's[1] that the only art that the natives of Africa have acquired from their five hundred years' acquaintance with the Portuguese, has been the art of distilling spirits from a gun-barrel ; and that the only permanent belief they owe to them is the belief that man may sell his brother man ; for this, he says emphatically, is not a native belief, but is only to be found in the track of the Portuguese.

A century and a half before the time of Dr. Livingstone, William Bosman, a chief factor of the Dutch at the castle of Elmina in 1705, and the author of a valuable work on the Coast of Guinea, remarked on the fatal results, which were even then apparent, of the introduction of spirits among the Negroes ; ex-

[1] Livingstone's 'Expedition to the Zambesi,' page 240.

cessive brandy drinking, he said, seemed to be the favourite vice of the Negro, but that of the Gold Coast exceeded all others whom he had ever met. Islam, it should be remembered, had not then approached the Gold Coast: if it had, his statement as to the extent of the evil amongst the Negroes of that part might have needed an important qualification ; and when we reflect on the havoc wrought by the 'desolating flood of ardent spirits' poured into Africa ever since by European merchants, what Christian should not rejoice that what a native African well calls a 'Total Abstinence Association' extends now, owing to the spread of Islam, right across Central Africa from the Nile to Sierra Leone?

The stopping of the Oceanic slave trade by England on the other hand is an enormous benefit to Africa. Like the suppression of slavery itself throughout the British dependencies, it is directly due to the noble exertions of genuine Christian philanthropists ; and it is one of the greatest triumphs which Christianity has ever won over the self-seeking and baser instincts of a great nation. It were to be wished that one could discern any immediate prospect of a wave of such philanthropy sweeping spontaneously through Musalman countries. Musalmans would, as I hope to show hereafter,[1] only

[1] See Lecture IV. p. 328.

be true to the spirit of their Faith in now at length striking the fetter from the slave, and in once and for ever branding the slave hunter and the slave seller as the worst of men. But, if we except the small number of converts made within the limits of their settlements, the suppression of the foreign slave trade has been the only benefit hitherto conferred by Europeans on Africa. The extension of African commerce is of more than doubtful benefit at present. The chief articles that we export from thence are the produce of slave labour, and, what is worse, of a vastly extended slave trade, in the inaccessible interior.[1] Nor is it wholly without reason that in spite of Krapf and Moffat, of Frere, and Livingstone, and of a score of other single-hearted and energetic philanthropists, the white man is still an object of terror, and his professed creed an object of suspicion and repugnance to the Negro race.

Here I must leave this, as I think, one of the most interesting and important parts of my subject. Do not let me be misunderstood. I contend here

---

[1] For the introduction, or rather the invention, of the Slave Trade by the Portuguese in the year 1444, see Helps' 'Spanish Conquest in America,' I. 35 *sq.* ; and the quotation there given from the Chronicle of Azurara, relating the capture of 200 Africans by a Portuguese company at Lagos, and their shipment to Portugal. A disastrous precedent from that time down to the end of the last century, only too fatally followed by all the Christian nations of Europe which had the chance !

only that Islam is a comparative benefit to Africa ; that Christendom till very lately has failed to influence it in any direction extensively for good ; that certain evils, such as drunkenness, always accompany European progress there; and that there is room enough, and degradation enough, amidst its barbarous races for any and for every elevating agency. Making every deduction for possible exaggeration in the accounts I have quoted ; granting freely, what I have never denied, that there is a vast amount of superstition, of impurity, of cruelty among African Mohammedans, as there is in every other semi-civilised, I might add among other highly civilised races, I yet think that enough has been demonstrated to any unbiassed mind to justify the view I have taken. A religion which indisputably has made cannibalism and human sacrifice impossible, which has introduced reading and writing, and, what is more, has given a love for them ; which has forbidden, and, to a great extent, has abolished, immodest dancing and gambling and drinking, which inculcates upon the whole a pure morality, and sets forth a sublime, and at the same time a simple theology, is surely deserving of other feelings than the hatred and the contempt which some portions of our religious press habitually pour upon it.

Truly, if the question must be put, whether it is

Mohammedan or Christian nations that have as yet done most for Africa, the answer must be that it is not the Christian. And if it be asked, again, not what religion is the purest in itself, and ideally the best, for to this there could be but one answer ; but which, under the peculiar circumstances, historical, geographical, and ethnological, is the religion most likely to get hold on a vast scale of the native mind, and so in some measure to elevate the savage character, the same answer must be returned. The question is, indeed, already half answered by a glance at the map of Africa. Mohammedanism has already leavened almost the whole of Africa to within five degrees of the Equator ; and, to the south of it, Uganda, the most civilised state in that part of Central Africa, has just become Mohammedan.[1] A few years ago, a Mosque was built on the shores of the Victoria Nyanza itself, and the Nile, from its source

---

[1] See some interesting remarks by Mr. Francis Galton at a meeting of the British Association at Leeds, on Sept. 22, 1873. I have also to thank him for giving me, in conversation, his experience of Mohammedanism in Africa, and for directing me to the best authorities on the subject. _ Along the coast-line Mohammedanism of a degraded kind has, of course, extended much further South, beyond Zanzibar to Mozambique and the Portuguese colonies. There are Mohammedans to be found even among the Kaffirs and in Madagascar. The original Portuguese settlers found the Arabs established along the coasts of Mozambique and in the interior. They exterminated the former ; but as they failed to dispossess the latter, it is possible, or rather it has lately been proved to be the case, that some of the *terra parum cognita* in the interior is still Mohammedan.

to its mouth, is now, with very few exceptions, a Mohammedan river.

That Mohammedanism may, when mutual misunderstandings are removed, as I hope to show in a future Lecture, be elevated, chastened, purified by Christian influences and a Christian spirit, and that evils such as the slave trade, which are really foreign to its nature, can be put down by the heroic efforts of Christian philanthropists, I do not doubt; and I can, therefore, look forward, if with something of anxiety, with still more of hope, to what seems the destiny of Africa—that Paganism and Devil-worship will die out, and that the main part of the continent, if it cannot become Christian, will become, what is next best to it, Mohammedan.

Anyhow, it is certain that the gains of Mohammedanism, in Africa alone, counterbalance its apparent losses from Russian conquests, and from Proselytism everywhere else; nor can I believe, notwithstanding predictions inspired by the wish, that its work is yet done, or nearly done, in any of the countries, except, perhaps, those of Europe, that have ever owned its sway.

I speak of the apparent losses from Russian conquest, for the onward march of the Russian Colossus through Central Asia, so far from carrying any form of Christianity with it, seems to intensify the

religious convictions of the half-conquered or threatened races.   What was dead in the religion before,
it revives ; to what was only half-alive, it gives fresh
vigour.   Islam has now become with them a patriotism as well as a creed ; and Mr. Gifford Palgrave, an
able and accurate observer, has lately described how
the distinctive precepts of the Mohammedan religion
—those enjoining the observance of the month of
Ramadhan, the reading of the Koran, the pilgrimage
of the Hajj, the abstinence from gaming, from tobacco, and from intoxicating drinks—are now much
more rigidly observed in the debateable territories ;
and, more than this, the Abkhasians with their
immemorial antiquity, and the heroic Circassians
driven from their homes after a desperate struggle by
Muscovite oppression and bad faith, dropping such
traces of Christianity as they had, but carrying with
them a legacy of immortal hate to the creed and
country of their tyrants, have crossed the frontier of
the more liberal Turkish Empire, and coalescing with
Kurds, Turkomans, and Arabs, have settled down in
the uplands of Armenia, and are there forming, as
Mr. Palgrave believes, the nucleus of a new, and
vigorous, and united Mohammedan nation.[1]

In India, again, where the two religions are brought

---

[1] Palgrave's ' Essays on Eastern Questions,' iv. and v.

face to face, and where, if anywhere, we may expect the great drama to play itself out, Mohammedanism gives no sign of yielding. Unlike Brahmanism, which the thousand influences of Western civilisation are sapping in every direction, Mohammedanism, on the contrary, seems to concentrate the strength it already has, and owing to the efforts of its zealous missionaries, is giving symptoms at once of a Revival and of a Reform that may, at any time, change the religious destinies of the country. The Faithful are as courageous, as sincere, as ardently monotheistic as they ever were; witness it the Indian Mutiny, the Wahhabee Revival, and the last terrible argument of assassination. The heroism and self-devotion of our missionaries seem to be wasted on them in vain, and, except in individual cases, I see no sign that it will ever be otherwise. Buddhism and Brahmanism may be driven out of India, but Mohammedanism never, except by the Mohammedan method of the sword.[1]

The most recent historian of India[2] remarks, that 'few impartial observers will deny the fact that, to all appearance, the people of India are drifting, slowly but surely, towards the religion of the Prophet of Arabia rather than towards that Christianity which is freely offered to them, but which they are not

[1] See Appendix to this Lecture.
[2] Talboys Wheeler, in the Preface to his 'History of India.'

prepared to accept.' And if this be true, or nearly true how profound the importance to England, even from an Imperial point of view, of a sympathetic study of the religion which, under her very rule, threatens to become dominant; and how far more profoundly important to the Christian and to the philanthropist to understand and to influence, while yet he may, a system which, long probably after the British Empire in India shall have passed away, will be the chief motive power—for in most Eastern countries religion and national feeling are one and the same thing— among its two hundred millions of inhabitants! Yet, probably, nowhere is there a more profound ignorance of Islam and its founder, and a greater indifference to what it is doing in the world, than in England. Popular preachers and teachers still call the Prophet of Arabia an impostor; and military officers, and even civil servants of the Crown, have gone out to India, passed years there, and returned again, still fancying that Musalmans are idolaters.

Such are the leading facts of Mohammedanism viewed from the outside; and now how are we to account for them?

One thing is certain, that the explanations so readily offered by historians and Christian apologists till within a very recent period will not suffice now. People who think they have nothing to do with a system except to attack it, are not those who can best explain the causes of its vitality or its success. One historian tells us that Mohammedanism triumphed by the mere force of arms ; another, by the use Mohammed made of the tendency so deeply planted in man to fall victims in masses to any well-conceived imposture ; a third traces his success to his skilful plagiarisms from faiths purer than his own ; and a fourth to the elevated morality, or to the lax morality, inculcated in the Koran ; for both of these are strangely enough urged almost in the same breath by the same people : while, lastly, others dwell on the inherent strength of the founder's character and the enthusiasm that must accompany a crusade against idolatry.[1] We feel that most of these have some truth in them ; some of them have much ; and one or two of them are not only not true, but they are the very reverse of the truth. But we also feel that none of them singly, nor all of them together, adequately account for the phenomena they profess to explain.

In treating of Mohammedanism, as remarked by M. Barthélemy St. Hilaire,[2] we have to try *in limine* to discard alike our national and our religious

---

[1] See some of these explanations admirably dealt with by F. D. Maurice, ' Religions of the World,' Lecture I.

[2] ' Mahomet et le Koran,' preface, p. 6.

prejudices. It was not till Mohammedanism had existed for eight hundred years that it was possible to discard the one ; and not till very lately that it was even attempted to discard the other. Since the conquest of Constantinople, or rather since the brilliant naval victory of Don John of Austria at Lepanto, and its final repulse by John Sobieski from the walls of Vienna two hundred and thirty years later, Moham- medanism has ceased, in Europe at least, to be an aggressive and conquering power ; and since then, it has been possible for the states of Christendom to breathe more freely, and to forget the infidel in the ally or the subject.

Religious prejudice is more difficult to overcome. Men who are ardently attached to their own religion find it difficult to judge another dispassionately, and from a neutral point of view. The philosopher who, according to Gibbon's famous aphorism, looked upon all religions of the Roman Empire as equally false, and the magistrate who looked upon all as equally useful, would be alike incapacitated for viewing the Musalman creed from the Musalman stand-point. Perhaps the populace who looked upon all religions as equally true would have been the best judges of the three ; but I doubt whether in this, as in most epigrammatic sentences, something of truth has not been sacrificed to the antithesis. Nature does not

arrange herself in antithetical groups for our conveni-
ence ; and I doubt whether the mass of any people,
at any time, have looked upon all religions as equally
true.

But the comparative study of religion is beginning
to teach, at all events, the more thoughtful of mankind, not indeed that all religions are equally true or
equally elevating, but that all contain some truth ;
that no religion is exclusively good, none exclusively
bad ; that any religion which has a real and continued hold on a large body of mankind must satisfy
a real spiritual need, and is so far good. God is in
all His works, and not the least so in the thoughts
and aspirations of His creatures towards Himself ;
and what we have to do is to feel after Him in
each and all, assured that He is there, even if haply
in our ignorance we can find no trace of Him.

Truly, when we are dealing with religion at all,
even though it be Polytheism or · Fetishism, we are
' treading upon holy ground ; ' and in order that we
may treat that creed, sublime in its simplicity, which
is our special subject, with that union of candour and
of reverence which alone befits it, it is necessary before concluding this introductory Lecture that I should
lay down clearly one principle which must guide us
in our investigation.

It is this, that for the purposes of scientific

investigation, religions must be regarded as differing from one another in degree rather than in kind. This is the one postulate, itself the result of a careful induction, upon which alone the existence of any true science of religion must depend. Without a clear perception of this truth you enter upon the study of the religions of the world, with a preconceived idea, which will colour all your conclusions, and will invalidate them the more gravely, the more favourable those conclusions are to your own creed. The ordinary distinctions of kind, therefore, drawn between true and false, natural and supernatural, revealed and unrevealed religions, are, for our present purpose, unreal and misleading. The fact is, that from one point of view all religions are more or less natural, from another all are more or less supernatural; and all alike are to be treated from the same standpoint, and investigated by the same methods. In the Science of Religion, to quote an expression of Max Müller's used in this place, Christianity ' owns no prescriptive rights, and claims no immunities.' It challenges the freest inquiry; and as it claims to come from God Himself, so it fears not the honest use of any faculties that God has given to man. Christianity is indeed a revelation, and what it really reveals is true; and, so far, if the alternative must needs be put in this shape, no Christian would have any doubt in which category to place his own creed.

But does Christianity claim any such monopoly
of what is good and true as is implied in this crude
classification, or will any one say that there is no
real revelation of God in the noble lives of Confucius
or Buddha, and no fragments of Divine truth in the
pure morality of the systems which they founded ?
Truth, happily for man, is myriad-sided, and happy
he who can catch a far-off glance of the one side of it
presented to him ! Claim, if you like, for the Bible
what the Koran does claim for itself and the Bible
does not—a rigid or a verbal inspiration. Grant that
the truth revealed passed mechanically through the
mind of the sacred writer without contamination and
without alloy, yet who can say,—since the Verities
with which religion deals are all beyond the world of
sense,—that the precise meaning attached by him to
any one word in his creed is the same as that attached
to it by any other ?—*quot homines tot sententiæ.* The
recipient subject colours every object of sensation or
of thought as it passes into it, and is conscious of that
object, not as it entered, but as it has been instantaneously and unconsciously transformed in the alembic
of the mind. In religion, as in external nature, the
human mind is, as Bacon says, an unequal mirror to
the rays of things, mixing its own nature indissolubly
with theirs. And this relative element once admitted
into religion at all, it follows that to divide religions

F

by an impassable barrier into true and false, natural and revealed, is like dividing music into sacred and secular, and history into sacred and profane. It is a division convenient enough for those—the majority of the human race—who are content with an artificial classification, and who care for no religion but their own ; but, for scientific purposes, it is a cross division, it begs the question at issue, and is as unphilosophical as it is misleading.[1]

Nor do Sacred Books, whatever be the theory of inspiration on which they rest, lend to the religion to which they belong any distinction of kind ; they fix the phraseology of a religion, and we are apt to believe that they also fix the thought. They do not do so, however. The 'poetic and literary terms thrown out,' to use Mr. Matthew Arnold's happy expression, by the highest minds at the highest objects of thought, as faint approximations only to the truth respecting them, become enshrined in the Sacred Canon. They are misunderstood, or half understood, even by those who hear them from the Psalmist's or the Prophet's own lips, and in a few years the misunderstanding grows till they become fixed and rigid.[2] Poetic imagery is mistaken for

---

[1] For a full discussion of the ordinary methods of classifying religion see Max Müller's ' Science of Religion,' pp. 123-143.

[2] For illustrations of this, see ' Literature and Dogma,' cap. II. and

scientific exactness, and dim outlines for exhaustive definitions. A virtue is attached to the words themselves, and the thought, which is the jewel, is hidden by the letter, which is only the casket. If it be true that man never knows how anthropomorphic he himself is, still less do sacred writers know the anthropomorphism and the materialism which will eventually be drawn even from their highest and most spiritual utterances. How little did the author of the prayer at the dedication of the temple of Solomon—the grandest assertion, perhaps, in the Old Testament of the infinite power and the infinite goodness of God, His nearness to us and His distance from us—imagine that the time would ever come when it would be held that in that temple alone, and by Jews alone, the Father could be worshipped!

Christians may and must rise from an impartial study of the religions of the world with their belief vastly deepened that their Sacred Books stand as a whole on a far higher level than other Sacred Books, and that the ideal life of Christianity, while it is capable of including the highest ideals of other creeds, cannot itself be attained by any one of them. But the value of this belief will be exactly proportioned

V. p. 123. This part of Mr. Arnold's work, it may be pretty confidently asserted, is done once for all; and its influence will be felt, avowedly or not, throughout the domain of Biblical criticism.

to the extent to which they have been able, for the
purposes of scientific study, to divest themselves of
any arbitrary assumption in the matter ; and they
must also acknowledge that it is possible and natural
for sincere Mohammedans or Buddhists to arrive at
the same conclusions concerning their own faiths.   It
is not easy to be thoroughly convinced of this, or to
act upon it ; for intolerance is the 'natural weed of
the human bosom,' and there is no religion which
does not seem superstitious to those who do not believe in it.[1]

But this belief is far from necessitating in practical
life a religious indifference, nor, however it may seem
so at first sight, is it averse to all missionary efforts.
Missionaries will not cease to exist, nor will they lose
their energy, their enthusiasm, and their self-sacrifice.
But they will go to work in a different way, will view
other religions in a different light, and will test their
success by a different standard.   They will no doubt
be forced to acquiesce in what seems the will of
Providence, that a national religion is as much part
of a man's nature as is the genius of his language, or
the colour of his skin ; they will admit that the pre-

[1] See Grote, VI. p. 156, sq., on the death of Socrates.   The boast
of Cicero, 'Majores nostri superstitionem a religione separaverunt'
(de Nat. Deorum, II. 28), is the natural belief of every one, even
of the Fetish-worshipper, concerning his own, and none but his own,
creed.

cise form of a creed is a matter of prejudice and of
circumstance with most of us, and that, in spite of the
rise of historical religions which have shattered other
faiths and risen upon their ruins, nine-tenths of the
whole human race have died, and will in all probability
continue to die, in the profession of that faith into
which they were born ; but this will no longer seem
to them, as it must seem now, a mysterious and
overwhelming victory of evil over good, which appals
the moral sense, and, if a man be not better than the
letter of his creed, must tend to shake at once his
belief in the Universal Fatherhood of God, and the
true brotherhood of humanity ; they will rather, in
proportion to the strength of their belief in the goodness of God, believe that His creatures cannot grope
after Him, even in the dark, without getting that
light which is sufficient for them ; they will not seek
to eradicate wholly any existing national faith, if only
it be a living one ; nor, as the phrase is, will they aim
at 'bringing its adherents over to Christianity ; ' they
will seek rather to bring Christianity to them, to infuse a Christian spirit into what is, at worst, not an
anti-Christian, but merely a non-Christian, or, it may
be, a half-Christian faith.

The Apostles did not cease to be Jews because
they became Christians, nor did they look up to
Moses less because they reverenced Christ more.

And yet the difference between Judaism and Christianity, between the forms and the ceremonies and the exclusiveness of the one, and the spirituality and the freedom and the universality of the other, is at least as great, as I hope to show, is the difference between a sincere believer in the teaching of the Prophet of Arabia and a humble follower of the character of Christ.

St. Paul, the one model given us in the New Testament of what a missionary should be in dealing with the faith of a cultivated people much dissimilar to his own, a faith, most people would say now, differing in kind as' well as in degree from Christianity, never thought himself of drawing so broad a distinction between the two. He might well have been disposed to do so, for the Polytheism of Athens had long ceased to be an adequate expression of the highest religious life of the people. It was in its decadence even when it had inspired the profoundest utterances of Æschylus or Sophocles; it could not have inspired them then, even had there existed genius like theirs to be inspired. Its oracles were dumb; and yet St. Paul dropped not a word of scorn for the echoes that still lingered, and the flames that were still flickering, on its shattered altars. He did not talk of false gods or of devil-worship, of imposture or of superstition. Those whom our translation calls 'superstitious' he calls 'God-fearing.' He quotes their great authors with sympathy and with respect. He professes only to give articulate utterance to their own thoughts, and to declare more fully to them that God whom, unknowingly, they already worshipped.

And so, again, in writing to the converts to be found even in the metropolis of the world, and, it must be added, the head-quarters of its vices, while he lashes its moral iniquities and its religious corruptions with an unsparing hand, yet, with a toleration wholly alien to the Jewish race, and without forfeiting his supreme allegiance to his Master, he strikes at the root of the impassable distinction between revealed and unrevealed religion, by pointing out that those who, not having the law, yet did by nature the things contained in the law, were in truth a law unto themselves. He showed that the Eternal could reveal Himself as well by His unwritten as by His written law, and that the voice of conscience is, in very truth, to everyone who follows it, the voice of the living God.

The missionaries of the future, therefore, will try to penetrate to the common elements which, they will have learned, underlie all religions alike, and make the most of those. They will be able, with a sympathy which is real because it is drawn from a knowledge of the history of their own faith, to point out the abuses which have crept, and always will creep, into an originally spiritual creed. They will inculcate in their teaching, and exhibit in their lives, as they do now, something of that highest morality which they have learned from their Master, and which they will then have learned is the very essence of their faith, and which, in its broad outlines at least, in the ' secret ' as well as in the ' method ' of Jesus,[1] may adapt itself to the wants of every nation and every creed.

They will never, therefore, think it necessary to present Christianity to those of an alien creed as a collection of defined yet mysterious doctrines which must be accepted whole or not at all, but will rather be content to show them Christ Himself as He appeared to His earliest disciples—before the mists of metaphysics had gathered round His head, and the watchwords of theology had half hidden Him from the view—glorious in His moral beauty, sublime in His

---

[1] ' Of the all-importance of righteousness there is a knowledge in Mohammedanism, but of the method and secret of Jesus, by which alone is righteousness possible, hardly any sense at all.'—' Literature and Dogma,' p. 343. There is substantial truth in this ; but few can read Mr. Arnold's own account of what he conceives the secret and method of Jesus to have been, without feeling that all the higher religions of the world,—any religion, in fact, which controlling the lower part of man's nature and stimulating the higher, makes him to be at peace with himself, which gives hope in adversity, and calmness in the prospect of death, must contain much both of the one and of the other.

self-surrender, Divine in His humanity and by reason
of it. And they may then leave it to the moral
sense of some, at least, in every section of the race
whose greatest glory and Ideal Representative He is,
to judge of Him aright, and to recognise in His person the supreme and the final Revelation of God.
Here, in the ambition to set before the eyes of all a
higher Ideal, and a more perfect example than any
they have yet known ; in the proclamation of the
truth, which Christ came to proclaim, of the universal
Fatherhood, and the perfect love of God—here is
ample work for the enthusiasm of humanity ; in this
sense Christ may live again upon the earth, and in
this sense, and only in this, is it likely that Christianity will overspread the world. I have premised
this much, even at the risk of anticipating some of the
conclusions to which we shall, I believe, ultimately
come, because I think it necessary to prevent any
misunderstanding as to my point of view.

ἐξ οἴων οἷος ; how far the way was prepared for
Mohammed by circumstances, and what part he himself bore in the great revolution that goes by his
name ; what we are to say on the nature of his mission,
on the much-disputed question of his sincerity, of the
inconsistencies in his career and the blots upon it,
this will form the subject of my next Lecture.

LECTURE II.

FEBRUARY 21, 1874.

MOHAMMED.

Μεγάλων ἑαυτὸν ἀξιοῖ ἄξιος ὤν.—ARISTOTLE.

There goeth the son of Abdallah, who hath his conversation in the heavens.—THE KURAISH.

A COMPLETE history of the opinions that have been held by Christians about Mohammed and Mohammedanism would not be an uninstructive chapter, however melancholy, in the history of the human mind. To glance for a moment at a few of them.

During the first few centuries of Mohammedanism, Christendom could not afford to criticise or explain ; it could only tremble and obey. But when the Saracens had received their first check in the heart of France, the nations which had been flying before them, faced round, as a herd of cows will sometimes do when the single dog that has put them to flight is called off ; and though they did not yet venture to fight, they could at least calumniate their retreating foe.

Drances-like, they could manufacture calumnies and victories at pleasure :—

> ' Quæ tuto tibi magna volant ; dum distinet hostem
> Agger murorum, nec inundant sanguine fossæ.'

The disastrous retreat of Charles the Great through Roncesvalles, and the slaughter of his rear-guard by the Gascons, is turned by Romance mongers and Troubadours into a signal victory of his over the Saracens ; Charles, who never went beyond Pannonia, is credited, in the following century, with a successful Crusade to the Holy Sepulchre, and even with the sack of Babylon ! The age of Christian chivalry had not yet come, and was not to come for two hundred years.

In the romance of 'Turpin,' quoted by Renan, Mohammed, the fanatical destroyer of all idolatry, is turned himself into an idol of gold, and, under the name of Mawmet, is reported to be the object of worship at Cadiz ; and this not even Charles the Great, Charles the Iconoclast, the destroyer of the Irmansul, in his own native Germany, would venture to attack from fear of the legion of demons which guarded it. In the song of Roland, the national Epic of France, referring to the same events, Mohammed appears with the chief of the Pagan Gods on the one side of him and the chief of the Devils on the other ; a curious anticipation, perhaps, of the view of Satanic inspiration taken by Sir William Muir. Marsilles, Khalif of Cordova, is supposed to worship him as a god, and his favourite form of adjuration is made to be ' By Jupiter, by Mohammed, and by Apollyon,'—strange metamorphosis and strange collocation! Human sacrifices are offered to him, if nowhere else indeed, in the imagination and assertions of Christian writers of the tenth and eleventh centuries, under the various names of Bafum, or Maphomet, or Mawmet ; and in the same spirit Malaterra, in his ' History of Sicily,' describes that island as being, when under Saracenic rule, 'a land wholly given to idolatry,'[1] and the expedition of the Norman Roger Guiscard is characterised as a crusade against idol worship. Which people were the greater idolaters, any candid reader of the Italian annalists of this time, collected by Muratori, can say. Even Marco Polo, the most charming and, where his religious prejudices or his partiality for the ' Great Khan ' do not come in, the most trustworthy of travellers, yet speaks of the Musalmans whom he met everywhere in Central Asia and in China as ' worshippers of Mahommet.'[2] It is not a little curious that both the English and French languages still bear witness to the popular misapprehension ; the French

[1] B. II. 1. ' Terram idolis deditam.'

[2] Marco Polo, II. 196, 200, 266. Colonel Yule, in his gorgeous and exhaustive edition of the Venetian traveller, quotes, in illustration

by the word 'Mahomerie'; the English by the word 'mummery,' still used for absurd or superstitious rites.[1] Nor has a Mohammedan nothing to complain of in the etymology and history, little known or forgotten, of the words 'Mammetry' and 'Paynim,' 'termagant' and 'miscreant';[2] but to these I can only refer in passing.

of the misconception, from Baudouin de Sebourg, where a Christian lady who is renouncing her faith before Saladin is made to say

'Mahom voel aourer, apportez le moi cha.'

= I wish to worship Mahommed; bring him to me here. Whereupon Saladin commanded

'Qu'on aportast Mahom; et celle l'aoura.'

He also remarks that even Don Quixote, who ought to have known better, celebrates the feat of Rinaldo, who carried off, in spite of forty Moors, a golden image of Mohammed! In keeping with Marco Polo's calling Musalmans 'Worshippers of Mahommet' are his other remarks on the subject (I. 70, 74, &c.): 'Marvel not that the Saracens hate the Christians; for the accursed law that Mahommet gave them commands them to do all the mischief in their power to all other descriptions of people, and especially to Christians. See then what an evil law and what naughty commandments they have! But in such fashion the Saracens act throughout the world.' Perhaps the best commentary on this, is, that Marco Polo himself passed unguarded through almost all Musalman countries, and came out unharmed in person and in property.

[1] Renan, 'Études d'Histoire Religieuse,' p. 223, note.

[2] Mammetry, a contraction of Mahometry, used in early English for any false religion, especially for a worship of idols, insomuch that Mammet or Mawmet came to mean an idol. In Shakespeare the name is extended to mean a doll: Juliet, for instance, is called by her father 'a whining mammet.' See Trench 'On Words,' p. 112. Paynim = Pagan or Heathen. Termagant, a term applied now only to a brawling woman, was originally one of the names given to the supposed idol of the Mohammedans. Miscreant, originally 'a man who believes otherwise,' acquired its moral significance from the hatred of the

In the twelfth century 'the god Mawmet passes into the heresiarch Mahomet,' [1] and, as such, of course he occupies a conspicuous place in the 'Inferno.' Dante places him in his ninth circle among the sowers of religious discord ; his companions being Fra Dolcino, a communist of the fourteenth century, and Bertrand de Born, a fighting Troubadour: his flesh is torn piecemeal from his limbs by demons who re-peat their round in time to re-open the half-healed wounds. The romances of Baphomet, so common in the fourteenth and fifteenth centuries, attribute any and every crime to him, just as the Athanasians did to Arius. 'He is a debauchee, a camel stealer, a Cardinal, who having failed to obtain the object of every Cardinal's ambition, invents a new religion to revenge himself on his brethren !' [2]

With the leaders of the Reformation, Mohammed, the greatest of all Reformers, meets with little sym-pathy, and their hatred of him, as perhaps was natu-ral, seems to vary inversely as their knowledge. Luther doubts whether he is not worse than Leo ; Melancthon believes him to be either Gog or Magog,

---

Saracens which accompanied the Crusades. The story of Blue Beard, the associations connected with the name 'Mahound,' and the dislike of European chivalry in Mediæval times for the Mare—the favourite animal of the Arabs—are other indications of the same thing.

[1] Renan, loc. cit.

[2] Renan, p. 224. According to Bayle (Dictionary, Art. 'Mo-hammed,') Benvenuti of Imola started this idea.

and probably both.[1]   The Reformers did not see that
the Papal party, fastening on the hatred of priestcraft
and formalism which was common doubtless to Islam
and to Protestantism, would impute to both a common
hatred of Christianity, even as the Popes had accused
the iconoclastic Emperors of Constantinople eight
centuries before.

The language of the Catholic Church, with the
accumulated wisdom and responsibilities of fifteen
centuries, was not more refined, nor its knowledge of
Islam more profound, than was that of the Protestants
of yesterday.   Genebrard, for instance, a famous
Catholic controversialist, reproaches Mohammed with
having written his Koran in Arabic, and not in Hebrew,
Greek, or Latin, 'the only civilised languages.'   Why
did he do so ? asks he.   'Because,' he replies to his

---

[1] See 'Quarterly Review,' Art. Islam, by Deutsch, No. 254, p.
296. Cf. Shakespeare's view of him,

> 'The prince of darkness is a gentleman :
> Modo he's call'd, and Mahu ' : *i.e.* Mahound.

and,

'five fiends have been in poor Tom at once : of lust, as Obidicut ;
Hobbididance, prince of dumbness ; Mahu, of stealing ; Modo, of
murder.'—King Lear, Act III. Scene IV. ; and Act IV. Scene I.

As a sample of the controversial works of the theologians of the
Reformed Church on this subject, take the following modest title-page
of a ponderous work written in 1666 :—'Anti-christus Mahometes:
ubi non solum per Sanctam Scripturam, ac Reformatorum testimonia,
verum etiam per omnes alios probandi modos et genera, plenè, fusè,
invictè solidèque demonstratur MAHOMETEM esse unum illum verum,
magnum, de quo in Sacris fit mentio, ANTICHRISTUM.'

own question, ' Mohammed was a beast, and only knew a language that was suited to his bestial condition !' Nor are some of his other arguments more convincing, however seriously they were meant.

Now, too, arose the invention, the maliciousness of which was only equalled by its stupidity, but believed by all who wished to believe it—of the dove trained to gather peas placed in the ear of Mohammed,[1] that people might believe that he was inspired by the Holy Ghost—inspired, it would seem, by the very Being whose separate existence it was the first article of his creed to deny ! In the imagination of Biblical commentators later on, and down to this very day, he divides with the Pope the credit or discredit of being the subject of special prophecy in the books of Daniel and Revelation, that magnificent series of tableaux, a part of which, on the principle that ' a prophecy may mean whatever comes after it,' has been tortured into agreement with each successive act of the drama of history ; while from another part, lovers of the mysterious have attempted to cast, and, in spite of disappointment, will always continue to cast, the horoscope of the future. He is Antichrist, the Man of Sin, the Little Horn, and I know not what

---

[1] A similar story is told of the great Shamil ; only in this case it is Mohammed himself who takes the form of a dove, and imparts his commands to the Hero.

besides; nor do I think that a single writer, with the one strange exception of the Jew Maimonides, till towards the middle of the eighteenth century, treats of him as otherwise than a rank impostor and false prophet.

Things did not much improve even when it was thought advisable, before passing judgment, or for the purpose of registering one already passed, to ascend as nearly as possible to the fountain-head. The Koran was translated into French by André du Ryer in 1649, and by the Abbé Maracci in 1698. Maracci, the confessor of a Pope, of course dealt with the Koran chiefly from a Romanist point of view: indeed he accompanies his translation with what he calls a ' Refutatio Alcorani,' and a very voluminous and calumnious one it is; and when a certain Englishman, named Alexander Ross, ventured to translate the French version of du Ryer into English, he thought it necessary to preface his work by what he calls ' a needful caveat or admonition,' which runs thus: ' Good reader, the great Arabian inpostor, now at last, after a thousand years, is, by the way of France, arrived in England, and his Alcoran, or Gallimaufry of Errors, (a Brat as deformed as the Parent, and as full of Heresies as his scald head was of scurf,) hath learned to speak English.' And one who has probably as much right to speak upon the subject as any

living Englishman,[1] after quoting this refined description of the Koran and its author, remarks that, 'though
the education of two centuries has chastened the style
of our national literature and added much to our
knowledge of the East, there is good ground for supposing that the views of Alexander Ross are in accordance substantially with the views still held by the
great majority of Englishmen.' That he is not far
wrong, I would adduce as evidence from amongst
Churchmen the tone habitually taken by a large
part of the religious press when dealing with any
subject connected with Islam ; and from among
Nonconformists the following hymn written by
Charles Wesley for 'believers interceding' for Mohammedans, and still, as I am informed, used by some
of them at their religious services :—

> 'The smoke of the infernal cave
> Which half the Christian world o'erspread,
> Disperse, thou heavenly light, and save
> The souls by that impostor led—
> That Arab thief, as Satan bold,
> Who quite destroyed thy Asian fold.

> 'Oh may thy blood once sprinkled cry
> For those who spurn thy sprinkled blood !
> Assert thy glorious Deity,
> Stretch out thine arm, thou triune God !
> The Unitarian fiend expel,
> And chase his doctrine back to hell.'

---

[1] Dr. G. P. Badger, in the 'Contemporary Review' for June 1875 ;
Art. Mohammed and Mohammedanism.

France and England may, however, in spite of the
'needful caveat or admonition' of Alexander Ross,
and the popular misconceptions which are still afloat
upon the subject, divide the credit of having been the
first to take a different view, and to have begun that
critical study of Arabian history or literature which,
in the hands of Gibbon and of Muir, of Caussin de
Perceval and of St. Hilaire, of Weil and of Sprenger,
has at length placed the materials for a fair and unbiassed judgment within the reach of everyone.
Most other writers of the 18th century, such as
·Dean Prideaux and d'Herbelot, Boulainvilliers and
Voltaire, and some subsequent Bampton lecturers
and Arabic professors, have approached the subject
only to prove a thesis. Mohammed was to be either
a hero or an impostor ; they have held a brief either
for the prosecution or the defence ; and from them,
therefore, we learn much that has been said about
Mohammed, but comparatively little of Mohammed
himself.

It is not unnatural that in some cases extravagant
detraction should have given rise to equally extravagant eulogy, and that the Prophet of Arabia should
have been, more than once, held up to admiration as
almost the ideal of humanity. But this is a length to
which it is quite unnecessary for me to go, and which is
inconsistent alike with what Mohammed claimed for

himself and with recorded facts. These facts are now all or nearly all before us ; and what is most needed now is, as has been well remarked by an able writer in the ' Academy,' the mind that can see their true meaning, 'that can grasp the complex character of the great man whose life they mark out, like a grand but intricate mosaic.'

The founder of the reaction was Gagnier, a Frenchman by birth, but an Englishman by adoption. Educated in Navarre, where he had early shown a mastery of more than one Semitic language, he became Canon of St. Geneviève at Paris ; on a sudden he turned Protestant, came to England, and attacked Catholicism with all the zeal of a recent convert. Having been appointed to the Chair of Arabic at Oxford, he proceeded to write a history of Mohammed, founded on the work of Abulfeda, the earliest and most authentic of Arabic historians then known.

The translations· of the Koran into two different European languages by Sale and Savary soon followed; and from these works, combined with the vast number of facts contained in Sale's Introductory Discourse, Gibbon, who was not an Arabic scholar himself, drew the materials for his splendid chapter, the most masterly of his 'three master-pieces of biography,' Athanasius, Julian, and Mohammed. 'He has de-

scended on the subject in the fulness of his strength,'
has been inspired by it, and has produced a sketch
which, in spite of occasional uncalled-for sarcasms
and characteristic innuendoes, must be the delight
and the despair even of those who have access, as
we now have, thanks especially to Sprenger and
Muir, to vast stores of information denied to him.
But Gibbon's unfair and unphilosophic treatment of
Christianity has, perhaps, prevented the world from
doing justice to his generally fair and philosophic
treatment of Mohammedanism ; and, as a consequence of this, most Englishmen, who do not condemn the Arabian prophet unheard, derive what
favourable notions of him they have, not from
Gibbon, but from Carlyle. Make as large deductions
as we will on the score of Carlyle's peculiar views on
' Heroes and Hero-worship,' how many of us can
recall the shock of surprise, the epoch in our intellectual and religious life, when we found that he
chose for his ' Hero as prophet,' not Moses, or Elijah,
or Isaiah, but the so-called impostor Mohammed !

And now, before we go further, let us leap back in
imagination to the times preceding the birth of Mohammed, and enquire what the country was like from
which he sprung, what were the aptitudes of the
Arabs, their tastes, their organisation, their religions ;
we shall then, perchance, be better able to approach

the proper subject of this and the succeeding Lectures, the character of the Prophet himself and of the creed which he founded; and to apply that historical and relative judgment to the matter which is essential to it. 'Man is the creature of circumstances,' says the English aphorism: if we know what the antecedents of Mohammed were, we shall be better able to judge how far the proverb is true or adequate—how far, that is, Mohammed was formed by circumstances, and how far he moulded them by his mighty will and his keen insight.

The most distinctive feature of the countless tribes who have, from time immemorial, wandered over the vast and arid plains of Arabia, and the one most difficult for us to realise, is their immobility.[1] Some few there were among them who, like the inhabitants of Mecca, lived, in the main, by legitimate commerce; some few also, like the inhabitants of Medina, who lived by the cultivation of the soil; but the vast majority were shepherds of the desert. This was the air in which alone they could breathe freely, here they could wander at will. Nowhere in the world, says Sprenger in a charming passage, is a man happier than in the desert: the sky is always clear;

---

[1] For an admirable account, to which I am much indebted, of the characteristics of the Arabs, see the first two chapters of Dozy's 'Histoire des Musalmans d'Espagne.'

the air, even in hot weather, is strengthening and refreshing ; every breath we draw makes us thank God for life. A native of the Alps himself, though he would often amidst the burning sands of Arabia dream of glaciers, and long for the echoes of the Jüdel, he confesses that neither the air of his own Alps nor that of the Himalayas was so strengthening or so vivifying as that of the desert. Such a climate, he goes on to remark, had a powerful influence, physical and intellectual, on its inhabitants. They were elastic and quick ; their horses were swifter than any other horses, and very healthy. No king of Hira, so their historians say, ever died of ill-health brought on by natural causes! and Ibn Chaldun seriously attributes the forty years' wanderings of the Israelites in the desert to the natural feebleness of a race born elsewhere. It required a new generation born in the desert and endowed with the strength which the desert alone can give to conquer Canaan![1]

The Camel, it has been said, is the Arab's ship of the desert ; the caravan is his fleet. Agriculture the Arabs looked down upon as tethering the cultivator, like a slave, to the soil on which he laboured. Commerce was in better repute with them, but only

[1] Sprenger, III., Preface, viii. ; and chap. xvii. 3. Compare also the testimony of Mr. Layard in his popular condensation of his works on Nineveh.

because it gave more material for plunder : the foolish
merchants toiled, and the wise and wandering Bedouins entered into their toils.   What the Arabs
were in the time of Abraham, that they were in the
time of Mohammed ; and that, be it remembered, the
bulk of those who cling to their native deserts are, in
spite of the vast impulse given by him to the Arab
nation, to this very day ; that also, it is not too much
to add, they will be hundreds of years hence.   They
feed on the same food, wield the same weapons of
war, water their cattle at the same springs as the
Patriarchs themselves.   The accounts of Niebuhr and
of Burckhardt, of Burton and of Layard, are thus the
best commentaries on much of the Koran, on much also
of the Book of Genesis.   The Bedouins of the desert
call themselves Musalmans, but they value freedom
too much to trouble themselves about obeying the
Musalman laws.   'They pray, many of them,' says
Burckhardt, 'not five times a day, but never.'   The
Bedouin, though not the noblest, is yet a noble type
of humanity.   A stranger to the idea of progress, he
despises the hurry and the flurry, the breathless race
for wealth, the luxuries and the appliances, and the
accumulated knowledge of facts, that go to make up
what we call our civilisation.   It is surely a relief to
turn, if only for a moment, to the supreme content-
ment of an Arab with his lot, to his carelessness of the

future, to his ineffable dignity of repose from the feverish activity, the constant straining after an ideal which can never be satisfied, the 'life at high pressure,' which is the characteristic of the more active, but hardly the more highly gifted, races of the West.

It is not that the Arab lacks the intelligence or the power to change his condition—he does not wish, or rather he wishes not, to do so. He looks upon himself as the highest type of creation,[1] upon his language as the most perfect language ; and in this, if Arabic scholars are to be believed, and if the music of the Koran is what they say it is, he is not so far wrong. Upon him, and upon him alone, as he proudly asserts, God has bestowed four privileges-- that their turbans should be their diadems, their tents their homes, their swords their entrenchments, and their poems their laws. Passionately fond of liberty, the Arab may well boast that, whatever the cause, his country has never been conquered by foreign foes. Alexander dreamed, but only dreamed, of conquering Arabia. Trajan struck medals to commemorate his conquests of it ; but what he conquered was not Arabia at all, but only an outlying province of it, and that he did not attempt to hold.

Nor are the individual and the social liberty of the Arabs less than their national. Split up into

[1] Dozy, Vol. I. p. 4.

innumerable tribes, constantly at war with each other, each tribe has a Sheik of its own, but that Sheik is elected by the members of his tribe, not for his birth or for his wealth, but for his individual merits. When elected, he has duties only, not rights; influence, not power. His tent is pitched on that side of an encampment on which an enemy is most likely to attack it, or a friend to visit it. To be the first to resist an enemy, or to do honour to a guest, this is at once his duty and his privilege. He can neither issue an order nor inflict a punishment of his own free will. He must summon the heads of all the families of the tribe, and, sitting in council with them, he is only *primus inter pares.* The tie most sacred in the eyes of the Arab is that which binds him to his tribe: he calls his fellow tribesmen his brothers, he will share his last morsel or kill his last sheep to relieve any one of them who is in distress.[1] He will avenge any insult or injury offered to him as if it were his own.

A true Bedouin despises wealth, for his only property consists of flocks and herds. The descent of a band of plunderers may hurry it all away, and the despoiled owner must wait patiently till his turn comes for reprisals. Amongst such a people hospitality and open-heartedness would be not only one of the higher, but also one of the easier and commoner

[1] Dozy, p. 10.

virtues. 'Let the torrent of your liberality escape from your hand,' says the Arab proverb, 'without the sound of it reaching your ear.' A man who had ruined himself by his open-handed generosity was held in high honour, while he who had amassed riches was despised and hated. 'From the hand of the greedy falls not even a grain of mustard seed,' says one Arab proverb. 'The miser puts a bridle even on the rats of his house,' says a second, meaning that he tries to guard even what cannot be guarded. 'The miser is like a glow-worm's spark, which gives neither light nor heat that is good for anything,' says a third.[1]

Next to the passion for liberty, the affection for their tribe, and the duty of hospitality, came, in the breast of a true-born Bedouin, the appetite for plunder, the respect for valour, the love of poetry and eloquence. The scanty sustenance which an arid soil yielded they were fain to eke out by plundering those who conducted caravans along the coast of Hedjaz to exchange the spices and precious stones of India, of Hadramaut, or of Yemen, with the manufactures of Bozra and Damascus; their hand was against every man, and every man's hand was against them; yet even in their plundering excursions

---

[1] Quoted by M. Scholl, 'L'Islam et son Fondateur,' p. 12, 13, from Meidani's collection of ancient Arabic Proverbs.

there was a contempt of danger and a sensibility of
honour which lends a charm to all we hear of their
loves and their wars, their greed and their hospitality,
their rapine and their revenge. The Bedouin has
been the same in these respects in all ages. ' Be
good enough to take off that garment of yours,' says
the Bedouin robber politely to his victim ; 'it is
wanted by my wife ; ' and the victim submits with as
good a grace as he can muster to the somewhat un-
reasonable demands of a hypothetical lady.   When a
woman is the victim, no Bedouin brigand, however
rude, will be ill-mannered enough to lay hands upon
her.   He begs her to take off the garment on which
he has set his heart, and he then retires to a distance
and stands with eyes averted, lest he should do violence to her modesty.[1]

El Mutanabi, a poet, prophet, and warrior, three
hundred years after the Hijrah, but who, no doubt, had
his prototypes before it, was journeying with his son
through a country infested by robbers, and proposed
to seek a place of refuge for the night : ' Art thou
then that Mutanabi,' exclaimed his slave, ' who wrote
these lines,—

> ' I am known to the night, and the wild and the steed,
>   To the guest and the sword, to the paper and the reed ? '

---

[1] See an exquisite story illustrating the true knightly courtesy of
Othman, son of Zalha, to Omm Salama, who afterwards became a wife
of the Prophet. (Sprenger, II. 535–538.)

The poet-warrior felt the stain like a wound, and throwing himself down to sleep where he then was, met his death at the hands of the robbers.[1] The passion indeed for indiscriminate plunder had, before the time of Mohammed, so far given way to the growing love of commerce that a kind of Treuga Dei, or Truce of God, was observed, in theory at least, during four months of the year. But what the law forbade then, *ex hypothesi* it allowed at other times, and it is likely that the enforced abstention gave, at once, the zest of novelty and a clear conscience to the purveyors of the trade when the four months were over.

Nor were the Arabs as uncivilised in other respects as has often been supposed. They were as passionately fond of poetry as they were of war and plunder. What the Olympic Games did for Greece in keeping up the national feeling, as distinct from tribal independence, in giving a brief cessation from hostilities, and acting as a literary centre, that the annual fairs at Okatz and Mujanna were to Arabia. Here tribes made up their dissensions, exchanged prisoners of war, and, most important of all, competed with one another in extempore poetic contests. Even in the 'times of ignorance,' each

---

[1] Burton's 'Pilgrimage to Mecca,' III. p. 60, where he tells this story and translates the Arabic lines. See the whole of chap. XXIV. for a graphic account drawn from personal observation of Bedouin knight errantry, and poetry, and generosity.

tribe produced its own poet-laureate ; and the most
ready and the best saw his poem transcribed in letters
of gold,[1] or suspended on the wall of the entrance of
the Kaaba, where it would be seen by every pilgrim
who might visit the most sacred place in the country.
But the Arab poetry, rich as it was in sparkling
gems, in melody, and in all the graces of style, and
passionately fond as the Arab was of it, never rose
to the dignity of the epic.   It was lyrical and descrip-
tive only : their amours and their love feuds, the
joys of the dice-box and the wine-cup, the heroic deeds
of their ancestors, the birth of a son or of a foal of
generous breed—these were the themes of their
greatest poets, and these the wild tribes of the
desert flocked to hear.   'The Kings of the Arabs,'
said the Khalif Omar, 'are their orators and poets,
those who practise and who celebrate all the virtues
of a Bedouin.'[2]

What those virtues were, the foregoing sketch may
indicate; perchance we may think some among them to
be vices; but there is a yet darker side to the picture,
which called aloud for the hand of a reformer, if such
could ever be found in so unchangeable a people.

---

[1] Called Moállacât. Sprenger and Deutsch agree that this word
means not 'suspended,' but 'strung loosely together,' and question
the truth of the story of the suspension in the 'Kaaba.' Some of these
poems, as, for instance, that of the poet Labyd, still survive, and are a
standing proof of the untaught poetic genius of the Arabs.

[2] Quoted by Dozy, p. 8.

To forgive an injury was with the Arabs the sign of a craven spirit; revenge was a religious duty; blood feuds were handed down from father to son as the most sacred of obligations; the crime, or it might be the misfortune, of an individual involved a whole tribe in its consequences; and the claim was sometimes not considered to be satisfied till the whole tribe had been swept away. Arab writers celebrate with patriotic pride this national characteristic, and attribute it to the flesh of the camel, that most surly and unforgiving of creatures, which forms the main animal food of the Bedouin.[1] Drunkenness was, as many poems which have been preserved to us indicate, very common, and very fatal in its effects. The passion for gambling was so reckless that a man would often stake all his possessions, and after losing them at a throw, would next stake his freedom, and, losing that also, become a slave.[2]

But the most barbarous practice of these 'times of ignorance,' for so the Arabs after the time of Mohammed call with proud humility the times before him, was the burying alive of female children as soon as they were born; or, worse still, as sometimes happened, after they had attained the age of six

---

[1] Sale, 'Preliminary Discourse,' I. 22.

[2] See 'Christian Remembrancer' for January 1855, by Dr. Cazenove, p. 68.

years. The father was generally himself the murderer. 'Perfume and adorn,' he would say to the mother, 'your daughter, that I may convey her to her mothers.' This done, he led her to a pit dug for the purpose, bade her look down into it, and then, as he stood behind her, pushed her headlong in, and then filling up the pit himself levelled it with the rest of the ground ! It is said that the only occasion on which a certain Othman ever shed a tear was when his little daughter whom he was burying alive wiped the dust of the grave earth from his beard.   This inhuman practice may have originated from motives of domestic economy, or from fear of dishonour to the tribe if a woman should be taken captive by the enemy, or, what is more likely, from the general disregard of female life and rights.   Anyhow it had once been very common, and in Mohammed's time it was still not rare, even among the Kuraish.[1]

Some women there were who, like the Arabian poetess El Khunsa, by sheer force of character or of genius managed to assert themselves even in 'the times of ignorance.'   But the majority were in the most degraded position, worse even than that in which they were under the laws of Manu in Hindustan, or than they are in Musalman states now.   A woman had no rights ; she could not inherit property ; her person

[1] Sale, 'Preliminary Discourse,' V. 92.

formed part of the inheritance which came to the heir of her husband, and he was entitled to marry her against her will.   Hence sprung the impious marriages of sons with their step-mothers and others of an even worse character which Mohammed so peremptorily forbade.   Polygamy was universal and quite unrestricted ; equally so was divorce, at least as far as the man was concerned.   We read of a certain woman Omm-Charijeh, who had distinguished herself, even amongst the Arabs, by having forty husbands.   A husband could dismiss his wife on the merest whim, and then, if he so pleased, might recall her again under the influence of a similar whim.   A few ancient Arab proverbs collected by an American Missionary in Syria, Dr. Jessup,[1] will perhaps illustrate, more forcibly than any statements of my own, the degradation of woman in the times preceding Mohammed.   Here are some of them :—

‘ To send women before to the other world is a benefit.’
‘ The best son-in-law is the grave.’
‘ Obedience to women will have to be repented of.’
‘ A man can bear anything but the mention of his wives.’
‘ The heart of woman is given to folly.’
‘ Leave not a girl nor a green pasture unguarded.’
‘ Women are the whips of Satan.’
‘ Our mother forbids *us* to err, and herself runs into error.’
‘ My father does the fighting, and my mother the talking about it.’

---

[1] ‘Women of the Arabs,’ cap. I.

H

Such then were the leading social characteristics of the nation from which Mohammed sprang. It is important for us to bear carefully in mind the difficulties that were in the Prophet's way, that we may be better able hereafter to appreciate the manner in which he dealt with them, and the extent to which he was able to overcome them.

Let us now turn to the religious systems and ideas which prevailed in Arabia before Mohammed's time, and which he, like every other reformer whose work is to last, would have to take into account.

The two highest religions of the world, Judaism and Christianity, were not unknown in Arabia. The destruction of Jerusalem by Titus had caused a very general migration of Jews from Palestine, southwards and eastwards, beyond the limits of the Roman Empire ; and from that time onwards the northern part of Arabia was dotted over by Jewish colonies. In the third century a whole Arabian tribe, even in the south of the peninsula, had adopted the Jewish faith, and the history of Mohammed proves that the neighbourhood of Yathrib[1] contained many Jewish tribes, which, though they maintained in the land of their exile that proud religious isolation which was

---

[1] Not called Medina, *i.e.* Medinat-an-Nabi, 'the City of the Prophet,' till after the Hijrah. The Arab capital of Malta (now Civita Vecchia) bore for several centuries the same name, Medina.

their national birthright, were not without their influence on Arab politics.

Christianity may have been introduced into Arabia by St. Paul himself. 'Neither went I up into Jerusalem to them which were apostles before me,' he says to his Galatian converts, 'but I went into Arabia.' Anyhow, the persecutions which sprang up in the Eastern Church in the third century drove large numbers of Christians, chiefly those of the Jacobite persuasion, into this land of liberty and free toleration. ' I reign,' said Marthan, a king of Yemen in the fourth century, ' over men's bodies, not over their minds. I require of my subjects that they should obey my government: of their opinions God alone will judge.' Noble words, but mistimed by above eleven centuries, and how imperfectly carried out even now ! Accordingly, we hear of several tribes of Yemen becoming to some extent Christianised. We hear of churches, and even of bishops, at Djafar and at Nadjran. But Christianity seems to have taken even less hold than Judaism of the Arab character. Controversies on the minutest points of Christian doctrine absorbed all the energies of those who never thought of leading a Christian life ; and the Khalif Ali was not far wrong when he said of a tribe in which Christianity seemed more than elsewhere to be the dominant religion,

' The Taglibites are not Christians: they owe nothing to Christianity except the custom of drinking wine.' [1]

Thus neither Christianity nor Judaism ever struck deep root in the Arabian soil. The people were not suited to them, or they were not suited to the people. They lived on, on sufferance only, till a faith, which to the Arabs should be the more living one, should sweep them away.

I have admitted in my first Lecture that the religion of Mohammed was in its essence not original. Mohammed never said it was : he called it a revival of the old one, a return to the primitive creed of Abraham ; and there is reason to believe that both the great religions of the Eastern world existing in his time, Sabæanism, that is, and Magianism, had been, in their origin at least, vaguely monotheistic. They had passed through the inevitable stages of spirituality, misunderstanding, decline, and, lastly, intentional corruption, till the God whom Abraham, according to the well-known Musalman legend, had been the first to worship, because, while He had made the stars and sun to rise and set, He never rose nor set Himself, had withdrawn behind them altogether ; the heavenly bodies, from being symbols, had become the thing symbolised ; temples were erected in their honour, and idols filled the temples.

[1] Dozy, p. 20.

And, as with Sabæanism, so with Magianism ;
Ormuzd and Ahriman were no longer the principles
brought into existence, or existing, by the permission
of the one true God, who, as Zoroaster had taught,
would tolerate neither temples, nor altars, nor symbols ; worshipped only on the hill-tops with the eye
of faith, quickened though it might be by the glory
of the rising or setting sun presented to the bodily
eye. Fire had itself become the Divinity ; and what
offering could be more acceptable to such a God
than the human victim, overwhelmed by the mysterious flame, whose divine power he denied ?

And, combined with these two religions which
had been spiritual in their origin, and, probably, more
prominent and popular than either, was the grossest
Fetishism. The idea indeed of one God was not
altogether lost ; but a number of inferior divinities
were worshipped as mediators with Him, or, as the
Koran indignantly expresses it, as ' companions ' to
Him. Stocks, stones, trees, shapeless masses of
dough—such were some of the objects of the Bedouins'
worship. Al-Lat, Al-Uzza, and Manah were worshipped as angels under female names, and were
called the daughters of God. ' They attribute,' says
Mohammed, in a noble Sura of the Koran, ' they
attribute daughters to God ; yet they wish not
daughters for themselves. When a female child is

announced to one of them, his face grows dark, and he is as though he would choke.'[1] Al-Uzza was worshipped under the form of a tree, Manah of a large stone, Yaghuth of a lion, Sawa of a woman, Ya'uk of a horse, Nasr of an eagle. Here was material enough for the withering scorn of the Prophet.

But the most famous and the most ancient sanctuary in the country was the Kaaba, called Beit-Allah, or House of God, built in the shape of a cube, and forming a veritable Pantheon of all Arabia. Here was the grim array of the three hundred and sixty idols, one for every day in the year. Here was the famous Hobal, the figure of a man carved in red agate and holding seven wingless arrows in his hand, like those used in divination. Here, strange to say, was a statue of Abraham ; and, stranger still, a statue of the Madonna. Here was Zemzem, the sacred spring which bubbled forth, as the Bedouins believed, from the sandy soil to save the life of Ishmael, their great progenitor, when perishing of thirst. Here was the white stone which was supposed to form his sepulchre ; and here, above all, was the black stone, that stone which had fallen from heaven in the time of Adam, once of dazzling whiteness, but long since turned black by the kisses of sinful mortals.

[1] Sura XVI. 59, with Rodwell's note ad loc.

The religious ideas or superstitions of the Arabs varied as much as did the objects of their worship. A father not unfrequently sacrificed his own child to appease an angry God ; a practice which, common amongst other branches of the Semitic races, the Phœnicians, the Moabites, the Carthaginians, and not unknown even amongst the Jews, need not occasion surprise when found amongst the Arabs. Divination by arrows was a favourite method of finding out the will of God. Seven of these pointless and featherless arrows were kept in the Kaaba, but the number most commonly employed was three : one of them marked with the words, ' My Lord hath commanded thee ; ' a second, ' My Lord hath forbidden thee ; ' the third being left blank. The Arab was always ready to consult these arrows, but not always so ready to abide by their decision. A certain prince was anxious to avenge the murder of his father. He consulted an idol of much repute by drawing from three arrows in his presence. On one of them was inscribed the word ' command,' on the second ' prohibition,' on the third ' delay.' He drew out ' prohibition : ' dissatisfied, he shuffled the arrows a second time, and the second time drew out the same. Twice again he shuffled them, and each time with the same result. In his anger he broke the arrows into pieces, and threw them at the idol's head, exclaiming :

'Wretch! if it were thy father who had been killed, thou wouldst not have forbidden his being avenged.'[1]

The fact is, that though there were many religions and many superstitions amongst the Arabs, they were, as a whole, in temperament, neither religious nor superstitious. They were careless, sceptical, materialistic. 'Let us eat and drink, for to-morrow we die,' is the Epicurean tone of the majority of the poems that have come down to us. What a contrast they were in this respect to Mohammed, and what a Herculean difficulty did this temperament of theirs place in the way of the religious reformer! Many of the Arabs believed that death was extinction: some few believed in a future life and a future judgment. By these last a camel was tethered to a dead man's grave, and was left to die of hunger, that the corpse might have an animal to carry it at the day of resurrection. There was a weird superstition too among them, that the soul of the dead hovered over his grave in the form of an owl, and that if the person had been murdered it might be heard crying 'Oscuni, Oscuni,' that is, 'Give me drink, give me drink ;' nor would it cease doing so till the blood of the murderer had been shed.[2]

Such then, very briefly, was the condition of the

[1] Caussin de Perceval, II. 310, quoted by Cazenove, p. 69.
[2] Sale, ' Preliminary Discourse,' p. 15.

Arabs, social and religious, when, to use an expression of Voltaire, quoted by Barthélemy St. Hilaire, ' The turn of Arabia' came ;[1] when the hour had already struck for the most complete, the most sudden, and the most extraordinary revolution that has ever come over any nation upon earth.

One of the most philosophical of historians has remarked that of all the revolutions which have had a permanent influence upon the civil history of mankind, none could so little be anticipated by human prudence as that effected by the religion of Arabia. And at first sight it must be confessed that the Science of History, if indeed there be such a science, is at a loss to find that sequence of cause and effect which it is the object and the test of all history, which is worthy of the name, to trace out.

The Emperor Justinian, not the least shrewd of the Byzantine Emperors, who, some forty years before, had thought it necessary to protect his empire from every possible and from many impossible dangers, had neglected to erect a line of fortresses on the side of his empire which, in defiance of nature, really was the most vulnerable.[2] ' By a precaution which inspired the cowardice it foresaw,' he had

---

[1] P. 211. See Cap. II., generally, for a description of Pre-Mohammedan Arabia.

[2] Cf. Gibbon, Vol. V. 102–111.

erected a fortress, even at Thermopylæ, where the *religio loci* would rather have called for a Spartan rampart of three hundred men, if only they had been forthcoming. He had kept the Sclavonians out of Constantinople by one long wall, and the Russians out of the Crimea by another; he had fortified Amida and Edessa against the fire-worshippers; had built St. Catherine's half-monastery and half-fortress in the wilderness of Mount Sinai; and had even taken precautions against the savages of Æthiopia: but he had trusted to the six hundred miles of desert which Nature had interposed between him and a set of robber tribes, intent only on molesting one another. What hostile force could pass such an obstacle?

But we can see now, and Mohammed himself perhaps saw, that the ground was in many respects prepared for a great social and religious revolution. 'It detracts nothing from the fame of a great man to show, so far as we can, how his success was possible.'[1] It is only another proof, if proof were wanting, that genius is little else than insight joined to sustained effort; the eye sees what it brings with it the power of seeing; and the great man differs from his contemporaries chiefly in this, that he can read the dark riddle of his time with an eye a few degrees less

[1] M. Barthélemy St. Hilaire, 'Mahomet et le Koran,' p. 51.

obscured than those around him. He is the greatest product of his age, but he is still its product, and he is only the father of the age that is to succeed in so far as he owns his parentage. He marches indeed in front of his age; but his influence will be permanent or fleeting precisely so far as he discerns the direction in which it would advance at a slower pace without him.[1] When he tries to go beyond this, and to force the world out of its groove, to adopt hobbies of his own, then begins the region of the remote, the selfish, the personal; in this the great man fails; and hence the commonplaces on the failure of greatness, and the greatness of failure, with which we are all familiar. 'Perish my name,' said Danton, 'but let the cause triumph;'[2] and personal failure of this kind is to the great man no failure at all—it is only another word for success. The truth is that greatness, so far as it is the truest greatness, rarely fails altogether of its object; and that failure is great, only when the end proposed is good, and the human means, though inadequate to its attainment, are yet a real advance towards it.

It must be remembered therefore as regards what

---

[1] Cf. Guizot's 'Lectures on History,' Vol. III. Lect. XX.; and Mill's Review of them in 'Dissertations and Discussions,' II. 249, 250.

[2] A similar saying is attributed to Cavour: 'Perish my name and memory, so that Italy be made a nation!'

seems the sudden birth of the Arabian nation, fully armed, like Athena from the head of Zeus, that the annual resort to Mecca for purposes of trade, poetry, and religion, had pointed to the Holy City as to a possible metropolis ; and to the Kuraish, the heredi‑ tary guardians of the Kaaba, as the potential rulers of a future people ; while as regards the new religion, there was the groundwork of Monotheism underlying all the abuses and corruption of Magianism and Sabæ‑ anism.   There was also a class of people, called Hanyfs, who prided themselves on preserving the original creed of Abraham, and even his sacred books ; while Ibn Ishak,[1] the earliest known historian

---

[1] See Sirat‑er‑raçoul. Weil's Translation, I. 107–108. Ibn Ishak died A.H. 151.   His work has been preserved for us in the Sirat‑er‑raçoul of Ibn‑Hisham, who died in the year of the Hijrah 213.   The fullest and most trustworthy historian, in the judgment of Muir and Sprenger, whose writings have come down to us, is the Katib al Wakidi, or secretary of the historian Wakidi : died 207 A.H.   The MS. was discovered by Sprenger at Cawnpore.   Among other discoveries of Sprenger may be mentioned a portion of the biography of Mohammed by Tabari, who died A.H. 310, and a complete biographical dictionary, termed Içaba, of the Companions of Mohammed, compiled by Ibn‑Hidjr, in the fifth century, from writers, whose names he gives, of earlier and incontestable authority.   It contains the biographies of some 8,000 people.   And it may be hoped that the Government of India, which numbers among its subjects more than fifty million Musalmans, may recognise, if they have not already done so, the imperial importance of publishing the three remaining folios of the work.   Sprenger brought out one volume, but an order of the Court of Directors suspended the publication of the rest. See Sprenger, Preface, p. 12, where it may be observed how modestly he passes over his own great discoveries, and does not even allude to the slight shown it by the

of Islam, records a meeting of four or five among the Kuraish at which it was resolved to open a crusade against idolatry, and to seek for the original and only true faith; and they straightway abandoned their homes and spread over the world in quest of this Holy Grail.[1]

Mohammedanism therefore is no real exception to the principle I provisionally laid down in my first Lecture as to the origin of the Historical Religions of the world, though, at first sight, it may appear to be so. To Mohammed's own mind it is quite true that the theological element was the predominant and inspiring one, but Mohammed's mind itself was the outcome, at least as much as it was the cause, of the great revolution which goes by his name. There was a general social and religious upheaving at the head of which the Prophet placed himself, and which partly carried him on with it, partly he himself carried it on : the train was already laid, and the spark from heaven was all that was needed to set the Arab world ablaze. In this sense it is perhaps true, as Renan has remarked and the Koran itself declares, that Mohammedanism

Directors. Learned and critical Mohammedans, it would seem, do not think so highly of Wakidi and his secretary as Muir and Sprenger do : they prefer Ibn-Hisham.—See Muir, I. 97-105, and B. St. Hilaire, p. 19-25. Syed Ahmed's 'Life of Mohammed,' Preface, p. 14, 18, etc. Syed Ameer Ali, Preface, p. 7.

[1] Sprenger, p. 81. These four 'enquirers' were Waraka, Othman, Abayd, and Zeid.

was preached before the time of Mohammed ; but there were Mohammedans before Mohammed, only in the sense in which there were Zoroastrians before Zoroaster, Lutherans before Luther, and Christians before Christ. Renan has himself remarked èlsewhere, though he seems to have forgotten it in dealing with Mohammedanism, that the glory of a religion belongs to its founder, and not to his predecessors or to his successors.[1] It is easy, he says himself, to try to awake faith, and it is easy to be possessed by it when once it has been awakened; but it is not easy to inspire it. It is the grandest gift, a very gift of God.

[1] It seems to me, though I would speak with the utmost diffidence in venturing to dissent from the greatest European authority on the subject, that Sprenger errs in the same direction as Renan, when he says in his volume, published at Allahabad (p. 171), that Abu Bakr did more for the success of Islam than the Prophet himself ; and again (p. 174), after enumerating all those who, merely from their vague Monotheism, he calls the predecessors of Mohammed, he says that even after Mohammed was acknowledged as the messenger of God, Omar had more influence on the development of the Islam than Mohammed himself. ‘ The Islam is not the work of Mohammed ; it is not the doctrine of the impostor . . . . it is the offspring of the spirit of the time, and the voice of the Arabic nation. . . . There is, however, no doubt that the impostor has defiled it by his immorality and perverseness of mind.’ It is fair to say that this tone seems somewhat moderated, or even altered, in the author's subsequent and greater work. Cf., however, Vol. I. 209, and II. 83-88. One is inclined to ask, if Islam was merely the spirit of the time, who proved himself best able to read that spirit ? Was it Abu Bakr and Omar, or was it Mohammed that produced the Koran ? And is it their personality, or his, which has stamped itself with ineffaceable clearness for all time upon the Eastern world ?

But though, as I have said, the hour had come, the
youth of Mohammed gave few signs that he was the
man. The portents which ushered in his birth, and
that attended his early youth, are the offspring of
another country and of a later age. The celestial
light that beamed in the sky and from his newly-
opened eyes; the Tigris overflowing its banks; the
palace of Chosroes toppling over to the ground ; the
sacred fire of Zoroaster, which had burned for one
thousand years, suddenly extinguished ; the mules
that talked, and the sheep that bowed to him, were
unknown to the contemporaries of Mohammed, and
Mohammed himself says nothing of them ! [1] He belonged to the family of Haschim, not the least distinguished family of the Kuraish, who were then the
leading tribe at Mecca. He was born on April 20,
575 A.D. His father Abd' Allah died before his
birth ; his mother Aminah was weak and sickly, and
was obliged to put him out to nurse with the wife of
a shepherd : thus the first few years of the Prophet's
life were spent in the tent of a nomad family. His
mother died when he was only six years old, and
his share of his father's property consisted of but five
camels, of a few sheep, and of a female slave. His
grandfather Abd'al Muttalib took charge of the orphan,

[1] They appear, however, in the Sirat-er-raçoul about A.H. 200. See
I. 77-81.

and on his death-bed committed him to the care of his uncle Abu Taleb; a charge which, though he never believed in his nephew's mission, he observed to the day of his death, with all the fidelity of an Arab to a member of his family. Abu Taleb himself, however, was very poor; the boy's small patrimony was soon spent; and then, as he loved to recall in after years, in order to support life he was obliged to tend sheep in the wilderness, a calling much despised among the aristocratic Meccans, who got their wealth by merchandise, but one which encouraged his fondness for solitude, and supplied him with the vivid descriptions of the scenery of the desert which we find in the Koran. 'God had never chosen anyone to be a prophet,' he used to say in his later days, 'who had not, like Moses, like David, or like himself, tended sheep in the wilderness.' [1] But Mohammed was not always to remain a shepherd. Hitherto a man of few words, and with few friends, he was yet notable within his own small circle for his truthfulness and good faith. Men called him 'Al-Amin, or the trusty.' A rich widow, named Khadijah, employed him to go on some trading journeys for her to Syria. The shepherd became a camel-driver, and the trust committed to him he discharged with such fidelity and prudence, that Khadijah offered him

[1] Sprenger, I. 148.

her hand in marriage. She was some fifteen years older than he ; old enough, that is, in that Eastern climate to be his mother ; yet the marriage was one of real affection and respect, and from that time to the day of her death, a period of twenty-four years, Mohammed remained faithful to her, and took no second wife, though the universal custom of his countrymen would have countenanced him in so doing.

Mohammed's married life was still, what men would call, an uneventful one. The birth of four daughters, and of two sons, both of whom, to the great grief of their father, died in childhood ; his famous vow to succour the oppressed ; and the skill with which he managed to reconcile conflicting claims in placing the Black Stone in the renovated Kaaba—these are the only noteworthy external incidents in the next few years of his life. Up to the age of forty, there is nothing to show that any serious scruple had occurred to him individually as to the worship of idols in general, and in particular of the Black Stone, of which his family were the hereditary guardians.

Of a nervous, excitable, imaginative temperament, Mohammed was susceptible to influences too subtle for robuster natures to feel. What a contrast in all respects to those who lived around him, and what a contradiction to Sprenger's theory that the Prophet was only the type of his time and nation, and that

I

Islam was only an impersonation of its tendencies! He was liable, too, to fits,[1] which, whether epileptic or not, involved strange physical phenomena, which at that time and place—like the so-called 'sacred disease' among the Greeks, or 'the possession of the devil' of the Jews—would suggest both to himself and to his friends influences that were not physical. The month of Ramadhan, like other religious Arabs, he observed with punctilious devotion; and he would often retire to the caverns of Mount Hira for purposes of meditation and prayer. As time passed on, solitude became a passion with him—that solitude which is 'the school of genius,' and in the silence of his own heart he held high converse with the unseen God of the universe. The sin of worshipping idols of wood and stone, which could neither hear nor regard, began to flash at times across him ; the crimes, too, of his countrymen weighed upon his spirit ; when he walked forth from his cave, he heard, or fancied that he heard, the rocks and

---

[1] Sprenger (Vol. I. 207) has described these fits most minutely, and with a great deal of curious learning. He thinks Mohammed suffered from hysteria, followed by catalepsy, rather than epilepsy ; for the Prophet does not seem to have lost all consciousness. It is worth remarking that Sprenger's medical knowledge is not very favourable in its result to Mohammed. He starts by saying, p. 210, that all hysterical people have a tendency to lying and deceit. This is his major premise. His minor is that Mohammed was hysterical, and the inference is obvious. Accordingly, we are not surprised to find him (Vol. I. Cap. IV. p. 306, note) speaking of the '*vision*' of the flight to Jerusalem as one 'lie,' and that to the seventh heaven as another lie.

the shrubs of the desert calling him the Apostle of God.[1]

It is possible that his interviews with Nestorian monks, with Zeid, or with his wife's cousin Waraka, may have turned his thoughts into the precise direction they took. Dejection alternated with excitement; these gave place to ecstasy or dreams; and in a dream, or trance, or fit, he saw an angel in human form, but flooded with celestial light, and displaying a silver roll. 'Read!' said the angel. 'I cannot read,' said Mohammed. The injunction and the answer were twice repeated.[2] 'Read,' at last said the angel, 'in the name of thy Lord, who created all besides Himself; who created man out of a clot of blood; read, in the name of the Most High, who taught with the pen; who taught man that which he never knew.' Upon this Mohammed felt the heavenly inspiration, and read, as he believed, the decrees of God, which he afterwards promulgated in the Koran. Then came the announcement, 'O Mohammed, of a truth thou art the Prophet of God; and I am his angel Gabriel.'[3]

[1] 'Sirat-er-raçoul,' I. 153.

[2] Cf. Sura XCVI. Deutsch (Islam, p. 306) renders the word usually translated 'Read' by 'Cry,' comparing Isaiah xi. 6.

[3] Strangely enough, Sir William Muir, Vol. II. p. 89–96, selects this period, above all others in Mohammed's life, as the one in which to suggest his peculiar view, that the Prophet's belief in his inspiration was Satanic in its origin; and he supports his view by a somewhat elaborate parallel with the temptations which presented themselves to Christ at the beginning of His work. Whether such a *Deus ex machinâ*

This was the crisis of Mohammed's life. It was his call to renounce idolatry, and to take the office of Prophet. Like Isaiah, he could not at first believe that so unworthy an instrument could be chosen for such a purpose. 'Woe is me, for I am undone, because I am a man of unclean lips, and I dwell in the midst of a people of unclean lips;' but the live coal was not immediately taken from the altar and laid upon his, as upon Isaiah's lips. Trembling and agitated, Mohammed tottered to Khadijah and told her his vision and his agony of mind. He had always hated and despised soothsayers, and now, in the irony of destiny, it would appear that he was to become a soothsayer himself. 'Fear not, for joyful tidings dost thou bring,' exclaimed Khadijah. 'I will henceforth regard thee as the prophet of our nation. Rejoice,' she added, seeing him still cast down; 'Allah will not suffer thee to fall to shame. Hast thou not been loving to thy kinsfolk, kind to thy neighbours, charit-

is required to untie the knot is hardly within my province to inquire, since the whole matter is alike incapable of proof and disproof; but it seems pertinent to remark, first, that the developed and quasi-scientific conception of such a being as Sir William Muir pictures is Persian rather than Jewish in its origin, and is found in Palestine only after the Captivity; and, secondly, that if the spirit of evil did suggest the idea to Mohammed, he never so completely outwitted himself, since friend and foe must alike admit that it was Mohammed's firm belief in supernatural guidance that lay at the root of all he achieved. Without this we should never have heard of him except as one of a thousand short-lived Arabian sectaries; with it he created a nation, and revivified a third of the then known world.

able to the poor, faithful to thy word, and ever a defender of the truth?' First the life, and then the theology, in the individual as in the tribe and the nation.

But the assurances of the good Khadijah, and the conversions of Zeid and Waraka, did not bring the live coal from the altar. A long period of hesitation, doubt, preparation followed. At one time Mohammed even contemplated suicide, and he was only restrained by an unseen hand, as he might well call the bright vision of the future, pictured in one of the earliest Suras of the Koran,[1] when the help of God should come and victory, when he 'should see the people crowding into the one true Faith, and he, the Prophet, should celebrate the praise of his Lord, and ask pardon of Him, for He is forgiving.' Three years, the period of the Fatrah, saw only fourteen proselytes attach themselves to him. His teaching seemed to make no way beyond the very limited circle of his earliest followers. His rising hopes were crushed. People pointed the finger of scorn at him as he passed by : 'There goeth the son of Abdallah, who hath his converse with the heavens!' They called him a driveller, a star-gazer, a maniac-poet. Thorns were strewn in his path, and stones thrown at him. His uncles sneered, and the main body of the citizens

[1] Sura CX.

treated him with that contemptuous indifference, which must have been harder to him to bear than active persecution. Well might he, to take an illustration suggested by Sir William Muir himself,[1] like Elijah of old, go a day's journey into the wilderness, and request for himself that he might die, and say, ' It is enough, O Lord ; now take away my life, for I am not better than my fathers :' or, again, ' I have been very jealous for the Lord God of hosts, because the people have forsaken Thy covenant, thrown down Thine altars, and slain Thy prophets with the sword ; and I, even I, only am left, and they seek my life to take it away.' At times his distress was insupportable :

> ' And had not his poor heart
> Spoken with That, which being everywhere
> Lets none, who speaks with Him, seem all alone,
> Surely the man had died of solitude.'

And, as the Kuraish said in their bitter scorn, the son of Abdallah did indeed 'have his converse with the heavens;' for out of weakness came forth strength at last ; out of doubt, certainty ; out of humiliation, victory. Another vision, in which he was commanded to preach publicly, followed ; and now he called the Kuraish of the line of Haschim together, those who had most to lose and least to gain by his reform, and boldly announced his mission.

[1] Muir, Vol. II., 228.

Content no longer with preaching in the abstract the one true God, he now ventured to denounce those who, as with righteous indignation he expressed it, 'gave companions' to Him. The Kuraish, the guardians of the Kaaba, perceived, like the silversmiths at Ephesus, that, if this went on, their position would be endangered, and their gains gone. Finding that bribes, and threats, and entreaties were alike powerless to deter him, they expostulated with Abu Taleb, his guardian. Abu Taleb, in his turn, expostulated kindly with his nephew. 'Should they array against me the sun on my right hand, and the moon on my left,' said Mohammed, 'yet while God should command me, I would not renounce my purpose.' These are not the words, nor this the course, of an impostor.

'Were there as many devils in Worms,' said Luther, 'as there are tiles on the houses, yet would I go there, putting my trust in God.' Luther knew somethihg of the Koran, and knew it only to malign it : had he known how exactly his own noble answer had been anticipated by the Prophet of Arabia, would he not have recognised a singleness and a sincerity of purpose in Mohammed which would have made him honour him as a man, even if he could not have welcomed him as a brother ? Like the Hebrew prophets, like St. Anthony and St. Benedict, like Joan of Arc and St. Theresa, like

Swedenborg,[1] like Luther himself, Mohammed had his visions. Luther's visions, as every one knows, were material enough, for he threw an inkstand at the devil which appeared to him at the Castle of Wartburg. But if an imposture theory is not needed to explain the visions of the one, why is it needed to explain the visions of the other? What Mohammed said he saw, he did see, even if they were only the 'subjective creations of his own brain ;' and if results are any test of truth, Mohammed's vision must have been in some sense a true one, for it gave him strength for his great work.

Ten more years passed away: his doctrine fought its way amidst the greatest discouragements and dangers by purely moral means, by its own inherent strength. But with the number of his disciples, increased also the persecutions they had to endure. Mohammed, unwilling to expose their newly awakened faith to too sore a trial, advised them to take refuge in Abyssinia. They did so to the number of fifteen, while Mohammed remained at his post. That they took his advice is not to be regretted; for first it is a convincing proof, if proof be needed, how throughout this period Mohammed's real strength lay in what the world

---

[1] I have to thank a friendly critic, Mr. I. de Maine Browne, for directing my attention to the analogy to be traced between the 'visions' of Mohammed and those of Swedenborg, as well as to one or two fine passages in the writings of the remarkable Swede on the founder of Islam.

would call his weakness; and secondly, because to
this, the first Hijrah, as it is called, we owe the
noblest summary of the Prophet's early teaching that
we now possess.

The Kuraish sent to the Nagashy of Abyssinia
demanding that the exiles should be given up for
death; but one of their number, Djafar, came forward,
and in the presence of the Christian bishops of the
country, who had been specially convened for the
purpose, and had 'brought their Bibles with them,'
explained the change in their religion as follows:

'O King! we were in ignorance and barbarism, we
prayed to idols, we eat animals that had died of themselves, we committed hateful things, we wounded the
love of our own relations, and violated the laws of
hospitality; the strong consumed the weak, till God
sent a messenger among us, of whose birth, faithfulness, and purity we were aware; he exhorted us to
worship God alone, and to turn ourselves from stones
and other gods, which we and our fathers had associated with Him. He commanded us to speak the
truth, to be faithful to our trusts, to love our relations,
and to protect our guests; not to consume the property of the orphan, or to slander virtuous women;
he bade us pray, give alms, and keep the fast. We
have obeyed Mohammed and have believed in his
message. Hence our people have maltreated us, and

have sought to bring us back to idolatry and their other abominations; we have come to thee for help; wilt thou not protect us?'

The Nagashy asked for a sample of the message which had wrought such wonders. Djafar read him a Sura from the Koran, not to our ideas one of the most remarkable; but the effect was such that all present burst into tears, and the Nagashy exclaimed, his tears gushing down over his beard, and those of all the Bishops upon their books, 'I will never deliver you up;' and the Kuraish messengers returned to Mecca discomfited.[1]

Warned afterwards in his solitude by these same Kuraish that they would not cease to oppose his preaching till either they or he had perished, Mohammed answered them only by fearlessly frequenting the approaches to the Kaaba, the stronghold of his enemies, and by delivering his message to the wild Arabs of the desert who resorted to the national fair or the pilgrims' festival there.[2] But a greater disaster than

[1] Sirat-er-raçoul, p. 219, 220.

[2] Sprenger (II. XVI.) thinks that verses 82, 83, &c., of Sura XVI. were delivered especially for the edification of these wandering tribes : 'Allah has given you tents for dwellings and animal skins for coverings ; and ye find them light to remove and easy to pitch again ; and He hath given you furniture made of their wool and fur ;—these pleasures last for a time ; and Allah hath given you places of shade and retreats in the mountains ; clothing also to protect you from the heat, and to cover you in the day of battle. He has made His benefits thus complete to you that ye may become Muslims.'

any Mohammed had yet experienced was at hand.
Khadijah, his faithful wife, died ; Abu Taleb, his uncle
and protector, died also. The Prophet was now alone
amongst his enemies, like Elijah amongst the prophets
of Baal ; and, persecuted in his own city even to the
death, he determined to fly to another. He had
already preached to pilgrims from Medina, and had received from them an offer of an asylum in case of need.
Accompanied by Abu Bakr he fled from the assassin's
knife and took refuge on Mount Thor, a league from
Mecca: for three days he lay concealed in a cavern
there ; the Kuraish pursuers scoured the country, thirst-
ing for his blood. They approached the cavern. ' We
are only two,' said his trembling companion. ' There is
a third,' said Mohammed ; ' it is God Himself.' The
Kuraish reached the cave : a spider, we are told, had
woven its web across the mouth, and a pigeon was sitting on its nest in seemingly undisturbed repose. The
Kuraish retreated, for it was evident the solitude of the
place was unviolated ; and by a sound instinct, one of
the sublimest stories in all history has been made the
era of Mohammedan Chronology.

It is unnecessary to follow connectedly and in
detail any other incidents in Mohammed's life. The
above may be found, with some variety in the details,
in any History of Mohammed ; but I have thought it
essential to dwell upon them, however familiar they

may be to some of us, as they seem to me, apart from their own intrinsic beauty, to supply the key to almost everything else in Mohammed's career.

With the flight to Medina the scene changes. The Prophet and his creed now take their place for good or evil on the theatre of the world.   Was it for evil or for good ?

On the one hand, it may be as fairly,[1] as it has been often, said that it might have been well for the Prophet's memory if he had died a simple Prophet, as he gave utterance to those grand words, ' There is a third with us, it is God Himself.'   The utterance itself would have been not less true, and the speaker would have died, not indeed a great hero, a great law-giver, or a great ruler, but he would have died as he had lived, and as so many men who were greater than their generation, and of whom the world was not worthy, have lived and died before and since.   But had he died then, his name would never have been known beyond the neighbourhood of Mecca.   His small band of followers would have melted away like the other thousand sects that Arabia has produced, leaving not a trace behind them, and Islam itself might have been strangled in its cradle.

And what would this have meant for the Eastern

---

[1] Cf. 'Academy' for June 6, 1874.

world, and for something too of the world which is not Eastern ?

The practices that Mohammed forbade, and not forbade only, but abolished, human sacrifices and the murder of female infants, and blood feuds, and unlimited polygamy, and wanton cruelty to slaves, and drunkenness, and gambling, would have gone on unchecked in Arabia and the adjoining countries. The Mongols, the Tartars, and the Turks would have devastated, as they did devastate, the fairest regions of the earth without gaining that which, in some degree, softened their national character, and alone prevented their conquests from being an unmitigated evil.[1] In Northern and Central Africa there would have been, not the semi-civilisation of the Moors or of the Mandingoes, but the brutal barbarism of the Fans and

---

[1] The Mogul invasion of Hindustan, for instance, gave the peninsula for nearly two hundred years, 1526-1707, a succession of princes who, in spite of their passion for war, were the ablest, the most enlightened, and the best whom, till within a very recent period, it has ever known. Baber, the conqueror of Delhi and the founder of the dynasty, is almost as famed for his poems and for his public works as for his military adventures. The administration of Akbar, one of the greatest monarchs of all time, need not shrink from comparison in any respect with that of his great contemporary Elizabeth of England. He introduced not only religious toleration, but entire religious equality among his subjects. Shah Jehan was a great organiser ; and Aurungzebe, with his energy and with his magnificence, filled a large place in the horizon of Europeans themselves. Even the less distinguished members of the dynasty may compare not unfavourably with most of their Christian contemporaries. The architecture of the Mogul emperors, like that of their co-religionists, the Moors of Spain, is the admiration and the despair of the whole world.

the Ashantees. The dark ages of Europe would have been doubly, nay trebly dark ; for the Arabs who alone by their arts and sciences, by their agriculture, their philosophy, and their virtues, shone out amidst the universal gloom of ignorance and crime, who gave to Spain and to Europe an Averroes and an Avicenna, the Alhambra and the Al-Kazar, would have been wandering over their native deserts. As to religion, a Christianity which, in the East, had long become a corrupt superstition, would have become yet more corrupt, and would have sunk to the condition in which it is in Abyssinia now. Over a seventh part of the earth's surface the Star-worshipper might have been worshipping stars, and the Fetish-worshipper Fetishes, to this very day. The answer therefore to the question whether it would have been well for the Prophet and well for the world, if he had died by the sword of the Kuraish before a wider field, with its greater dangers and temptations, opened before him, is not a simple one ; and in the remainder of this and the subsequent Lectures I hope to give, not indeed a full answer to it—for that would be as much beyond my powers as beyond my limits—but at least to indicate the direction in which, as I think, the answer lies.

The question of the sincerity of Mohammed has been much debated, but to me, I must confess, that to question his sincerity at starting, and to admit the above indisputable facts relating to his early life, is very like a contradiction in terms. Nor could anyone have done what Mohammed did without the most profound faith in the reality and goodness of his cause. Fairly considered, there is no single trait in his character up to the time of the Hijrah which calumny itself could couple with imposture : on the contrary, there is everything to prove the real enthusiast arriving slowly and painfully at what he believed to be the truth.

It has been remarked by Gibbon that no incipient prophet ever passed through so severe an ordeal as Mohammed, since he first presented himself as a prophet to those who were most conversant with his infirmities as a man. Those who knew him best, his wife, his eccentric slave, his cousin, his earliest friend— he who, as Mohammed said, alone of his converts, 'turned not back, neither was perplexed '—were the first to recognise his mission. The ordinary lot of a prophet was in his case reversed ; he was not without honour save among those who did not know him well. Strange that Voltaire, who himself wrote on Mohammed, and even made him the subject of a drama, should, with Mohammed's example before him, have ventured on his immoral paradox that 'No man is a hero to his valet!' Explained in one sense that a

small mind cannot fully understand or appreciate a
great one, it is a feeble truism ; explained in another,
which was the sense Voltaire meant, that the hero is
only a hero to those who see him at a distance, and
that there is no such thing as true greatness, it is an
audacious falsehood.   It is almost equally strange
that Gibbon, who has done such full justice to Mohammed in the general result, should say at starting,
' Mohammed's religion consists of an eternal truth,
and a necessary fiction—There is one God, and Mohammed is His prophet.'   It was, as I have endeavoured to show, no fiction to Mohammed himself or
to his followers ; had it been so, Mohammedanism
could never have risen as it did, nor be what it is now.

But before we go on to consider those points in
Mohammed's career which are really open to question, it may be well to recall a few prominent characteristics of the man who has stamped his impress
so deeply on the Oriental world.   Minute accounts of
his appearance and of his daily life have been preserved to us ; they may be found in most of the
biographies, and Sir William Muir in particular has
given us copious extracts from the writings of the
secretary of Wakidi.[1]

Mohammed was of middle height and of a strongly

---

[1] Muir, Vol. IV., Supplement to Chap. XXXVII. ; cf. also
Deutsch's ' Islam,' pp. 302-304.

built frame ; his head was large, and across his ample forehead, and above finely arching eyebrows, ran a strongly marked vein, which, when he was angry, would turn black and throb visibly. His eyes were coal black, and piercing in their brightness ; his hair curled slightly ; and a long beard, which, like other Orientals, he would stroke when in deep thought, added to the general impressiveness of his appearance. His step was quick and firm, 'like that of one descending a hill.' Between his shoulders was the famous mark, the size of a pigeon's egg, which his disciples persisted in believing to be the sign of his prophetic office ; while the light which kindled in his eye, like that which flashed from the precious stones in the breast-plate of the High Priest, they called the light of prophecy.

In his intercourse with others, he would sit silent among his companions for a long time together, but truly his silence was more eloquent than other men's speech, for the moment speech was called for, it was forthcoming in the shape of some weighty apothegm or proverb, such as the Arabs love to hear. When he laughed, he laughed heartily, shaking his sides, and showing his teeth, which 'looked as if they were hailstones.' He was easy of approach to all who wished to see him, even as 'the river bank to him that draweth water therefrom.' He was fond of ani-

K

mals, and they, as is often the case, were fond of him.
He seldom passed a group of children playing together without a few kind words to them ; and he was
never the first to withdraw his hand from the grasp of
one who offered him his.   If the warmth of his
attachment may be measured, as in fact it may, by the
depth of his friends' devotion to him, no truer friend
than Mohammed ever lived.   Around him, in quite
early days, gathered what was best and noblest in
Mecca ; and in no single instance, through all the
vicissitudes of his chequered life, was the friendship
then formed, ever broken.   He wept like a child over
the death of his faithful servant Zeid.   He visited his
mother's tomb some fifty years after her death, and
he wept there because he believed that God had forbidden him to pray for her.   He was naturally shy
and retiring ; ' as bashful,' said Ayishah, ' as a veiled
virgin.'   He was kind and forgiving to all.   ' I served
him from the time I was eight years old,' said his
servant Anas, 'and he never scolded me for anything,
though I spoiled much.'   The most noteworthy of
his external characteristics were a sweet gravity and
a quiet dignity, which drew involuntary respect, and
which was the best, and often the only, protection he
enjoyed from insult.

His ordinary dress was plain, even to coarseness ;
yet he was fastidious in arranging it to the best ad-

vantage. He was fond of ablutions, and fonder still of perfumes; and he prided himself on the neatness of his hair, and the pearly whiteness of his teeth. His life was simple in all its details. He lived with his wives in a row of humble cottages, separated from one another by palm branches, cemented together with mud. He would kindle the fire, sweep the floor, and milk the goats himself. Ayishah tells us that he slept upon a leathern mat, and that he mended his clothes, and even clouted his shoes, with his own hand. For months together, Ayishah is also our authority for saying that he did not get a sufficient meal. The little food that he had was always shared with those who dropped in to partake of it. Indeed, outside the Prophet's house was a bench or gallery, on which were always to be found a number of the poor who lived entirely on his generosity, and were hence called the 'people of the bench.' His ordinary food was dates and water, or barley bread; milk and honey were luxuries of which he was fond, but which he rarely allowed himself. The fare of the desert seemed most congenial to him, even when he was sovereign of Arabia. One day some people passed by him with a basket of berries from one of the desert shrubs. 'Pick me out,' he said to his companion, 'the blackest of those

berries, for they are sweet—even such as I was wont
to gather when I fed the flocks of Mecca at Adgad.'

Such were some of the characteristics of the man
whom the Arabs were now called upon to recognise
as the prophet of their country, and as a messenger
direct from God.

Monotheism, pure and simple, if it is to be a life
as well as a creed, almost postulates the prophetic
office. The Creator is at too great a distance from
His creatures to allow of a sufficiently direct communication with them. The power, the knowledge,
the infinity of God overshadow His providence, His
sympathy, and His love. Renan has remarked that
in only two ways can such a gap be bridged over :
first, if, as in the Indian Avatar, from time to time,
or, as in Christianity, once for all, there is an actual
manifestation of the Godhead upon earth ; or, secondly, if, as in Judaism or in Buddhism, the Deity
chooses a favoured mortal, who may give to his
brother men a fuller knowledge of the Divine mind
and will.[1] The latter would seem the form most
congenial to the Semitic mind, if one may be allowed
to use that convenient, but since the bold generalisa-
tions in which Renan has indulged respecting them,
somewhat misleading word. The Arabs themselves
looked up to Adam, Noah, Abraham, and Moses as

[1] Renan, p 278.

prophets ; Mohammed did the same, and added Christ to their number. He held that each successive revelation had been higher than the preceding one, though each was complete in itself, as being adequate to the circumstances of the time. Was there, Mohammed might ask, any reason to suppose that Christ had been the last of the prophets, and that His revelation was absolutely as well as relatively final ; and were there not evils enough in Arabia and in the world to call for a further communication from heaven ? To say that Arabia needed renovation was to say in other words that the time for a new prophet had come, and why might not that prophet be Mohammed himself ? Sprenger, the most recent and exhaustive writer on the subject, has shown that for some hundred years before Mohammed the advent of another prophet had been expected and even predicted. So strong was the general conviction on the subject that the Arab tribes were guided by it even in their politics.[1]

But, if we admit the sincerity of Mohammed and the naturalness of his belief up to the time of the Hijrah, what are we to say of him during his first

[1] Sprenger, I., p. 245, quotes a saying of the Arabs that the children of Shem are prophets, of Japhet kings, of Ham slaves. We are told that the Arab women were at this time in the habit of praying for male children, in the hope that of them the long-expected prophet might be born.

years of exile at Medina, and again of his subsequent successes ?

It is unquestionably true that a change does seem to come over him. The revelations of the Koran are more and more suited to the particular circumstances and caprices of the moment. They are often of the nature of political bulletins, or of personal apologies rather than of messages direct from God. Now appears for the first time the convenient but dangerous doctrine of abrogation, by which a subsequent revelation might supersede a previous one.[1]

The limitation to the unbounded license of Oriental polygamy which he had himself imposed, he relaxes in his own behalf;[2] it is a blot, and, in the Christian view, an indelible blot, upon his memory; but it is possible, on the one hand, that he may have justified himself to his own mind by the Ethiopian marriage not condemned in the case of Moses,[3] whom he always regarded as, in a peculiar sense, his predecessor, and it is certain on the other, that if, in accordance with Eastern notions, he claimed for himself as Prophet exceptional privileges in this one direction, he imposed upon himself exceptional privations, in the way of prayers, fasting, and poverty, in every other. He was certainly, therefore, not a

---

[1] Sura XVI. 103, II. 100.   [2] Sura XXXIII. 49, and LXVI. 1.
[3] See Lecture IV. p. 262.

sensualist or a voluptuary in the ordinary meaning of
that term. His marriage with Maria, a Christian, an
Egyptian, and a slave, caused an uproar among his
lawful wives ; but it does not seem to have been any
violation of the Harem law, and it was certainly not
condemned by the Arabs themselves. His marriage
with Zeinab, the wife of Zeid, his freedman and
adopted son, after her divorce from him, bears on the
face of it a worse complexion ; but I am satisfied,
after a close examination of the circumstances of the
case, that it does not bear the interpretation usually
placed upon it by Christians. It raised an outcry
among the Arabs of the Ignorance, not because they
suspected an intrigue on the Prophet's part to secure
a divorce ; but because they looked upon an adopted
as though he were a real son, and considered, therefore, that the marriage fell within the prohibited
degrees. This restriction, which Mohammed, for
whatever causes, considered to be an arbitrary one, he
abolished by his marriage, not for his own benefit
only, but for that of the Arabs at large. In the view
indeed usually taken of the whole transaction, there is
a strange compound of fact and fiction ; and much that
was comparatively innocent has been made to wear the
appearance of deep guilt ; but it must be admitted
with sorrow that in the matter of his marriages Mohammed laid himself open to much misconception and

to much blame even on the part of the most temperate and most truth-loving of his opponents.[1]

Whether, indeed, the various explanations of the Prophet's conduct that have been suggested by the piety or the admiration of his followers are quite consistent with the facts or not, matters now comparatively little: but it matters very much, and should be a subject of rejoicing to every Christian, that pious Musalmans, instead of justifying an act

---

[1] It should be remembered, however, that most of Mohammed's marriages may be explained, at least, as much by his pity for the forlorn condition of the persons concerned, as by other motives. They were almost all of them with widows who were not remarkable either for their beauty or their wealth, but quite the reverse. May not this fact, and his undoubted faithfulness to Khadijah till her dying day, and till he himself was fifty years of age, give us additional ground to hope that calumny or misconception has been at work in the story of Zeinab? There are some indications on the face of it, besides those mentioned in the text, that this is the case. For example, Zeinab was the Prophet's cousin, and there was nothing to prevent his having married her himself when both he and she were younger, instead of giving her in marriage to his freedman. An able and a friendly Muslim critic, Mir Aulad Ali, Professor of Oriental Languages at Trinity College, Dublin, suggests to me that the marriage of Zeinab, one of the Kuraish and first cousin to the Prophet, with a freedman, was distasteful to her; and that it was an unhappy one for the husband as well as for the wife, as is shown by Zeid's continuing to demand a divorce, when the Prophet advised him against it. Mohammed by his subsequent marriage with her removed, he goes on to suggest, a restriction which he thought unnecessary; and showed that he at all events saw nothing degrading in a marriage connection with a freedman. Anyhow it is certain that Zeid, if he had suspected, as Christians have done, anything in the nature of an intrigue on the Prophet's part to alienate his wife's affection from him, could not have served him as he did even to the day of his death with all the loyalty and devotion of a zealous disciple.

which, if it was in reality what it has often been represented to have been, they, no less than we, know to be wrong, are able to explain it to themselves in a way which does not impute a crime to the founder of their creed, nor involve them in condoning it.

The free toleration of the purer among the creeds around him, which the Prophet had at first enjoined, gradually changes into intolerance. Persecuted no longer, Mohammed becomes a persecutor himself; with the Koran in one hand, the scymitar in the other, he goes forth to offer to the nations the threefold alternative of conversion, tribute, death. He is once or twice untrue to the kind and forgiving disposition of his best nature; and is once or twice unrelenting in the punishment of his personal enemies, especially of the Jews, who had disappointed his expectation that they would join him, and of such as had stung him by their lampoons or libels. He is even guilty more than once of conniving at the assassination of inveterate opponents; and the massacre of the Bani Koraitza, though they had deserted him almost on the field of battle, and their lives were forfeit by all the laws of war, moved the misgivings of others than the disaffected. He might, no doubt, believing, as he did, in his own inspiration, have found an ample precedent for the act in the slaughter of the Midianites by Moses or the Canaanites by Joshua two thousand years before, or even in the wars of Saul and David with neighbouring tribes ; but, judged by any but an Oriental standard of morality, and by his own conspicuous magnanimity on other occasions, his act, in all its accessories, was one of cold-blooded revenge.

Can we explain away or extenuate these blots on his memory, or, if we cannot, are they inconsistent with substantial sincerity and singlemindedness? Here is a problem of surpassing interest to the psychologist, and I have only time to touch lightly upon it.

In the first place, the change in his character and aims is not to be separated from the general conditions of his life. At first he was a religious and moral reformer only, and could not, even if he would, have met the evils of his time by any other than by moral means. If he was without the advantages, he was also free from the dangers, of success. A religion militant is, as all ecclesiastical history shows, very different from a religion triumphant. The Prophet in spite of himself became, by the force of circumstances, more than a prophet. Not, indeed, that with him height ever begot high thoughts. He preserved to the end of his career that modesty and simplicity of life which is the crowning beauty of his character; but he became a temporal ruler, and, where the Koran did not make its way unaided, the civil magistrate

naturally used temporal means. Under such circumstances, and when his followers pressed upon him
their belief in the nature of his mission, who can
draw the line where enthusiasm ends, and self-decep-
tion or even imposture begins ? No one who knows
human nature will deny that the two are often perfectly consistent with each other. Once persuaded
fully of his divine mission as a whole, a man unconsciously begins to invest his personal fancies and
desires with a like sanction : it is not that he tampers
with his conscience ; he rather subjects conscience
and reason, appetite and affection, to the one domi-
nating influence ; and so, as time goes on, with perfect good faith gets to confound what comes from
below with what comes from above. What is the
meaning of the term 'pious frauds,' except that such
acts are frauds in the eyes of others, acts of piety in
the eyes of the doer ? The more fully convinced a
man is of the goodness of his cause, the more likely
is he to forget the means in the end ; he need not
consciously assert that the end justifies the means,
but his eyes are so fixed upon the end that they
overlook the interval between the idea and its realisa-
tion. He has to maintain a hold over the motley
mass of followers that his mission has gathered round
him. Must he not become all things to all to meet
their several wants ? Perhaps he does become so

and, in the process, what he gains in the bulk of his influence he loses in its quality. Its intensity is in inverse proportion to its extension. No man—I quote here, with only such slight alteration as adapts them to my subject, the noble words of George Eliot: 'No man, whether prophet, statesman, or popular preacher, ever yet kept a prolonged hold over a mixed multitude without being in some measure degraded thereby. His teaching or his life must be accommodated to the average wants of his hearers, and not to his own finest insight. But, after all, we should regard the life of every great man as a drama, in which there must be important inward modifications accompanying the outward changes.'[1] Rigid consistency in itself is no great merit, rather the reverse: what one has a right to demand in a great man is that the intensity of the central truth he has to deliver should become, not less, but more intense ; that that flame shall burn so clear as to throw into the shade other objects which shine with a less brilliant light ; that the essence shall be pure even if some of the surroundings be alloyed ; and this, I think, if not more than this, with all his faults, we may affirm of Mohammed.

On the whole the wonder is to me not how much, but how little, under different circumstances, Mo-

[1] Romola, Vol. II., Chap. V. p. 5.

hammed differed from himself. In the shepherd of the desert, in the Syrian trader, in the solitary of Mount Hira, in the reformer in the minority of one, in the exile of Medina, in the acknowledged conqueror, in the equal of the Persian Chosroes and the Greek Heraclius, we can still trace a substantial unity. I doubt whether any other man, whose external conditions changed so much, ever himself changed less to meet them : the accidents are changed, the essence seems to me to be the same in all.

Power, as the saying is, no doubt put the man to the test. It brought new temptations and therefore new failures, from which the shepherd of the desert might have remained free. But happy is the man who, living

> ' In the fierce light that beats upon a throne,
> And blackens every blot,'

can stand the test as well as did Mohammed. A Christian poet has well asked :—

> ' What keeps a spirit wholly true
> To that ideal which he bears ?
> What record ? not the sinless years
> That breathed beneath the Syrian blue.'

But it is a current misconception, and, subject to the above explanation, a very great one, that a gradual, but continuous and accelerating moral de-

clension is to be traced from the time when the
fugitive unexpectedly entered Medina in triumph.
'Truth is come—let falsehood disappear,' he said,
when, after his long exile, and after the temptations
of Medina had done their worst for him, he re-entered
the Kaaba, and its three hundred and sixty idols, the
famous Hobal amongst them, vanished before him;
and in his treatment of the unbelieving city he was
marvellously true to his programme.   There was now
nothing left in Mecca that could thwart his pleasure.
If ever he had worn a mask at all, he would now
at all events have thrown it off; if lower aims had
gradually sapped the higher, or his moderation had
been   directed,   as   Gibbon   supposes,   by   his   selfish
interests, we should now have seen the effect; now
would have been the moment to gratify his ambition,
to satiate his lust, to glut his revenge.   Is there anything of the kind?   Read the account of the entry of
Mohammed   into   Mecca,   side   by   side with that of
Marius   or   Sulla   into   Rome.   Compare   all   the   attendant   circumstances,   the   outrages   that   preceded,
and   the   use   made   by   each   of   his   recovered   power,
and we shall then be in a position better to appreciate
the   magnanimity   and   moderation   of   the   Prophet   of
Arabia.   There were no proscription lists, no plunder,
no wanton revenge.

The chief blots in his fame are not after his undisputed victory, but during his years of chequered warfare at Medina, and, such as they are, are distributed very evenly over the whole of that time. In other words, he did very occasionally give way to a strong temptation ; but there was no gradual sapping of moral principles, and no deadening of conscience —a very important distinction. One or two acts of summary and uncompromising punishment; possibly, one or two acts of cunning, and, after Khadijah was dead, the violation of one law which he had from veneration for her imposed on others, and had always hitherto kept himself, form no very long bill of indictment against one who always admitted he was a man of like passions with ourselves, who was ignorant of the Christian moral law, and who attained to power after difficulties, and dangers, and misconceptions which might have turned the best of men into a suspicious and sanguinary tyrant.[1]

As regards the relaxation of the marriage law in his own favour it must be remembered that, according to the notions of the Jewish Rabbis, a prophet who was properly commissioned might supersede any

[1] Yet Sprenger (I. p. 359), on no more grounds than those here mentioned, can say of Mohammed, that when he attained to power in Medina, ‘er wurde zum wollüstigen Theokraten und blutdürstig Tyrannen, Pabst und König.’ What Christian Pope or King—to say nothing of Oriental rulers, with whom alone is it fair to compare him —had as great temptations and succumbed to them as little as did Mohammed?

law ;[1] when Christ broke through the sabbatarian restrictions of the Pharisees, it was his mission only, and not his right, if he was so commissioned, which they called in question. The answer 'He is a Prophet' was a sufficient one to all who could receive it as true. The Arab notions seem to have been substantially similar, and this must be carefully borne in mind in estimating the blame we attribute to the Prophet of Arabia.

It is no doubt true that some of the revelations of the Koran, particularly the later ones, bear the appearance of having been given consciously for personal and temporary purposes, and these have led, with some show of reason, even such impartial writers as Sir William Muir to accuse Mohammed of 'the high blasphemy of forging the name of God.' But it would be strange indeed if, viewed in the light of what I have said above as to Mohammed's unfaltering belief in his own inspiration, he had not occasionally,

---

[1] See Farrar's 'Life of Christ,' I. 83, *seq.*   Mir Aulad Ali, whom I have quoted above, writes to me on this subject as follows :—'We Muslims are not bound to follow or accept as law any of the deeds of any of the Prophets ; we are only bound to accept what they give us as law.   Mohammed has not enjoined polygamy, he has only allowed it under certain conditions.   This permission has often been abused ; but whatever its abuses, it has lessened the immorality, the illegitimate births, and the child-murder which are rife in monogamous countries.   One Prophet may be right according to us Muslims in practising polygamy, while another may be right in remaining celibate, but it may not be right in others to follow the example of either ; still less is it right to make their example binding.'

or even often, revealed in the Koran the mental pro-
cesses by which he justified to himself acts about
which he may have, at first, felt scruples, or which
his contemporaries may have called in question.[1] Is
not this the true explanation of what is commonly
considered to be the deepest stain upon Mohammed's
memory, the production of a Sura[2] in which he
legalises in God's name his marriage with Zeinab, a
divorced wife of his adopted son? The production
of this Sura, whatever else it proves about Mohammed, seems to me to prove not his conscious insin-
cerity, but the reverse; he had already attained his
end, why then blazon his shame if shame he felt it to
be? why 'forge the name of God?' Why lay himself open to the crushing retort which his enemies
would at once bring against him? Surely a single
act of conscious imposture in the matter of the Koran
would have sapped all his strength; it would have
been like

> 'The little rift within the lover's lute,
> Or little pitted speck in garner'd fruit,
> That rotting inward slowly moulders all.'

It would have made such a speech as that wherein, at
the very close of his life, Samuel-like, he boldly
challenged all Musalmans to mention aught that they

---

[1] Cf. the view of Mohler in his treatise 'on the Relation of Islam to
the Gospel,' p. 20–22.

[2] Sura XXXIII. 37.

L

had against him, impossible : moreover, such an act, if successful, would have been repeated again and again ; the path would have been too slippery and the descent have seemed too easy and inviting for him to recall his footsteps. It seems pertinent also to ask, by way of rebutting the charge, whether he was not at least equally ready, when occasion required, to blame himself for what he had said or done, and to call the whole Musalman world to be witnesses of his self-condemnation ? [1]

But what are the facts ?   Take two samples.

On one occasion, in a moment of despondency, he made a partial concession to idolatry.   He thought to win over the recalcitrant Kuraish to his views by allowing that their gods might make intercession with the supreme God.

'What think ye of Al-Lat, and Al-Uzza, and Manah, the third besides? They are the exalted Females, and their intercession with God may be hoped for.'

The Kuraish, overjoyed, signified their adhesion to Mohammed, and it seemed that they would bring over all Mecca with them.   His friends would have passed the matter over as quietly as possible.   So great was the scandal among the Faithful that some of his earliest historians omit it altogether.   But the

---

[1] Cf. Sura XLVIII. 2, 'that God may forgive thee thy preceding and thy subsequent sin.'

Prophet's conscience was too tender for that. In an hour of weakness Mohammed had mistaken expediency for duty, and having discovered his mistake, he would recall the concession, at all hazards, as publicly as he had made it, even at the risk of the imputation of weakness and of imposture. The amended version of the Sura ran thus:

'What think ye of Al-Lat, and Al-Uzza, and Manah, the third besides? They are nought but empty names which ye and your fathers have invented.'[1]

I will give one more instance. It is a memorable one. Mohammed was engaged in earnest conversation with Wallid, a powerful Kuraish, whose conversion he much desired. A blind man in very humble circumstances, Abdallah by name, happened to come up, and, not knowing that Mohammed was otherwise engaged, exclaimed, 'Oh, Apostle of God, teach me some part of what God has taught thee.' Mohammed, vexed at the interruption, frowned and turned away from him. But his conscience soon smote him for having postponed the poor and humble to the rich and powerful, and the next day's Sura showed that this 'forger of God's name' was at least as ready to forge it for his own condemnation as in his defence.

[1] Sura LIII.; cf. also XVII. 75, and XXII. 51; see Muir, II. p. 149-158, and Sprenger, II. 17, where there is a curious dissertation on the word Gharânyk, used for Females—'swans which mount higher and higher towards God.'

The Sura is known by the significant title ' He frowned,' and runs thus :

> ' The Prophet frowned, and turned aside,
>   Because the blind man came unto him.
> And how knowest thou whether he might not have been cleansed from
>   his sins,
> Or whether he might have been admonished, and profited thereby ?
>   As for the man that is rich,
>   Him thou receivest graciously ;
> And thou carest not that he is not cleansed.
> But as for him that cometh unto thee earnestly seeking his salvation,
> And trembling anxiously, him dost thou neglect.
>   By no means shouldst thou act thus.'

And, ever after this, we are told that, when the Prophet saw the poor blind man, he went out of his way to do him honour, saying ' The man is thrice welcome on whose account my Lord hath reprimanded me,' and he made him twice Governor of Medina.[1]

Mohammed never wavered in his belief in his own mission, nor, what is more extraordinary, in his belief as to its precise nature and well-defined limits. He was a prophet charged with a mission from God ; nothing less, but nothing more. He might make mistakes, lose battles, do wrong acts, but none the less

---

[1] Sura LXXX., with Sale's note ad loc. ; and Muir, II. p. 128. Sir William Muir tells the story much as I have related it, but seems quite unable to see its grandeur, for he only remarks upon it, ' This incident illustrates at once the anxiety of Mohammed to gain over the principal men of the Kuraish, and when he was rejected, the readiness with which he turned to the poor and uninfluential.' Was ever moral sublimity so marred, or heroism so vulgarised? How Mohammed towers above even his best historians !

did he believe that the words he spoke were the very words of God. To every Sura of the Koran he prefixed the words 'In the name of God, the Compassionate, the Merciful,' even as the Hebrew prophet would open his message with his 'Thus saith the Lord;' and before every sentence and every word of the Sacred Book is to be read, between the lines, the word 'say,' indicating that Mohammed believed, what Moses and Isaiah only believed on special occasions, that in his utterances he was the mere mouthpiece, and therefore the unerring mouthpiece, of the Infinite and the Eternal. He might win his way against superhuman difficulties, preserve a charmed life, do deeds which seemed miracles to others, gain the homage of all Arabia, and present in his own person an ideal of morality never before pictured by an Arab; and yet he never forgot himself, or claimed to be more than a weak and fallible mortal.

As his view of his own mission is an all-important point in estimating his character, let us deal, in concluding this Lecture, with facts alone, and watch his conduct at a few critical epochs which I have purposely selected, as throwing light upon the matter, in its different aspects, away from their chronological order and from very different periods of his life.

When the Persian monarch Chosroes was contemplating with pride, like Nebuchadnezzar of old,

the great Artemita that he had built and all its fabu-
lous treasures, he received a letter from an obscure
citizen of Mecca, bidding him acknowledge Mohammed as the Prophet of God.   Chosroes tore the letter
into pieces.   'It is thus,' exclaimed the Arabian Prophet when he heard of it, 'that God will tear his kingdom and reject his supplications.'   No prediction could
have seemed at the time less likely to be accomplished,
since Persia was at its height, and Constantinople at
its lowest.   But Mohammed lived to see its fulfilment,
and yet never claimed in consequence, as others might
have done, the power of prophecy.

While he had as yet only half established his position, a powerful Christian tribe tendered their submission, if only he would leave their chief some remnant
of his power.   'Not one unripe date,' replied Mohammed.[1]   We remember how the French rhetorician the
other day, knowing that his nation, if they are slaves
to nothing else, are always slaves to an epigram, prolonged resistance to the bitter end by his famous de-
claration that not 'an inch of their territory nor a stone
of their fortresses' would the French surrender.   And
we may imagine the effect produced upon the handful
of Mohammed's Meccan followers who were still in
exile at Medina by such an answer, coming from one
who was certainly no vapid rhetorician, who preferred

[1] Muir, Vol. IV. p. 59.

silence to speech, and who never said a thing he did not really mean.

· Moseilama, the most formidable of the rival prophets whom Mohammed's success stirred up, thinking that Mohammed's game was a merely selfish one, and that two might play at it, sent to Mohammed to offer to go shares with him in the good things of the world, which united they might easily divide. The letter was of Spartan brevity : ' Moseilama the apostle of God to Mohammed the apostle of God.—Now let the earth be half mine and half thine.' Mohammed's reply was hardly less laconic : ' Mohammed the apostle of God to Moseilama the liar.—The earth is God's, He giveth it to such of His servants as He pleaseth, and they who fear Him shall prosper.'

Again mark his conduct under failure or rebuff. He had lost, within three days of each other, Abu Taleb his one protector, and his venerable wife Khadijah, that toothless old woman, as Ayishah long afterwards in the bloom of her beauty called her ; the wife who, as Mohammed indignantly replied, ' when he was poor had enriched him, when he was called a liar had alone believed in him, when he was opposed by all the world had alone remained true to him.' [1] What was he to do ? Silence and

---

[1] Sprenger characteristically remarks (I. 151) that Mohammed's faithfulness to Khadijah to her dying day was due probably not to his

the desert seemed the one chance of safety, but what
did he do ? Followed only by Zeid, his faithful
freedman, he went to Tayif, the town after Mecca
most wholly given to idolatry ; and, like Elijah in
Samaria, he boldly challenged the protection and
obedience of the inhabitants. They stoned him out
of the city. He returned to Mecca defeated, but not
disheartened ; cast down, but not destroyed ; quietly
saying to himself, ' If thou, O Lord, art not angry, I
am safe; I seek refuge in the light of thy countenance
alone.' [1]

After the tide had turned in his favour, and the
battle of Bedr had, as it seemed, put the seal to his
military success, he was signally defeated and
wounded almost to the death at Mount Ohud.
People began to desert him ; but a Sura, Mohammed's ' order of the day,' appeared : ' Mohammed is
no more than a prophet. What if he had been
killed, needs ye go back? He that turneth back

---

inclination, but to his dependence on her. Why, then, the interval
before Mohammed married again ? And why, long afterwards, his
noble burst of gratitude to her memory when Ayishah contrasted her
own youth and beauty with Khadijah's age and infirmities, and asked,
' Am not I much better than she ? ' ' No, by Allah,' replied Mohammed ; ' no, by Allah ; when I was poor she enriched me,' &c. Was
Mohammed dependent upon the dead ? For cynical remarks of a
similar kind see, amongst many other instances, Sprenger, II.
19, 23, 86.

   [1] See the story in full in Muir, Vol. II. p. 198–203.

injureth not God in the least, but himself.'[1] The spell of his untaught eloquence recalled them to themselves, and we are assured that his defeat at Ohud advanced his cause as much as did his victory at Bedr.

Here is a story which illustrates the nature of the revenge which the Prophet lived to take. He was one day sleeping under a tree, alone, and at a distance from his camp, when he awoke and beheld Durthur, his deadly foe, standing over him with a drawn sword. ' Oh Mohammed,' cried he, ' who is there now to save thee?' 'God,' said the Prophet. Struck with awe, Durthur dropped his sword; Mohammed seized it, and exclaimed in his turn, ' Oh Durthur, who is there now to save thee?' 'No one,' replied Durthur. ' Then learn from me to be merciful ;' and with these words he gave him back his sword, and made him his firmest friend.

Ayishah, his favourite wife, one day asked of him, 'O Prophet of God, do none enter Paradise but through God's mercy?' ' None, none, none,' replied he. 'But will not even you enter by your own merits?' Mohammed put his hand upon his head and thrice replied, 'Neither shall I enter Paradise unless God cover me with His mercy.'[2] There was

---

[1] Sura III. 138. [2] Mishkat-ul-Masibeh, I. Book IV. 280.

no 'false certitude of the Divine intentions,' the besetting temptation of spiritual ambition ; no facile
dogmatising upon what he had only to hint to be
believed—his own preeminent position in the unseen
world.   It would have been safe to do so : ἐς ἀφανὲς
τὸν μῦθον ἀνενείκας οὐκ ἔχει ἔλεγχον :[1] and how few
could have resisted a like temptation !

And at the last grand scene of all, when the Prophet had met his death, as he had always told his
doubting followers he must, and Omar, the Simon
Peter of Islam, in the agony of his grief drew his
scymitar and wildly rushing in among the weeping
Musalmans swore that he would strike off the head
of any one who dared to say that the Prophet was
dead—the Prophet could not be dead—it was by a
gentle reminder of what the Prophet himself had
always taught, that the venerable Abu Bakr, the
earliest of the Prophet's friends, and his successor in
the Khalifate, calmed his excitement : 'Is it then
Mohammed, or the God of Mohammed, that we have
learned to worship ?'

---

[1] Hdt. II. 23.

LECTURE III.

MOHAMMEDANISM.

Hear, O Israel, the Lord our God is one God. . . . Now
therefore go and I will be with thy mouth, and teach thee what
thou shalt say.—THE HEBREW BIBLE.

Allahu Akbar—God is most great—there is no God but God, .
and Mohammed is His messenger.—THE CREED OF ISLAM.

IN the concluding part of my last Lecture I discussed
at length the question of the character of Mohammed,
and we arrived, I think, at the conclusion that, on the
one hand, he had grave moral faults which may be
accounted for, but not excused, by the circumstances
of the time, by the exigencies of his situation, and by
the weaknesses of human nature. And on the other,
we saw reason to believe that he was not only passionately impressed with the reality of his divine
mission in early life, but that the common view of a
great moral declension to be traced in his latter years.
is not borne out by the evidence, and that to the end.

of his career, amidst failures and successes, in life and in preparation for death, he was true to the one principle with which he started. He became indeed, by the force of circumstances, general and ruler, law-giver and judge of all Arabia ; but above all and before all, he was still a simple prophet delivering God's message in singleness of heart, obeying, as far as he could, God's will, but never claiming to be more than God's weak and erring servant.

And now, perhaps, it is time to ask what was the essence of Mohammed's belief, that which made him what he was, which has given his religion its inexhaustible vitality? How did it resemble, and how did it differ from, the religions which it overthrew, and one of which at least we are accustomed to look upon, and shall, in its pure form as it came from Christ's own lips, and can still be read in Christ's own acts, and even to some extent in the character of His servants, always continue to look upon, as immeasurably superior to Mohammedanism?

The essence of Mohammedanism is not merely the sublime belief in the unity of God, though it is difficult to us to realise the tumult of the feelings, and the intensity of the life, which must be awakened in a Polytheistic people, who are also imaginative and energetic, when, on a sudden, they recognise the One in and behind the Many. Mohammed started indeed

with the dogmatic assertion that there was but one
God, the Creator of all things in heaven and earth, all
powerful, knowing all things, everywhere present.
He reiterates this in a thousand shapes as the fore-
front of his message ;[1] and sublimely confident that
it need only be stated to ensure ultimate acceptance,
he deigns not to offer proof of that which, in his judgment, must prove itself.

But it was more than the unity of God, and the
attributes which flow from that conception, which
Mohammed asserted.   A theoretic assent to this
might have had but little influence on practice.
What is by its nature immeasurably above man, may
also be immeasurably removed from him ; and accordingly Mohammed reasserted that which had been
the life of the old Hebrew nation, and the burden of
the song of every Hebrew prophet—that God not
only lives, but that He is a righteous and a merciful
ruler ; and that to His will it is the duty and the
privilege of all living men to bow.[2]   Nor was the

---

[1] See especially Suras I. and CXII., the beginning and end of the
Koran in the orthodox arrangement ; also Sura XXXV. 41-44. Cf.
also Sura II. 19-20, 109 ; VI. 1-6 ; XIII. 10, 11 ; XVI. 12-17 ;
LIII. and XCVI.

[2] See this well drawn out in Maurice's ' Religions of the World,' p.
21-24. The passage is a most suggestive one. I owe much to it, and
it seems to me that here, and in many other passages of his writings,
Mr. Maurice did far more, and penetrated far deeper, than is allowed
in a very brilliant passage of a recent work (see ' Literature and
Dogma,' p. 345). When the unacknowledged debts of the nineteenth

sublimity of this doctrine marred in its application by the old Hebrew exclusiveness. The Arabian nation was first called indeed ; but as in Christianity, and as it was not in Judaism, the obligations of the Arabs were to be measured by their privileges, and the call was to be extended through them to the world at large.   The Jew surrendered his birthright if he imparted his faith to other peoples.   The Arab surrendered his if he did not spread his faith wherever and however he could.

But Mohammed's assertion of the unity of God and of His rule over every detail of man's life, was no mere plagiarism from an older faith.   The Jewish people at large had, even in their best days, rushed wildly after the worship of alien gods ; at last, indeed, the iron of the Captivity had entered into their souls ; they learned much during their sojourn in the East, but they unlearned more ; they unlearned there, once and for ever, the sin of idolatry.   But though they never henceforward worshipped other gods, the higher teaching of their prophets they still too much ignored, and the period which might have been the culmination of their glory ended in that tragedy of tragedies which was the immediate precursor of their

century to its great writers come to be added up, I am convinced that it will be fully recognised that the mental powers of Mr. Maurice rank as high as did the purity and nobility of his life ; and more can hardly be said.

fall. The sceptre departed from Judah, but the Jewish exiles in Arabia still clung desperately to the phantom of those proud religious privileges when all which had given some claim to them had disappeared. Christians too, such Christians as Mohammed had ever met, had forgotten at once the faith of the Jews, and that higher revelation of God given to them by Christ which the Jews rejected. Homoousians and Homoiousians, Monothelites and Monophysites, Jacobites and Eutychians, making hard dogmas of things wherein the sacred writers themselves had made no dogma, disputing fiercely whether what was mathematically false could be metaphysically true, and nicely discriminating the shades of truth and falsehood in the views suggested to bridge over the abysmal gulf between them ; turning figures into facts, rhetoric into logic, and poetry into prose, had forgotten the unity of God, while they were disputing about it most loudly with their lips. They busied themselves with every question about Christ except those which might have led them to imitate Christ's life. Now Mohammed came to make a clean sweep of such unrealities. Images : what are they? 'Bits of black wood, pretending to be God ;'[1] philosophical theories, and theological cobwebs. Away with them all ! God is great, and there is nothing else great.

[1] Carlyle, 'Heroes,' p. 226.

This is the Musalman Creed. 'Islam,' that is, man must resign his will to God's, and find his highest happiness in so doing. This is the Musalman life.

Was there anything in these two principles, an objector may ask, that was either original or new? There was nothing; they were as old as the time of Moses, as old, in reality, even as Abraham; again and again Mohammed asseverates that he has been sent to bring the Arabs nothing new; he has come only to republish the creed of Abraham which had always existed, however it had been forgotten or neglected. Amongst sullen and isolated Jews, amongst wrangling tritheistic Christians, amongst Fetish-worshippers of every grade, came a camel driver, not to teach them what was new, but to remind them of what was old. On Arabian soil more than two thousand years before, there had come to one who was tending his father's flock in the desert, the simple but the startling message, 'I am that I am. Hear, O Israel: the Lord our God is one God; now therefore go and I will be with thy mouth, and teach thee what thou shalt say;'[1] and at the words, from Africa the chosen people had passed into Asia, slaves had become freemen, and a family a nation. On that same Arabian soil now came the same voice to another shepherd of the desert, and that with effects not less

[1] Exodus III. 14, IV. 12; Deut. VI. 4.

striking, and hardly less fraught with benefit to the world at large: 'Allahu Akbar, God is most great, there is no God but God, and thou, Mohammed, art the Prophet of God.' The mission was accepted and the message proclaimed, and within a century its echoes were heard, and its truth recognised, from Aden to Antioch, and from Seville to Samarkand.

And I would remark here, and would particularly beg those who are doing me the honour to attend these Lectures to bear in mind, that though I have, in compliance with European custom, often spoken of Mohammedanism and Mohammedans, the name was never used by Mohammed himself, or by his earlier disciples, and, in spite of the reverence paid to their Prophet, it has always been rejected by his followers themselves as a rightful appellation. To quote once more the noble words of Abu Bakr, it was not Mohammed, but the God of Mohammed, that the Prophet taught his followers to worship. The creed is ' Islam,' a verbal noun, derived from a root meaning ' submission to' and ' faith in God,' and the believers who so submit themselves are called Muslims, a participle of the same root, both being connected with the words ' Sàlam,' or ' peace,' and ' Salym,' or ' healthy.' [1] There was nothing, therefore, theoretically new in what I have described as the central truth of Islam,

[1] Sprenger, Vol. I. p. 69.

M

for it was this belief that lay at the root of the greatness of the Jewish nation, and their separation from all other nations. Certain forms of Christianity have asserted it as strongly as did Mohammed. It is this principle which has been the strength of Calvinism and of Puritanism, and in this direction perhaps lies the explanation of the fact that those forms of religion which have been theoretically most fatalistic have by their acts given the strongest practical assertion of free-will. This was the spark from heaven which lit the train. In his assertion of this, lay the religious genius of Mohammed. This gave the Arabs 'unity as a nation, discipline and enthusiasm as an army.'[1] This sent them forth in their wild crusade against the world; and, armed with this, they swept away before them every creed, or memory of a creed, which did not then contain any principle so inspiring.

Such then were the two leading principles of the new creed; the existence of one God, whose will was to be the rule of life, and the mission of Mohammed to proclaim what that will was. The one doctrine as old, if not older than the time when the father of the faithful left his Chaldean home in obedience to the Divine will; the other sanctioned indeed, in its general assertion of the prophetic office, by the

---

[1] Maurice, loc. cit.

traditionary belief of both Jews and Arabs; but startling enough in the time at which the revelation came, in the instrument selected, and in the way in which he proclaimed it. In this consists the originality, such as it is, of Mohammedanism. The other articles of faith, added to the two I have already discussed— the written revelation of God's will, the responsibility of man, the existence of angels and of Djinn, the future life, the resurrection, and the final judgment —are to be found, either developed or in germ, in the systems, either of Jews, or Zoroastrians, or Christians. Even in the times of ignorance, the camel tethered to a dead man's grave was an indication that the grave was, even to the wild Arab, not the end of all things.[1]

Nor was there anything much more original in the four practical duties of Islam—in prayer and alms-giving, in fasting and in pilgrimage. Prayer is the aspiration of the human soul towards God, common to every religion, from the rudest Fetishism to the most sublime Monotheism. But it occupies in Islam

[1] Sprenger says (I. 4, 301) that the reason why Mohammed refers so often, e.g., in the very first Sura in chronological order, to the 'clot of blood' from which man was created, is because he looked upon it much as Christians have done to the emerging of the butterfly from the chrysalis, as a proof or illustration of the resurrection. In Sura LIII. Mohammed says he took not the doctrine merely, but the illustration also, from the roll of Abraham. Cf. Sura LXXV., entitled 'The Resurrection,' ad fin. : 'Is not the God who formed man from a mere embryo powerful enough to quicken the dead ? '

a more prominent place both theoretically and practically than it does in any other religion. Some of the
characteristics of Musalman prayer are almost peculiar
to it, and render it sometimes, perhaps, more profoundly devotional, and sometimes more purely
mechanical, than is to be found amongst the followers
of any other creed.

Almsgiving is the most easy and obvious method
of evidencing that love to man which leads up to, and
is, in its turn, the result of love to God. Fasting is
an assertion, though a superficial one, of the great
truth that self-denial is a step towards God ; but
it is peculiarly liable to abuse as fostering the belief,
so common among the ruder of the Semitic nations,
and still commoner among ascetics in modern times,
that God is to be feared rather than loved, and that
there is something pleasing to Him in pain as such ;
pain, that is, apart from its effect upon the will, and
so upon the character. Pilgrimage is a concession to
human feelings, not to say to human weakness,
common again, in practice, to all the religions of the
world. But this last calls, perhaps, for some special
remark here, since its actual influence has been so
great, while in theory and in reality it is alien alike
to Mohammedanism and to Christianity.[1]

---

[1] A high authority, Dr. Badger, has remarked with reference to
this passage, that he is at a loss to understand how the Hajj can be

'The hour cometh when ye shall neither in this mountain, nor yet at Jerusalem, worship the Father.' 'God is a spirit, and they that worship Him must worship Him in spirit and in truth.' But from the time the words were spoken, even to this day, a continuous living stream has poured towards the Holy Land. For nineteen centuries Christian Pilgrims have been seen to leave their homes and kindred, facing, now privations, now dangers, and now ridicule, that they might enjoy the sacred luxury, the ineffable religious rapture, of beholding the city over which the Saviour wept, of standing on the spot which gave Him birth, of gazing on the lake whereon He taught,

---

spoken of as in any way alien to Islam, seeing that it is enjoined in the Koran : he has a much greater right to speak on the subject than I have, but I still think that a careful examination of the twenty-second Sura of the Koran, entitled the Pilgrimage, compared with other passages, will justify me in the way in which I have spoken here of it as alien in reality to so spiritual a religion as Islam, even though it is enjoined in the Koran ; as a concession, and an inconsistent concession, to natural weakness rather than as a part of the inner belief of the Prophet, who so emphatically said, 'There is no piety in turning your faces towards the East or West, but he is pious who believeth in God.' The gist of the Sura seems to me to be this (cf. Sprenger, II., xvi. 531) : the chief ceremony of the faithful is the pilgrimage, which it is well to observe with all its peculiarities as an historical commemoration (v. 25). Every people has religious rites and ceremonies of its own, and their use will depend on the spirit in which they are performed. 'By no means can the flesh of camels which ye sacrifice reach unto God, neither their blood ; but piety on your part reacheth Him' (v. 38). But ceremonies are externals (v. 66) ; the essence of the matter consists in prayer, in giving alms to the poor, in 'cleaving fast to God, to Him who is your liege Lord, a goodly Lord and a great helper' (v. 77).

and of worshipping in the shrine which covers the rock wherein His body lay. And far be it from me to say, spite of the invention of the true Cross, spite of St. Andrew's lance and the relics of the Apostles, spite of the Crusades themselves, spite of the keys of the Holy Sepulchre, and even of the imposture of the Holy Fire, that the evils belonging to this reverence for places have altogether predominated over the good. A scientific and unimaginative age laughs at the weaknesses and the follies involved, but it forgets the dauntless faith and the heroic endurance, the sacrifice of self, and the romance of danger; it forgets that it is the office of religion to deal with these very human weaknesses and follies, and make the best of such materials as it has to work upon.

Christ swept away some of the abuses of the temple worship, and looked forward to its ultimate abolition; but He did not sweep away the temple itself. He rather paid it its customary honours. Mohammed saw the dangers of the Kaaba worship, and, once and again, proposed to destroy it altogether; but he had to deal with an historical faith, and with a shrine of immemorial antiquity, one which Diodorus Siculus, a hundred years before the Christian era, tells us, was even then 'most ancient, and was exceedingly revered by the whole Arab race.' The traditions of the Kaaba ran back to Ishmael and

Abraham, nay even to Seth and Adam ;[1] and, as its very name, 'Beit Allah,' shows, it might, in its first rude shape, have been erected by some such ancient patriarch as he who raised a pillar of rough stone where in his sleep he had seen the angels ascending and descending, and called it ' Bethel or Beit Allah : this is the house of God, and this the gate of heaven.' Arab poets went further back still, and assigned to the holy city a date to be reckoned rather by astronomical or geological time than historical : even 'before Sirius was created,' so says a patriotic poem which commemorates the miraculous repulse of Abrahah, the Christian King of Abyssinia, from the Kaaba, ' even before Sirius was created, was Mecca a holy place : therefore should even the mightiest among men yield it homage. Ask the Nagashy of Abyssinia about it : sixty thousand of them returned not again to their homes ; they quitted life : God sent a mighty wind which scattered them like a flock of sheep.'[2] Now Mohammed cherished all the family associations of a Haschimite,[3] as well as all the local

---

[1] Cf. Sura III. 90. 'The first temple that was founded for man-kind was that in Becca (place of resort, *i.e.*, Mecca)—Blessed, and a guidance to human beings. In it are evident signs, even the stand-ing-place of Abraham, and he who entereth it is safe. And the pilgrim-age to the temple is a service due to God from those who are able to journey thither.' This sentence is still woven into the covering of the Kaaba, sent annually by the Sultan.

[2] Sirat-er-raçoul, I. 29.

[3] See a curious conversation between Mohammed and Ayishah on

affections of a Meccan patriot ; and the family, and
the place, and the country, the historical lore, and the
religious imagination, combined to save the sacred
shrine.   Mohammed swept away the idols of the
Kaaba ; he abolished the nude processions [1] and the
other abuses of its worship ; but he retained the
Kaaba itself ; and the quaint rites, which were old in
Mohammed's time, are still religiously observed by
the whole Mohammedan world.   Seven times the
pilgrim walks around the sacred mosque, seven times
he kisses the Black Stone ; he drinks the brackish
water of the sacred well Zemzem, buries the parings
of his nails, and the hair he has at length shaved, in
the consecrated ground ; he ascends Mount Arafat
and showers stones on the three mysterious pillars.[2]
Nor is the Kaaba present to the mind at those times
only when the prescribed pilgrimage is near at hand,
in prospect or in retrospect.   The first architectural
requisite of every Musalman house of prayer is the
niche or arch which points with mathematical pre-

the Kaaba, illustrating the strong family feelings of the Prophet.
Sprenger, I. iv. 315.

[1] Sura VII. 27 sq.   Cf. XXII. 27-40, and Mishkat-ul-Masibeh, I.
Book XI. 619.

[2] A plan of the Kaaba, as taken by Ali Bey, and a full description
of the Pilgrim ceremonies, which he himself went through, may be
seen in Burton's 'Pilgrimage,' III. 61.   Burckhardt and Burton have
both described the Black Stone minutely from personal observation ;
and a picture of it, the size of the original, is given in Muir, II. 18.

cision to the sacred pile; and, guided by this, every devout Musalman turns five times a day towards the Kiblah of the world, in earnest prayer to God. 'That man,' says Dr. Johnson, 'has little to be envied whose patriotism would not gain force on the plains of Marathon, or whose piety would not grow warm among the ruins of Iona.' The ceremonies of the Kaaba may perhaps seem to us ridiculous, but the shrine is one which kindled the feelings of the Arab patriot, and roused the hopes of the Bedouin of the desert, ages before Miltiades fought, and tens of ages before Columba preached. It has been consecrated in its later history by its connection with the grandest forward movement that the Eastern world has ever known; and, in spite of the mummeries and the abuses which have grown round the pilgrimage of the Hajj in the course of ages, I should be slow indeed to assert that the feelings which still draw, year after year, Musalmans by myriads from the burning sands of Africa, from the snows of Siberia, and the coral reefs of the Malays, towards a barren valley in Arabia, do not, on the whole, elevate rather than depress them in the scale of humanity. In their own rough and imperfect way, they raise the mind of the nomad and the shepherd from the animal life of the present to the memories of the distant past, and the hopes of the far future. They are a living testimony

to the unity of God, and a homage paid by the unprogressive nations of the world to that Prophet who
softened the savage breast, and elevated the savage
mind, and taught them what, but for him, they had
never learned at all.

It will be apparent, from what I have already said,
that of the previous faiths existing in the world, the
one which influenced Mohammed most was, beyond
all question, Judaism. Insomuch, that one whose loss
all who take interest in Eastern questions are now
deploring, the late Emanuel Deutsch, summed up
the connection between them in the celebrated dictum,
that 'when the Talmud was gathered in, the Koran
began—*post hoc ergo propter hoc.*' And he went on
to endorse and to develope what Dean Milman had
hinted before him, that Islam was little else than
a republication of Judaism, with such modifications
as suited it to Arabian soil, *plus* the important
addition of the prophetic mission of Mohammed.
The gifted author was, perhaps, from the very extent
of his knowledge of Talmudical literature, prone to
trace its influence everywhere; and the proposition
is, perhaps, stated a little too nakedly, and, as he,
no doubt, would have been the first to admit, needs
some important qualifications;[1] but nobody would

[1] It must be remembered also that in the new form of the faith the
ceremonialism which marked Judaism for the time almost entirely

deny that it is substantially true. Indeed, the general connection between race and creed has been proved by the Science of Comparative Religion to be so intimate, that it could hardly in any case have been otherwise. It seems a cruel destiny that allows a man of great original genius to accumulate such vast stores of recondite learning, and then snatches him away before he has had time to do more than leave the world dimly and sadly conscious of what it has lost in losing him !

Anyhow, the Koran teems with ideas, allusions, and even phraseology, drawn not so much from the written as from the oral Jewish law, from the traditions that grew round it, and the commentaries on it. The Talmud, in its two divisions of Halacha and Haggada, sums up the intellectual, and social and religious life of the Jews during a period of nearly a thousand years. It is the meeting point of the three Monotheistic creeds of the world ; and, even with the imperfect information that Eastern scholars have yet given respecting it, it has done much to throw light upon them all. Mohammed was never

disappeared ; and its exclusive spirit permanently and completely. The propagandist and missionary spirit of Islam is a point in which it compares most favourably with Judaism. For a full account of the influence of the Essenic communities and their doctrines on the rise of Islam, see Sprenger, I. 17-21, and 30-35 ; and for that of the Ebionites or Judaising Christians to the East of the Jordan, p. 21-28.

backward to acknowledge the intimate connection between his faith and that of the Jews. And in more than one passage of the Koran he refers with equal respect to their oral and to their written law. Nor did Christ really draw so broad a distinction between these two as might be imagined from the sweeping way in which He sometimes denounces the Scribes and Pharisees. 'Whatsoever they that sit in Moses' seat bid you observe, that observe and do.'[1] And it is incontestable that the Pharisees, as a body, contained some of the best and noblest— Hillel and Shammai, Gamaliel and St. Paul—as it contained some of the worst and meanest, of their nation.

And, accordingly, Mohammed, during the early years of the Hijrah, struggled hard, and, as it might have seemed to him, with every prospect of success, to secure the adhesion of the Jewish tribes who dwelt round Medina. He appealed to their Scriptures, which, he said, he came not to destroy, but to fulfil, and which, as he argued, for those who had eyes to see, pointed to him. 'A prophet shall the Lord your God raise up unto you of your brethren like unto me; to him shall ye hearken.' Was he not like unto Moses? he asked again and again ; and did he not

---

[1] St. Matt. XXIII. 2 and 3. See this well argued in an article on the Talmud, *Edinburgh Review* for July 1873.

spring from their brethren, the children of Ishmael ?
' In thee shall all families of the earth be blessed : '
were Abraham's descendants by Ishmael, he asked,
to be altogether excluded from this blessing, and had
they not now their part of the prophecy to fulfil, as
Abraham's descendants by Isaac had already fulfilled
theirs? 'The Lord came from Sinai, He rose up
from Mount Seir unto them, He shined forth from
Mount Paran.'[1] From Sinai had come the law of
Moses, so argued others for Mohammed, if he did not
argue for himself, from Mount Seir the Gospel; and
now from Paran, the hills round Mecca, had come the
Koran.[2] He adapted the fasts and the feasts of the
new religion to the Jewish model. He took from
them the law of usury and the law of inheritance.
He owes to them some of his regulations respecting
ablutions and unclean animals. He even, till he
could hope no longer, made Jerusalem the Kiblah of
the world for the five daily prayers.

It must have surprised Mohammed, with his half

---

[1] Deut. III. 2.

[2] Other passages of Scripture taken by Mohammed himself, or by
Musalman doctors, to refer to Islam, are Gen. XVII. 20 ; Isa. XXI. 7,
XLII. LXIII. 1-6; Habakkuk III. 3 ; John I. 21, 'art thou *that*
Prophet?' John XIV. 16 ; Rev. VI. 4. The treatment of the passage
in Isa. XXI. 7 is interesting : the watchman, according to the right
translation of the Hebrew original, 'saw a chariot with a couple of riders,
the one a rider on an ass, the other on a camel :' if, as Christian controversialists maintained, the Prophet of Nazareth was one, is not, so
argue the Musalman doctors, the Prophet of Mecca the other ?

knowledge of their history, that the Jews should be
unable to enter into his views of a great Catholic
creed, or Religion of Humanity—the creed of
Abraham—embracing Jews, Arabs, and Christians
in one body. But it can surprise no one who has
ever in any degree entered into the religious genius
of the Jewish race, or who has reflected on the
almost insuperable difficulties which lay in the way
of the Jews accepting that higher creed, the Author
of which it is their eternal honour to have produced,
and their tragic destiny to have rejected. And the
Bani Kainucaa, and the Bani Nadhir, the Bani
Kuraitza, and the Jews of Kheibar, bitterly experienced in Mohammed's subsequent treatment of
them the truth of the now-all-too-familiar maxim in
ecclesiastical history, that they who differ least in
religious matters hate the most.

It is impossible to gain for oneself, and almost
equally so to give to others within a short space of
time, anything like an adequate idea either of the
form or of the contents of the book of which Mohammed, whatever the general influences brought to bear
upon his mind, was the undisputed author, and which
still underlies the life of the vast fabric of the
Mohammedan world. In my First Lecture I compared and contrasted the Koran with the Bible ; but
it is necessary, perhaps, to say something more of its

leading characteristics, or the want of them. The Koran defies analysis, for that presupposes something like method in the thing to be analysed. It can hardly be characterised by any one epithet, for there is not·a single Sura of any length which sustains a uniform character throughout. It has often been remarked that there is no more striking proof of the discrepancies of national taste than the diametrically opposite opinions held by the cultivated classes of East and West on the literary merits of the Koran. Having performed repeatedly, for the purpose of these Lectures, a task which Bunsen and Sprenger and Renan all pronounce to be almost impossible—that of reading the Koran continuously from beginning to end, both in the orthodox and chronological order —I have acquired a better right, perhaps, than most people to endorse the superficial opinion that dulness is, to a European who is ignorant of Arabic, the prevailing characteristic of the book as a whole until he begins to make a minute study of it. The importance of the subjects it handles, the unique interest attaching to the speaker, and the unaffected reverence with which every utterance is still regarded by so large a portion of the world, are insufficient to redeem it from this general reproach.

Endless assertions as to what the Koran is, and what it is not, warnings drawn from previous

Arabian history, especially the lost tribes of Ad and Thamud ; Jewish or Arab legends of the heroes of the Old Testament, stories told, and, it must be added, often spoiled in the telling of them ; laws, ceremonial and moral, civil and sumptuary ; personal apologies ; curses showered upon Abu Lahab or the whole community of the Jews ; all this alternates with sublime revelations of the attributes of the Godhead, bursts of admiration for Christ Himself, though not for the views held of Him by His so-called followers, flights of poetry, scathing rebukes of the hypocrite, the ungrateful, the unmerciful.

That the book as a whole is a medley, however it may be arranged, will seem only natural when we remember the way in which it was composed, pre-served, edited, and stereotyped. Dictated from time to time by Mohammed to his disciples, it was by them partly treasured in their memories, partly written down on shoulder-bones of mutton or oyster-shells, on bits of wood or tablets of stone, which, being thrown pell-mell into boxes, and jumbled up together, like the leaves of the Cumean Sibyl after a gust of wind, were not put into any shape at all till after the Prophet's death by order of Abu Bakr. The work of the editor consisted simply in arranging the Suras in the order of their respective lengths, the longest first, the shortest last ; and, though the book once after-

wards passed through the editor's hands, this is substantially the shape in which the Koran has come
down to us. Various readings, which would seem,
however, to have been of very slight importance,
having crept into the different copies, a revising com-
mittee was appointed by order of the Khalif Othman,
and, an authorized edition having been thus prepared
'to prevent the texts differing, like those of the Jews
and Christians,' all previous copies were collected
and burnt!

Nor is it to be wondered at that the principle of
arrangement, combined with the impossibility of
keeping the rhyme or rhythm in any translation, have
prevented European critics, as a body, from endorsing
the judgment, not merely of Mohammed himself, for
that, if it had stood alone, might be looked upon as
partial, but also of the whole Eastern world.

'If ye be in doubt as to our revelation to our servant, then produce a Sura like unto it, and summon
your witnesses, God and all, if ye be men of truth.'[1]

And again, 'If men and genii were assembled together that they might produce a book like the Koran,
they must fail.'[2]

It is to be remarked that Mohammed and Mohammed's enemies are quite at one as to the merits of
the book. The Arabs said that the Koran could not

---

[1] Sura II. 21.   [2] Sura XVII. 90.

be Mohammed's work because it was too good. Mohammed replied to the effect that they were both right
and wrong. They were right, for it was too good for
Mohammed uninspired; they were wrong, for it was
too good to have come originally from any one but
the All-Merciful.[1]

Of course, by the existing arrangement, even such
psychological development as there was in the Koran
has been obscured; for, as a rule, what the editor put
last comes really first. These are the burning utterances of the Prophet who knows no influence but the
inspiration pent within him; in these are the pith and
poetry of the whole; while the elaborate and laboured
arguments, the *apologiæ pro vitâ suâ*, are the product
of the mind which the force of circumstances and the
love of spiritual power, that most exquisite and most
dangerous of fascinations, had driven to become conscious of itself. The very titles of the earlier Suras,
the imprecations with which they abound, the imagery
they employ, suggest the shepherd of the desert, the
despised visionary, the poet and the prophet. 'The
folding up,' 'the cleaving in sunder,' 'the celestial
signs,' 'the unity,' 'the overwhelming,' 'the striking,'
'the inevitable,' 'the earthquake,' 'the war-horses,'
tell their own story. There are passages in these,
though it must be admitted they are rare, which may

[1] Sura XVI. 105, compared with XXV. 5, etc.

be compared in grandeur even with some of the sublimest passages of Job, of David, or of Isaiah.

Take, for instance, the vision of the last day with which the eighty-first Sura, 'The folding up,' begins :

'When the sun shall be folded up,
And when the stars shall fall,
And when the mountains shall be set in motion,
And when the she-camels with young shall be neglected,
And when the wild beasts shall be huddled together,
And when the seas shall boil,
And when souls shall be joined again to their bodies,
And when the female child that had been buried alive shall ask for
    what crime she was put to death,
And when the leaves of the Book shall be unrolled,
And when the Heavens shall be stripped away like a skin,
And when Hell shall be made to blaze,
And when Paradise shall be brought near,
Every soul shall know what it has done.'

Allusions to the monotony of the desert; the sun in its rising brightness; the moon in its splendour; are varied in the Koran by much more vivid mental visions of the Great Day when men shall be like moths scattered abroad, and the mountains shall become like carded wool of various colours, driven by the wind. No wonder that Labyd, the greatest poet of his time, forbore to enter the poetic lists with Mohammed when he recited to him the description of the infidel in the second Sura.

'They are like one who kindleth a fire, and when it hath thrown its light on all around him, God taketh away the light and leaveth him in darkness, and they cannot see.'

' Deaf, dumb, blind, therefore they shall not retrace their steps.'

' They are like those who, when there cometh a storm-cloud out of heaven big with darkness, thunder and lightning, thrust their fingers into their ears because of the thunder-clap for fear of death. God is round about the infidels.'

' The lightning almost snatcheth away their eyes : so oft as it gleameth on them, they walk on in it ; but when darkness closeth upon them, they stop ; and if God pleased, of their ears and of their eyes would He surely deprive them ; verily God is almighty.'

And at the end of the same Sura, which, it is to be remembered, appeared quite late in the Prophet's life, at a period when it might have been expected that the cares of government would dim the brightness of the Prophet's visions, we find the sublime description of Him whom it had been the mission of his life to proclaim, and which is still engraved on precious stones, and worn by devout Musalmans.

' God ! there is no God but He, the Living, the Eternal. Slumber doth not overtake Him, neither sleep ; to Him belongeth all that is in heaven and in earth. Who is he that can intercede with Him but by His own permission? He knoweth that which is past and that which is to come unto them, and they shall not comprehend anything of His knowledge but so far as He pleaseth. His throne is extended over heaven and earth, and the upholding of both is no burden unto Him. He is the Lofty and the Great.'

Such is the theology of the Koran; and here, in the same grand Sura, is perhaps the best summary of its morality :—

'There is no piety in turning your faces towards the East or the West, but he is pious who believeth in God, and the Last Day, and the Angels, and the Scriptures and the Prophets; who for the love of God disburseth his wealth to his kindred, and to the orphans, and the needy, and the wayfarer, and those who ask, and for ransoming; who observeth prayer, and payeth the legal alms, and who is of those who are faithful to their engagements when they have engaged in them, and patient under ills and hardships and in time of trouble; these are they who are just, and those who fear the Lord.'

Almost equally well too, as a proof of his poetic inspiration, might have Mohammed quoted that other description of Infidelity also produced late in his life, and pronounced by Sir William Muir and by Emanuel Deutsch to be one of the grandest in the whole Koran.

'As to the Infidels, their works are like the Serab on the plain,[1] which the thirsty traveller thinketh to be water, and then when he cometh thereto, he findeth it to be nothing ; but he findeth God about him, and He will fully pay him his account ; for swift in taking an account is God ;

'Or as the darkness over a deep sea, billows riding upon billows below, and clouds above ; one darkness on another darkness : when a man stretcheth forth his hand he is far from seeing it ; he to whom God doth not grant light, no light at all hath he.'[2]

Strange and graphic accounts have been preserved to us by Ayishah of the physical phenomena attending the Prophet's fits of inspiration. He heard as it were the ringing of a bell ; he fell down as one dead ; he sobbed like a camel ; he felt as though he were being rent in pieces, and when he came to himself he felt as though words had been written on his heart. And when Abu Bakr, 'he who would have sacrificed father and mother for Mohammed,' burst into tears at the sight of the Prophet's whitening hair, 'Yes,' said Mohammed, 'Hud and its sisters, the Terrific Suras, have turned it white before its time.'[3]

---

[1] i.e. the Mirage of the Desert.

[2] Sura XXIV. 39, 40. See Muir, III. 308 ; and Deutsch, 'Islam,' in 'Quarterly Review,' No. 254, p. 346.

[3] Suras XI., Hud ; LVI., 'The Inevitable ;' CI., 'The Striking.' See Muir, II. 88.

But in order to make the general outline of Mohammed's system, which I am attempting to draw, as
little imperfect as it is possible for me to make it within
the limits I have prescribed myself, it is necessary to
touch upon three difficult questions, which have acquired different degrees of prominence at successive
periods in the history of Mohammedanism—questions
which have been much misunderstood, and sometimes
intentionally misrepresented, and which call more
loudly even than other matters which we have been
considering for a laborious investigation and a candid
judgment. They need also above all things the historical sense, which does not apply the standard of the
nineteenth century to the seventh, ot Europeans to
Asiatics, or of a high civilisation to semi-barbarism ;
and which is content to balance the evil against the
good, without requiring a verdict either for an absolute
acquittal or an uncompromising condemnation. The
three questions I refer to are the relation of Mohammedanism to Miracles, to Fatalism, and to wars for
the sake of Religion. I propose in the remainder of
this Lecture to deal with these in succession ; not
I hope consciously shirking any difficulty, or glossing
over what is unquestionably bad, but, of course, not
professing in any degree to exhaust the subject.

First, then, Miracles. Mohammedanism is a
system in many respects unique, but in none more

so than in this, that alone of the great religions of
the world it does not, in its authoritative documents,
rest its claims to reception upon miracles ; and yet
the attitude of Mohammed towards the miraculous
has been made the ground by different people of very
conflicting accusations.   Superficial observers up to
the middle of the last century, and Christian missionaries of later times, whose zeal has not always been
tempered by accurate knowledge of their subject,
fastening on the fantastic character of the few miracles
attributed to Mohammed by the pious credulity of his
followers or the ' successors,' have triumphantly torn
the mask from the ' impostor,' and have gone on to
contrast, as well they might from their point of view,
the purposeless character and impossibility of his
supposed miracles, with the sober nature and the
moral purpose which underlie the miracles of the New
Testament, however supernatural they may be.
Other writers—White in his ' Bampton Lectures,'
and Paley in his ' Evidences of Christianity,' and
Butler in his ' Analogy'—preferring to appeal to
what Mohammed said of himself, rather than to what
was said of him by others, have driven home the
contrast between Mohammedanism and Christianity
by pointing out that Christianity is attested by supernatural manifestations, and is therefore Divine, while
Mohammedanism is neither the one nor the other.

Let us enquire what the Koran itself, the only trust-worthy authority on the subject, says, and then make one or two remarks on the general question.

In the thirteenth Sura we read,—

'The unbelievers say, Unless a sign be sent down with him from his Lord, we will not believe. But thou art a preacher only, O Mohammed !'

Mohammed replies that God alone can work miracles; and, after specifying some of them, he says :—

'God alone knoweth that which is hidden, and that which is revealed. He is the great and the Most High.'

In the seventh Sura the Infidels ask why Mo-hammed had not been sent with miracles, like previous prophets? Because, replied Mohammed, miracles had proved inadequate to convince. Noah had been sent with signs, and with what effect? Where was the lost tribe of Thamud? They had refused to receive the preaching of the prophet Sahleh unless he showed them a sign, and caused the rock to bring forth a living camel. He did what they asked. In scorn they had cut off the camel's feet, and then, daring the Prophet to fulfil his threats of judgment, were found dead in their beds next morning, stricken by the angel of the Lord. There are some seven-teen places in the Koran in which Mohammed is

challenged to work a sign, and he answers them all
to the same effect.

There are in the whole of the sacred book only
two supposed exceptions to the attitude thus assumed
by him ; and those who know how large a part
the Miraj, or miraculous journey on the Borak,[1] bears
in popular conceptions of Mohammedanism will learn
with surprise, if they have not gone much into the
matter, that there is only one passage in the Koran
which can be tortured into an allusion to the journey
to heaven.

‘ Praise be to Him who transferred His servant by
night from the sacred temple to one that is more
remote.’[2]

To make this refer at all to the Miraj, we have to
insert the word ‘ Mecca ’ in one place, and Jerusalem
or ‘ seventh heaven ’ in another, and this, though in
the sixtieth verse of the same Sura Mohammed tells
us he was not sent with miracles, because people
would not believe them ; and in the sixty-second
verse express mention is made of a vision he had
had, beyond doubt of this very journey ! So, too, in
the verse : ‘ The hour hath approached and the moon
hath been split in sunder : ’[3] people were so anxious

---

[1] Borak after all means only Lightning ; the Barak of the Jews ; the
Barca of the Carthaginians.

[2] Sura XVII. 1.   [3] Sura LIV. 1.

to see an allusion to their own extravagant invention of the moon's descending on the Kaaba, and entering Mohammed's sleeve, that they forgot that 'the hour' means 'the hour of judgment,' and that the tense used is the prophetic preterite. To the eye of the Semitic ' nabi,' whether Jewish or Arab, the future is as the past.[1]

Without discussing the question of miracles at length, I would make three remarks on the general subject :—First, that in a new religion the real cause for wonder is, not that it claims to be founded on miracles, but that it should ever be able to profess to do without them. In certain stages of the human mind there is no natural phenomenon which will not bear a supernatural interpretation. In fact, the supernatural is then the rule ; the natural, the exception. Gibbon, I think, has somewhere asked whether there exists a single instance in ecclesiastical history of a Father of the Church claiming for himself the power of working miracles, and I am not aware that the question has ever been answered in the affirmative. And yet we know that during many centuries there was hardly a Father of the Church who did not have miracles attributed to him by other men of equal, or

---

[1] Cf. the past tense used in Sura XCVIII., called 'The Victory'—' Verily, we *have* won for thee an undoubted victory,' believed to point to the conquest of Mecca two years later.

even greater, reputed sanctity. Among many others
I need only mention the names of St. Benedict and '
St. Martin of Tours, of St. Bernard and St. Francis of
Assisi. They attribute even to inanimate remains,
and to relics, which were often fictitious, powers which
they would never dream of claiming for themselves.
St. Augustine, whose honesty is above suspicion, tells
us gravely that he had ascertained, on certain evidence, that some small fragments of the disinterred
relics of St. Stephen had, in his own diocese, within
two years, performed no less than seventy miracles,
and three of them raisings from the dead! St. Bernard was believed by his admirers to have excommu-
nicated some flies which teased him, and 'they
straightway fell down in heaps.' And if such be the
mental atmosphere of a Church in its adolescence,
à fortiori will an age which is capable of producing
or receiving a new religion throw a mystic halo of
supernaturalism round the supreme objects of its
reverence. Even if the founder himself disclaims the
power of working miracles, they will be thrust upon
him in the most perfect good faith by the warm
imagination of his disciples.

Secondly, and what would seem to follow from
my first remark: in proportion as exact knowledge
advances, the sphere of the supernatural is narrowed;
and therefore a proof which is fitted for an imaginative

and creative age is not best suited for a critical and
scientific one. Many minds, no doubt, will always
crave the supernatural, and they will always find
plenty of it ; but to many, also, in an age like this,
miracles have been a stumbling-block, and have seemed
a reason for rejecting the religion which is made to
rest mainly on them. Where there is a choice, it is at
least wise to select the strongest ground we have; nor
is there any fear that Science will ever explain too
much. Behind what she explains, there will always
remain the unexplained and the unexplainable. Let
her classify and explain the phenomena of Mind and
Matter as she will, but will she ever be able to tell us
what Mind and Matter are themselves? Let her
analyse the springs of human action, and dissect the
complex anatomy of the human conscience ; but the
religious instinct will still remain, as an ultimate fact
of human nature ; and that instinct will find without,
or supply from its own resources, the verities with
which it deals, the verities which supplement and
explain to it the facts of Nature, and are not explained
by them ; which assure us that this life is not the only
life, nor death extinction ; and that love, the main
source of human happiness, is not given us to make
all real happiness impossible ; which, in a word, supply
the soul with the supreme objects for its worship and
its aspirations.

Thirdly, I would remark that the answers given by Mohammed himself to those who demanded miracles, that God gave the power of working miracles to whom He pleased; that other prophets had wrought miracles, and had not been believed; that he who could not know even himself adequately, could not know what God had hidden; that there were greater miracles in nature than any which could be wrought outside of it; that the Koran itself was a miracle, find at least one line of thought in a greater than Mohammed, which is not opposed to, but identical with them. People have raised questions about the authenticity and meaning of much that is in the Gospels, but by the rules of all critical interpretation, what they can least question is the genuineness and accuracy of those passages which the Disciples have, in their undoubted honesty, recorded, as it were, in spite of themselves, and which appear to run counter to other and loftier conceptions of that majestic character on whose partially-preserved utterances all Christendom still hangs. He who said he could of His own self do nothing; it was the spirit which quickened, the flesh profiteth nothing; the words that He spake unto them, they were spirit and they were life; He who, when His Disciples wondered at the withered fig tree, told them that the trust in God which underlay His act would enable even them to do greater things; who, we are

told, *could* not, in certain places, work miracles because
of their unbelief; and when people declined to accept
His teaching on higher grounds, told them, with a
touch of scorn, that they might do so if they liked on
the lower ground, for ' His *very* works' sake ; ' and,
lastly, who said it was an evil and adulterous generation which sought after a sign, and that no sign should
be given it; and that if a man believed not Moses
and the Prophets, not even would he repent though
one rose from the dead ; in one aspect, at all events,
of His teaching agreed with the Arabian Prophet
whom Christians have so much discredited. He, at
all events, treated the miraculous as subordinate to
the moral evidences of His mission, and struck upon
a vein of thought and touched a chord of feeling
which, it seems to me, is reconcilable at once with the
onward march of Science, and all the admitted weaknesses of human nature.

II. Fatalism. I have spoken above of the extraordinary impulse given to the earlier followers of
Mohammed by their vivid sense of God's personal
presence with them. Inspiring, indeed, this principle then was ; for it must never be forgotten, as I
hope now to prove, that the belief in an absolute
predestination, which turns men into mere puppets,
and all human life into a grim game of chess, wherein
men are the pieces, moved by the invisible Hand of

but a single Player, and which is now so general in
Mohammedan countries, was, all appearances to the
contrary, no part of the creed of the Prophet himself
or of his immediate successors;[1] and I venture,
therefore, to think that Gibbon is wrong in tracing
the desperate valour of the primitive Musalmans
mainly to the notion that since there was no chance,
there need be no fear: the germ, indeed, of fatalism
was there, but its effects were as yet anything but
fatalistic.

It is of course true that there are many passages
in the Koran which assert in the strongest way the
foreknowledge of God. For instance, 'The fate of
every man have we bound about his neck;' and the
relations of the slain at the battle of Ohud are com-
forted by the assurance that every one must die at
his appointed time, whether it be in his own bed or
on the field of battle.   Nor is it possible to any religion to reconcile the conflicting dogmas of the foreknowledge of God and of the free will of man.   The
New Testament does not try to do so.   St. Paul's
simile of the potter, for instance, in the Romans is as
fatalistic as is any passage in the Koran.   It asserts
an absolute predestination as strongly as many other
passages in his Epistles assert free-will.   It is not
likely that Fathers of the Church or controversialists

[1] Cf. 'National Review' for July, 1858, p. 154.

will succeed in doing what an Apostle found it necessary to leave undone, and the maxim of John of
Damascus, '*illud scire oportet, Deum omnia prœscire sed
non omnia prœfinire,*' does not get over the difficulty,
though he appears to have imagined that it did. Most
assuredly our own Articles of Religion, however successful they may be in finding a compromise between
opposing views on other things, fail to effect a compromise here. Press to its logical result either the
omnipotence or the omniscience of God, and what
becomes of man's free will? But logic is not the
only criterion of truth, nor is it the only rule of life ;
and consequently there is hardly a religion which
does not, in words at all events, assert as strongly
as possible God's foreknowledge ; in acts, at all events,
man's freedom. Sometimes one will be the more prominent, sometimes the other.

The Prophet of Arabia naturally dwelt most on
those attributes of God which, throwing the widest
gulf between the Creator and His creatures, would,
once and for all, rescue the Arabs from worshipping
what their own hands had made.[1] He inculcates
hope in adversity, and humility in success, on the
ground that there is a supreme Ruler who never leaves
the helm ; who knows what is really best for man

[1] Cf. Gobineau, 'Les Religions et les Philosophies dans l'Asie
Centrale.' See the whole passage on this subject, p. 72, 73.

when man himself does not ; and whose supreme will
and power, where He asserts them, cannot be crossed
by the efforts of the creatures of His hand.   But this
is not the only side to his teaching.   He asserts that
man is a free agent ; free to refuse or to accept the
Divine message, responsible for his acts, and therefore
deserving, now of punishment, now of reward.   The
future, in fact, is in his own hands, and Mohammed
incessantly urges him to use his opportunities.   Ali,
the most saintly, I would almost say the most Christian, of all Musalmans, pronounces those who say the
will is not free to be heretics.[1]   There are at least
four sects among Mohammedans that differ from one
another on the one point of predestination and free
will.   One of them, the Mutazalites, almost assert
what philosophers have called the 'liberty of indifference ;' and there is little doubt that Mohammed
himself, if the alternative had been clearly presented
to him, would have had more in common with Pela-
gius than with Augustine, with Arminius than with
Calvin.

It is difficult to believe that if Mohammed had
been the consistent fatalist he is often represented to
have been, he would have made prayer one of the
four practical duties enjoined upon the faithful, and
that on an equal or even a higher footing than alms-

---

[1] Quoted by Gobineau, loc. cit.

giving, fasting, and pilgrimage. He is said to have
called it the Pillar of Religion and the Key of Paradise. He told a tribe which, after its conversion,
begged for a remission of some of the daily prayers enjoined upon them, that there could be no good in the
religion in which there was no prayer ; and, according
to one of his successors, prayer of itself lifts men half
way to heaven.[1] Now, if all events are absolutely
fixed by the Divine will, and foreseen by the Divine
mind, then there is no possibility, I do not say of
altering the fixed laws of nature, for that is a power
which few would claim for prayer, but even of a
man's improving in the smallest degree, by any
acts or petitions of his, his own spiritual condition.

[1] As to the reality of Prayer amongst Mohammedans, see the testimony of Lieutenant Wood, the intrepid explorer of the Oxus, who gave
a signal proof of his high Christian character by resigning his post under
the Indian Government on finding that it had employed him to make
promises of friendship to the Afghans which it was not prepared to
keep. He says ('Journey to the Source of the Oxus,' p. 93), after
mentioning a remarkable proof of the importance which his Mohammedan guides attached to prayer, 'Often since that time have I observed
that the Mohammedans, both old and young, however worn out by
fatigue or suffering from hunger and thirst, have postponed all thought
of self-indulgence to their duty to their God. It is not with them the
mere force of habit ; it is the strong impression on their minds that the
duty of prayer is so important that no circumstances can excuse its
omission.' Nor did their dependence on God make them less ready to
help themselves. As they neared the dangerous whirlpools of the
Indus below Attock (p. 77), 'the crew went to prayers : then, steering
the oars, they fixed their eyes upon the steersman, watching for his
signal when they were to exert themselves.' (Cf. Walpole's 'Ansayrii,'
I. 56-59. Curzon's 'Monasteries,' p. 56, &c.)

Prayer would thus be a superfluity and delusion if
explained in any other way than as an aspiration of
the heart towards God, which, being an end in itself,
necessarily brings its own answer with it.   Now,
whether this last is a true view of prayer or not, it
was certainly not Mohammed's view.   In neither case
would he have been quite a consistent fatalist ; but it
is not likely that he could have overlooked the
glaring inconsistencies involved between an absolute
predestination on the one hand, and material answers
to prayer on the other.   The prayers that he enjoined
five times a day [1] are still offered with full confidence
in their efficacy by all devout Musalmans, and the
cry of the Muezzin, before daybreak, from a myriad
mosques and minarets—' Prayer is better than sleep,
prayer is better than sleep'—is a living witness,
wherever the influence of the Prophet of Arabia has
extended, more vivid than the letter of the Koran
itself, overpowering even the lethargy and quietism of
the East, to Mohammed's belief in God's providen-
tial government of the world, and in the freedom of
man's will.

Mohammed, on one occasion, complains of the

---

[1] It is worth noticing, in passing, that the five daily prayers, like
the rite of circumcision, though universally observed by Musalmans, are
not enjoined in the Koran itself.   Circumcision is not even mentioned
in the Koran : it is one of the many Pre-Islamitic practices which
Mohammed tacitly sanctioned.

Jews, that 'if good fortune betide them, they say it is from God ; if evil betide them, they say it is from Mohammed :' say rather, he suggests, all is from God. But what, he asks in the very next verse, has come to these people that they are not near to understanding what is told them ?

'Whatever good betideth thee is from God, and whatever betideth thee of evil is from thyself.' [1]

There are the two contradictories brought face to face, and left fronting one another for all time ; and can any religion do more, and, perhaps, I may add, less, than this ?

It is not difficult to see how one and the same doctrine of God's 'foreknowledge on the one hand, and of His actual intervention in human affairs on the other, may have diametrically opposite effects in different natures, or in even the same natures under different circumstances.

> 'There is a tide in the affairs of men,
> Which taken at the flood, leads on to fortune ;
> Omitted, all the voyage of their life
> Is bound in shallows and in miseries.'

The early Musalmans in the new burst of life breathed into them by Mohammed, it inspired with double energy and double enthusiasm, as in their best days it inspired the Puritans, the Covenanters, the

[1] Sura IV. 80, 81.

Pilgrim Fathers. But to their descendants in their more normal state—the dreamy Sufi, the brooding Sepoy, the insensate Turk; I would add, to those religious people who refuse to prevent the miseries and the diseases which Nature they think has attached to guilt—it furnishes with a new excuse for that life of inactivity to which they are already too much disposed, since they believe that they are acquiescing, as in duty bound, in the immutable decrees of God.[1]

III. One more question remains to be discussed to-day—the wars of Islam and the relation they bear to Mohammed's religion. It is true that it was not till the Prophet found himself, to his surprise, in a position of power at Medina, that we hear even a whisper of the sword as an instrument of conversion. It is then, and not till then, that we are told that other prophets have been sent by God to attest His different attributes in their own person and by their miraculous acts; but that men had closed their eyes to the character, and denied the miracles, even of Moses and of Christ. What remained to the last of the prophets except that he should try the last argument of the sword? Was the sword then an after thought and an accidental appendage merely to Mohammed's religion, or was it

---

[1] See an eloquent passage on this subject in an article of the 'National Review' for October, 1861, entitled the Great Arabian, p. 312.

an essential part? I am inclined to think that the
nature of the case itself and the verdict of subsequent
experience will tend to show that, however absent it
was from Mohammed's thoughts at first, and however
alien to his gentle and forgiving nature, it came in the
progress of events to some extent in his own life, and
still more so in the lives of his successors, to be the
latter. How this came about requires careful explanation.

Mohammed's notion of God had never been that of
a great moral Being who designs that the creatures
He has created should, from love and gratitude to
Him, become one with Him, or even assimilated to
Him. Mohammed believed in God, feared, reverenced,
and obeyed Him after his light, as few Jews or
Christians ever did ; but he could hardly be said in
the Christian, or even the Jewish sense of the word, to
love God. It is possible that repeated acts of obedience
to a God whom he always represents as compassionate
and merciful might imply or result in love ; but at all
events with him love was not, as it is in Christianity,
the fulfilling of the law, the inspiring motive to
action, the sum of its theology as of its morality.
Had it been so, Mohammed would have seen more
reason to doubt whether the sword could ever be its
best ally ; but though he must in any case have seen
that it was impossible to force men to love God, it

may have crossed his mind that it was possible to force men to abstain from idolatry, to acknowledge one God with their lips, to fear and to obey Him, at all events in their outward acts.

Had Mohammed remained master of himself— had he remained, that is to say, the simple Prophet throughout his career—it is possible, on the one hand, that his message would never have spread in his life-time beyond the walls of Mecca and Medina ; and it is more than probable, on the other, that his character might now be held up to the world as that which we feel the Founder of a religion ought to be ; that which Confucius and Buddha were, and that which Mo-hammed himself, throughout his life at Mecca, unques-tionably was—a perfect model of the saintly virtues. There is one glory of the founder of a religion, another of the founder of a nation, another of the founder of an empire. They are better kept distinct ; and the limits of the human faculties are an adequate security against their being often found united in one person. It is the uncongenial mixture of earthly needs and heavenly aspirations which has made Mohammed at once a smaller and a greater man—at once more and less commanding than he would otherwise have been. What he gains as a ruler of men, he loses as a guide and as an example ; and people are, naturally enough, led to condemn the prophet for the drastic energy of

the leader, and the leader for the shortcomings of the
prophet. It is, perhaps, inevitable that Christians
should do so ; for the image of Him whose kingdom
was not of this world, who did not strive nor cry,
whose servants were never to draw the sword in
His defence, forces itself upon the mind, in silent
and reproachful antithesis to the mixed and sullied
character of the Prophet-soldier Mohammed. The
trumpet-call is not the still small voice ; it is immeasurably below it : but there has been room for
both in the development of humanity.

Now, on a sudden, Mohammed found himself in a
position he had not courted, which was forced on him
by his enemies ; and the exigencies of his exiled
followers—the need of sustenance, the appetite for
plunder, the desire of revenge, and the longing for
their homes, no less than the impending attack of the
Kuraîsh—drove the Prophet for the first time to
place himself at their head ; and, for temporal purposes only, to unsheath the sword. Mohammed thus
became a general by accident ; and the extraordinary
success of his first ventures deepened the impression,
already half natural to an Arab, that the sword might
be a legitimate instrument of spiritual warfare, and
that God had put into his power a new means, where
all other means, as in the case of previous prophets,
had failed. At all events the sword, originally drawn

for temporal purposes only, was found to have, half-unexpectedly, answered another end as well. It was found that the religion, once started by the sword, was soon able to throw the sword away. The march of the Faith anticipated the march of the army of the Faithful, and the all but uniform success of the armies, when they had to fight, seemed to stamp the means used with the Divine approbation ; and so it was that Mohammed felt less and less scruple as to the use of the sword where it seemed to him to be wanted ; and at the close of his life, in one of the last Suras of the Koran we are hardly surprised to find the stern command and the ' magnificent presentiment :'

' Fight on, therefore, till there be no temptation to idolatry, and the religion becomes God's alone.' [1]

The early Khalifs obeyed the precepts and imitated the example of the warrior-Prophet, and went forth on their enterprise in all the plenitude of autocratic power ; there was no rivalry between Church and State to tie their hands, for the Khalif was the head of both in one ; the State, so far as it had any separate existence at all, being simply a creature of the Church. And let us here turn aside for a moment to examine the relation then subsisting between the spiritual and temporal power, first in the Western,

---

[1] Sura VIII. 40. Cf. also XXII. 40, and IX. *passim* : perhaps the last Sura Mohammed composed.

and then in the Eastern Empire, and to contrast it
with the extraordinary concentration of all the energies of a new-born enthusiasm, placed in the hands of
the Khalif. We shall then see, on the one hand, from
what a vantage-ground the Arabs, at that precise
moment, entered the lists to contend with Christendom;
but, on the other, we shall note how few are the men
who, even under the most exceptional circumstances,
can, in the exercise of power, afford to dispense
with those checks which are a condition of its permanence, and which alone can prevent it from deve-
loping into unbridled tyranny, or dying of inanition.

The Christianity of the West then had, centuries
before this, organized an *imperium in imperio* which
afforded a substantial check to the tyranny of the
Emperors, and, by its moral majesty, could restrain a
savage barbarian even in the full career of conquest.
Ambrose had sternly rebuked Theodosius ; Innocent
had mitigated the horrors of the sack of Rome by
Alaric ; Leo had turned back Attila, and half-dis-
armed Genseric. The transference of the seat of
Empire to Constantinople forced the Bishops of Rome
into a political prominence which would not otherwise
have belonged to them ; and, in process of time,
the spiritual power thus fortified began to contend,
on something like equal terms, with the temporal.
Gregory the Great, whose pontificate ended shortly

before the 'call' of the Prophet of Arabia, was the virtual sovereign of Rome, able to protect it alike from the ferocity of the Lombards, and from the pretentious weakness of the Exarchs. Before long the sacerdotal monarchs who reigned on the Tiber were to be seen deposing by right Divine one Frankish dynasty which ruled upon the Rhine ; setting up another of their own creation; and, finally, in the person of Charles the Great, giving new body to the phantom of the ancient Roman Empire which had never ceased to flit before the mind of Europe, and fancying, in their superb audacity, that a breath might overthrow what a breath had made. And by the time that the Eternal City itself heard the dreaded Tecbir at their gates, it was to a Pope, and not a Cæsar—a Pope, too, elected in hot haste, without even the formal sanction of the Cæsar—that Rome owed her safety ! [1]

But the religion of the Eastern Empire, to quote Gibbon's epigram, could teach men only ' to suffer and to yield.' The Patriarch of Constantinople, unlike the Patriarch of Rome, was the puppet of the Emperor, endorsed his worst deeds, or was swept away if he objected to them.[2] And the Saracens who besieged

[1] Leo IV.

[2] See the history of the Iconoclastic Emperors generally, A.D. 717–841, and their dealings with the Patriarchs of Constantinople. Read especially, on the one hand, the account of the dastardly submis-

the 'ceremonious' Emperor of the East in his own
capital must have enjoyed, if they could read, the
form of service, prescribed by Church and State
together, for the day on which the Emperor should
trample on the necks of the captive Musalmans, while
the singers were to chant, 'Thou hast made mine
enemies my footstool,' and the people were to shout
forty times the 'Kyrie Eleeson.'[1] The crusading
spirit which might have been evoked by a proposition
of the great Emperors, Nicephorus and Zimisces, to
give a martyr's crown to those who fell in battle with
the infidels, was checkmated by a counter-proposition
of the Patriarch to exclude from the highest rites of
the Church all those who took up arms even in self-
defence.[2] Had it been otherwise, the period of the
Crusades might have been anticipated by more than
a hundred years! We see, therefore, that in the West,
by the time that the tide of Arab conquest had spread
from Mecca to Gibraltar, the spiritual power was independent of the temporal, and was often able to control
or neutralise its action, even in temporal affairs; while
in the East, on which the storm was first to burst, it

sion of the Patriarch Anastasius to Leo, and, on the other, the horrible
cruelties inflicted on the Patriarch Constantine by Copronymus.
Milman, II. Chap. VII.

[1] See the 'De Ceremoniis Aulæ et Ecclesiæ Byzantinæ' of Constantine Porphyrogenitus, II. 19; quoted by Gibbon, Chap. LIII. 116,
and note.

[2] See Gibbon, loc. cit.

was almost non-existent; and if ever it did·cause
its voice to be heard, the cry it uttered was that
·of Phocion, not of Demosthenes—of Jeremiah, not of
Isaiah; that of submission to the inevitable, not of
resistance to the bitter end.

But with the Saracens the case was different. The
God of Mohammed, like the God of the wanderers of
the wilderness, and unlike the God of Christendom,
was pre-eminently the God of battles. The early
Musalmans shed tears' when held back within their
leashes from the battle and the Emperor Leo, who
condemned the Mohammedan idea of God, must have
secretly envied the vigour that it brought. Military
zeal under a tried leader is a strong passion, so is
religious enthusiasm; and never probably in the
history of the world have these two passions burned
with so consuming a flame as they did in the breasts
of the early followers of Mohammed. The civil, the
religious, and the military were as indissolubly blended
together in his system as they were in mediæval
chivalry. It was not so much religion that became
warlike, as war, the normal condition of the Arabs on
a small scale, now itself became religious, with the
whole world for its battle ground. Probably in no
army in the world, not even among the Scotch
Covenanters, nor among Cromwell's Ironsides, did
religious exercises so form part of the military dis-

cipline, and religious enthusiasm so infuse an esprit
de corps.

The early battles of Islam, Bedr and Ohud, Kade-
sia and Nehavend, the Yermuk and Aiznadin; its
early sieges, Bozra and Damascus, Jerusalem and
Aleppo, Memphis and Alexandria, are more than
Homeric in the reckless valour and the chivalrous
devotion that they exhibit. And it is to be remembered that they are in the main historical.
Khaled is the Achilles of the siege of Damascus, Amru
of that of Memphis, Dames of Aleppo. At Bedr,
Omeir, a mere stripling, who, fearing that he might be
rejected on account of his youth, had managed to join
the small army of the Faithful unknown to Mohammed,
flung away the dates he was eating, with the vow that
he would eat the next in the presence of God. 'Paradise is before you, the devil and hell-fire in your
rear,' was the exhortation of the generals at the battle
of Yermuk. The Faithful courted death with the
ecstasy of martyrs, and received a martyr's reward.
At Aiznadin, Derar maintained a flying fight single
handed against thirty infidels, and killed seventeen of
their number. To Khaled, after he had been fighting
long, he cried, 'Repose yourself: you are tired of
fighting with this dog.' 'He that labours to-day,'
replied Khaled, 'shall rest in the world to come.'
'God is victorious,' said Ali, four hundred times in a

conflict, and each time he laid low an unbeliever.
At the siege of Damascus, a Saracen heroine, who
had followed her husband, Aban, to the holy
war, saw him killed by her side, stopped to bury him,
and then fought on in the post of danger till she
slew the famous archer who had killed her husband.
Nor is there any period in the history of Mohammedanism, late or early, in which the intensity of the
crusading spirit does not on occasion manifest itself.
It is God's battle that each Muslim is fighting ; and
as God may will, he is ready for either event, for victory
or defeat, for life or death.   In the Crusades themselves, when Christendom seemed to be seized with a
double portion of the Mohammedan spirit, by the
confession of the Christians, the generosity, the reckless valour, the self-sacrifice, and the chivalry were
not all on one side.   Richard of England and
Frederick Barbarossa found their match in Saladin ;
and even the history of our own Empire in India
teems with proofs that the vital spark of fanaticism
is latent only, not extinct.

Whenever hitherto, in the history of Mohammedanism, the belief has grown feeble that the Faithful
hold a commission from on high to put down evil,
wherever it shows itself, with a strong hand, it must
be admitted that the religion itself has proportion-
ately failed to do its proper work, both as a com-

pelling and as a restraining power. In the Middle
Ages the vitality and energy of Mohammedanism
evidenced itself most clearly, not in Arabia, or
Persia, or Northern Africa, where its success was most
complete, but in the Christian border lands, in Spain,
in Palestine, in Asia Minor, where the crusading spirit
was most evoked. Where there was no outlet for an
active, and even a material warfare, against what was
believed to be evil, there corruption crept in, and
stealthily paralysed all the energies of Musalman
society. '*Corruptio optimi fit pessima.*' Ommiade, and
Abbasside, and Fatimite Khalifs; Ghaznevide, and
Seljukian, and Ottoman Sultans passed through the
same dreary stages of luxury and decay; and the
government that now represents, or misrepresents, the
Khalifate, and is by most people foolishly supposed
to be the main support of Islam, originally in the
hands of men like Abu Bakr, or Omar, the best,
the simplest, and the most republican of all absolute
governments, has, in the hands of the Ottoman Turks,
ever since their faith ceased to be militant, become
the most hopeless of despotisms, since the abject
submission to the ruler remains, while all reason for
submission has vanished.[1]

---

[1] See this line of thought developed by Maurice, 'Religions of the
World,' p. 29 sq. I have done little more in this paragraph than con-
dense and illustrate his argument.

P

In the eyes of many the admission I have frankly made that the propagation of religion by the sword has been an essential part of Mohammedanism will serve to condemn it at once, and so in the abstract and from the highest point of view it ought. The sword is a rough surgical instrument in any case; but the doctrine that religion can ever be propagated by it, paradoxical as it sounds now, has seemed a truism in more ages than one; and though the Arabs were semi-barbarians, the conquered nations were constrained to admit that in their conquests they were not barbarous. Their wars were not mere wars of devastation like those of Genseric or Attila in earlier times, or of Chenghis Khan or Tamerlane in later. It was the savage boast of Attila, the genius of destruction, the 'scourge of God,' that the grass never grew where his horse had once trodden; and the proverb has, in later times, been applied by their enemies to the conquests of the Turks, to those rich provinces whose resources, from whatever causes, have been so long wasted, and whose inhabitants have been so misgoverned under the sway of the Othmanlis.

The saying that the grass never grows in the footprints of a Turk is, it must be admitted, not without some truth. The system of government, never an enlightened one, has at all events since the so-called 'reforms' of the Sultan Mahmoud been rotten at the

core. Stambul has become an asylum for the rascality
of West and East alike; the finest peasantry in the
world, the inhabitants of Asia Minor, are dying by
starvation, partly, no doubt, owing to bad harvests,
but still more owing to the neglect of the most ordinary
precautions and duties of government. Roads un-
made, bridges broken down, mines unworked, unprin-
cipled and exorbitant provincial Pashas, wastefulness
and disorder and excessive centralisation ; such is the
picture which travellers give us of those fair regions
of the earth,[1] and unfortunately we know it to be a
true picture. But it is easy, for all this, to be too
hard upon the Turk—to forget how much there is that
is fine in his character, to forget that many of the vices
of which we complain are not Turkish, but European
in their origin—to forget that those governments which
are loudest in their complaints are the very governments which by the injurious privileges they have
claimed in the ' Capitulations '[2] for the most worthless
of their subjects resident at Stambul; by their
usurious loans, and by their incessant interventions; by

---

[1] See Admiral Slade's 'Turkey, Greece, and Malta,' Vol. I. 295–
353, &c. Layard's ' Nineveh and Babylon,' I. i. p. 5, 11-13, &c.
'Quarterly Review,' Oct. 1874, Art. Provincial Turkey.

[2] See Walpole's ' Ansayrii,' I. ii. 23, 24 ; ' East and West,' Essays
I. and II ; and compare Curzon's 'Monasteries of the Levant,' p. 69,
for the like deleterious effects produced by Western influences on Cairo.
See also the dignified protest of General Kheredine, Prime Minister of
Tunis, ' Reforms of Musalman States,' p. 34 *seq.*

the funeral orations they have so frequently pronounced upon the sick man, and by their ill-disguised eagerness to divide his effects even before his death, have done most to render anything like good government impossible.

The genuine Othmanli has many noble social and national characteristics: he is, or was, till the example and the precept of the Western money-makers influenced him, eminently a man of his word; his word was his bond, and a bond which was a first-rate security. He is still sober, temperate, dignified, and courageous. Terribly cruel as he is when his passions are aroused, he is at other times gentle, hospitable, and humane. Nowhere in Christendom, with the one exception perhaps of Norway, are beasts of burden and domestic animals treated with such unvarying kindness and consideration as they are in Turkey, and nowhere probably, in spite of all the depressing influences of polygamy and the degradation of women generally, does the mother retain more hold on her children, or do children regard their mother with such constant and indissoluble veneration. It was not a Musalman, but a Christian Missionary, and he a zealous and successful one, who in rebuking some younger missionaries at Stambul who were speaking contemptuously of the Turks, remarked, 'You will see practised here the virtues we talk of in Christendom ;'[1] an over statement, no doubt, but still with some truth in it, and truth which we should do well to bear in mind as a makeweight against the official corruption and the misgovernment and the vices with which the Turks may be justly charged, and which those who most admire what is fine in their national character have the best right to deplore. With all their vices, the Turkish Sultans, as a whole, compare favourably with many of the Christian Cæsars who preceded them ; nor is it certain that, taking differences of time and circumstances into account, they compare unfavourably with the Pontiffs of more than one century of the Papacy.

But whatever may be said or thought of the conquests of the Ottoman Turks and of their rule now, of the early Saracen conquests it would rather be true to say that after the first wave of invasion had swept by, two blades of grass were found growing where one had grown before ; like the thunderstorm, they fertilised while they destroyed ; and from one end of the then known world to the other, with their religion they sowed seeds of literature, of commerce, and of civilisation. · And as these disappeared, in the lapse of years, in one part of the Musalman world, they reappeared in another. When they died out, with the dying of the Abbasside Khalifate, along the

---

[1] Dr. Gooddall, an American, ' East and West,' p. 141.

banks of the Tigris and Euphrates, they revived again
on the Guadalquivir and Guadiana. To the splendours
and civilisation of Damascus succeeded Bagdad; to
Bagdad, Cairo; to Cairo, Cordova.

Mohammedanism has been accused of hostility to
the growth of the human intellect. It may have been
so in its earliest days, when Omar, as the story goes,
condemned the Alexandrian Library to the flames by
his famous dilemma: 'If these books agree with the
Book of God, they are useless: if they disagree, they are
pernicious; and in either case they must be destroyed.'
It may be so whenever there is a passing outburst of
fanaticism; but it is not so in its essential nature,
nor has it been so historically not even in its wars.
The Prophet himself, it has been objected, was not a
learned man; he was scarcely able to read or write;
but even if the story be true, what does it prove?
Theodoric the Great, the patron of art and science and
philosophy, was only able to sign his own name by
drawing a pen round the first four letters of it, which
having been carved in brass were placed on the paper
which was to receive the signature; Charles the Great
strove laboriously in his later years to acquire the
simple arts, which, by the foundation of schools and
colleges throughout his vast empire, he took care that
his subjects should, as far as possible, acquire in their
youth: Nor was Mohammed less eager than the

Ostrogothíc King or the Frankish Emperor to promote the studies of which he felt that he had all too little. ' Seek for science, even though it be in China,' is one of the sayings attributed to him. ' A learned man is as superior to a worshipper as the full moon to stars,' is another. ' One learned man is harder on the devil than a thousand ignorant believers,' is a third. To impart knowledge to others was in Mohammed's view as imperative a duty as to acquire it. ' He who concealeth his knowledge shall be reined with a bridle of fire at the day of resurrection.' ' The wise are more exalted than those who pray. The latter hope to attain by prayer their own desires, the former learn themselves, that they may instruct the ignorant.' [1] The story of Balaustion, romantic as it is in itself, and sung as it has been by a great poet, is known to all the world; but no poet has sung, and few have ever heard of a story less romantic perhaps, but certainly not less suggestive or less beautiful, of the great Arabian. The Greeks, who, to gratify their artistic tastes, allowed a shipwrecked maiden to purchase the lives of her companions in misfortune by reciting a tragedy of Euripides, did well; but the illiterate Prophet, who, when in exile at Medina, allowed the Meccan prisoners who could write Arabic

[1] For these sayings and others of a like tendency see Mishkat-ul-Masibeh, Book II. Cap. II. and III.

to go free so soon as they should ·have taught twelve
lads of Medina the art of which he and they were
ignorant, did better.[1]

Nor have the best portion of Mohammed's followers
been unworthy of him. The religion which has
declared that ' the ink of the learned is as precious as
the blood of the martyrs ; '[2] and which declares that
at the Day of Decision a special account will be given
of the use made of the intellect, cannot fairly be
accused of obscurantism. It was not so when, during
the darkest period of European history, the Arabs for
five hundred years held up the torch of learning to
humanity. It was the Arabs who then ' called the
Muses from their ancient seats ; ' who collected and
translated the writings of the great Greek masters ;
who understood the geometry of Apollonius, and
wielded the weapons found in the logical armoury of

[1] Sprenger, XVIII. 131.

[2] Quoted by Gobineau, p. 26. So, too, Abulpharages, in his
' Dynasties,' says that Almamun, Khalif of Bagdad, invited learned men
to his court because they were the elect of God, whose lives were
devoted to the development of the mind. (See Gibbon, VII. 34.)
Against the destruction of the Alexandrian Library by Omar may fairly
be set the destruction by the Crusaders of an immense library at
Tripoli, in Palestine. The General, finding that the first room of the
library contained the Koran only, ordered the whole library to be
burnt. So, too, Cardinal Ximenes, on entering the Moorish capital,
showed that a crass fanaticism is not the prerogative of one religion only,
by his order to destroy the vast collection of Arabic MSS. there, with
the exception of 300 medical works, which he reserved for his own
university.

Aristotle. It was the Arabs who developed the sciences of Agriculture and Astronomy, and created those of Algebra and Chemistry ; who adorned their cities with colleges and libraries, as well as with mosques and palaces ; who supplied Europe with a school of philosophers from Cordova, and a school of physicians from Salerno. When we condemn the Mohammedan wars, let us at least remember what of good they brought with them.

Nor is Mohammedanism the only religion which has tried to propagate itself by the sword. It is true, of course, that a holy war waged by Christians is in direct contravention of the spirit of their Founder, while one waged by Mohammedans is in accordance with both the practice and the precept of the Prophet, and so far there is no parallel at all between the two religions. The means authorised by Christ for the spread of His religion were moral and spiritual only. The means authorised by Mohammed were persuasion and example first ; but, failing these, the sword.

Yet, historically speaking, the contrast between the practice of Christians and Mohammedans has not been so sharp as is often supposed. The Saxon wars of Charles the Great were avowedly religious wars, and differed chiefly from the Syrian wars of Omar and of Ali, from the African wars of Amru and Akbah, and the Spanish wars of Mussa and of Tarik, in that

they were much more protracted and vastly less successful.   Otto the Great, the best of Charles's successors, used the sword with vigour to extend the external profession of Christianity among the Sclavonian
tribes who dwelt along the shores of the Baltic.   The
Mediæval Papacy, whatever its other services to progress, was never backward to unfurl the standard of a
religious war, whether against the common enemy of
Christendom, or, as more often happened, against a
sect of heretics, the Albigenses or the Waldenses,
nearer home.   Nor, in point of ferocity, is it clear that
religious wars waged by Christians will compare
favourably with those of Mohammedans.   The Mohammedan wars were never internecine.   Even on
the field of battle the conquering Musalman allowed
his conquered foe the two other alternatives of conversion or of tribute.   When Abu Bakr first invaded
Syria, he charged his troops not to mutilate the dead,
not to slay old men, women, and children, not to cut
down fruit-trees, nor to kill cattle unless they were
needed for food ; and these humane precepts served
like a code of laws of war during the career of Mohammedan conquest.   And this, be it remembered, among
Orientals, who had always been remarkable for their
disregard of human life.   When we remember, on the
other hand, the massacre of 4,500 Pagan Saxons in
cold blood by Charles the Great—when we remember

the famous answer by which the Papal Legate, in the
Albigensian war, quieted the scruples of a too conscientious general, 'Kill all, God will know His own'
—when we recall the Spanish Inquisition, the Conquest of Mexico and Peru, the Massacre of St. Bar-
tholomew, and the sack of Magdeburg by Tilly, we
shall be disposed never, indeed, to justify religious
wars, but to point out that, of the religious wars
which the world has seen, the Mohammedan are certainly not the worst—in their object, in their methods,.
or in their results.

Nor is the extermination of moral evil in all cases.
an unworthy object of war. There are occasions even
in our modern civilisation, and in an era of non-inter-
vention, when one longs to feel that the sword a
nation wields may be, in their eyes at all events, the
sword of the Lord and of Gideon. An unselfish war
to put down the slave trade or the opium traffic, to
counteract some 'Holy Alliance' of Emperors against
the rights of peoples, to prevent a giant iniquity like
the partition of Poland, is perhaps the only kind of
war, except those of self-defence, to which the spirit of
Christianity is not opposed. Christianity *is* opposed
to wars of aggression, to dynastic wars, and, above
all, to religious wars; for a religious war rests upon
the irreligious assumption that one fallible man holds.
a fiat from Omnipotence to step between another

human soul and God ; and to enforce his partial views of truth upon a fellow-mortal, who, for aught he knows, may have as wide a prospect, and as deep an insight, as he has himself. '*Deorum injuriæ Deis curæ.*' The sword may silence ; it cannot convince : it may enforce hypocrisy ; it can never force belief. But this has not always seemed so self-evident ; and I say it deliberately and with all the force of conviction, compared with the war of the Confederate States in the nineteenth century for the perpetuation of slavery, compared with our own Japanese wars for the extension of our trade, our Chinese wars for the sale of our opium, and our miserable African wars waged for the possession of a territory which we bought, and had no moral right to buy, from those who sold what they had no moral right to sell,[1] the Mohammedan wars for the propagation of a comparatively pure religion and a higher morality were, in their time and according to their light, inasmuch as they were not purely selfish, I do not say excusable, but they were at least intelligible and natural.

Here I must close for to-day. What of good and what of evil the world owes to Mohammed ; what is the condition and what the prospects of Mohammedanism now ; what, as a matter of fact, is the historical connection between Mohammedanism and Chris-

---

[1] See Appendix to Lecture III.

tianity—its points of difference as well as of resemblance ; finally, and most important of all, how that connection ought to be regarded by Christians, and under what conditions or modifications the two great creeds may work together, or, if needs be, apart, for their common object, the general good of humanity— these are some of the points I hope to be able to discuss in my fourth and concluding Lecture.

LECTURE IV.

MARCH 7, 1874.

MOHAMMEDANISM AND CHRISTIANITY.

Say unto the Christians, their God and my God is one.—
THE KORAN.

'Ο δὲ Ἰησοῦς εἶπε, Μὴ κωλύετε αὐτόν· ὃς γὰρ οὐκ ἔστι καθ' ἡμῶν, ὑπέρ ἡμῶν ἐστιν.—ST. MARK.

IT may have been observed that in attempting, in my last Lecture, to deal with some of the questions connected with Mohammedanism, such as miracles, fatalism, religious wars, which have much perplexed the Christian mind, I omitted to say anything on a point which, more even than any of these, has scandalised those who view Mohammedanism from a distance: I mean the notions Mohammedans have formed of a future state. The omission was not altogether accidental, for I am inclined to think that too much stress has been laid upon these notions, no less by Mohammed's apologists than by his critics ; more stress than the Koran itself, and more even than the current Mohammedan belief, will warrant. But, remembering a remark of Sprenger's,[1] that, although Islam has been described in many books, yet educated people have not got much further in the knowledge of it than that the Turks are Mohammedans, and allow polygamy, I think it will be well to add a few words to counteract the common notion, which I should be disposed to place on a par with this, that the Paradise of the Mohammedans is nothing more than the enjoyment of polygamy, with its earthly drawbacks and limitations removed.

So much has been said and written about the gross nature of Mohammed's Paradise, the black-eyed Houris, the perfumes and the spices, the cushions and the carpets, with which his imagination furnished it, that ordinary people may be excused for believing that it was mainly, if not wholly, sensual.   But this is not, in the main, a true, and still less is it an adequate account of the matter.   The passages are few in number in which Mohammed dwells much on these aspects of the future, and, even in these, much of what is said is explained by orthodox Mohammedans to be merely Oriental imagery, while some of it is especially suitable—the bubbling fountains and the shady gardens above all—to the inhabitants of a dry and thirsty land, such as Arabia is.[2]

[1] Sprenger, Vol. II. Chap. XI. p. 18.
[2] See Sale's 'Introduction,' p. 73 ; and Lane's ' Modern Egyptians,' I. Chap. III. 84.

Few people now put a literal interpretation upon the gorgeous imagery and the glowing colours used in the Book of Revelation to describe the Celestial City ; and every one will admit that in all religions, even the most spiritual, the circumstances of this life must necessarily, to some extent, lend both form and colour to the views of the life to come. The Red Indian dreams of a heaven behind the cloud-topped hills, embosomed in woods, wherein his faithful dog will bear him company. The fierce Norseman hoped to be admitted after death to the Hall of Odin, and there, reclining on a couch, to drink ale for ever from the skulls of his enemies whom he had slain in battle. The earnest Methodist pictures to himself a place

> ' Where congregations ne'er break up,
>   And Sabbaths never end, '

for the simple reason that he finds his highest spiritual happiness in these things on earth. A polygamous people could hardly have pictured to themselves a heaven without polygamy. It would never even have occurred to them that such a thing was possible, since few of them had ever known a society on earth which was without it ; nor do I suppose that any individual Christian who has ever known the luxury of home affection, has been able to accept in any literal sense the doctrine that, in the future world, there are to be no exclusive attachments,[1] for the simple reason, again, that without individual love no human heart can conceive of the possibility of any happiness as complete or real.

Again, it is to be remembered that much that is material, or even gross, in the Mohammedan conception of a future life is due, not to Mohammed, but to Mohammed's successors; and it is not the least of the enigmas that attach to the extraordinary and unique character of the Prophet, that his views of a future state are never more spiritual than at the time when, according to the common theory, he had most entirely, and, in fact, he had to some extent, fallen away from his austerely moral life. Contrast the tone of the Suras, referring to this subject, which were written at Mecca early in his life,[2] with the third, for instance, which was written at Medina many years later.

'Fair,' says he, 'in the sight of men are the pleasures of women and children; fair are the treasured treasures of gold and silver; and fine horses; and flocks; and corn-fields! Such is the enjoyment of this world's life. But God! goodly is the home with Him!

'Shall I tell you of better things than these, prepared for those who fear God in His presence? Theirs

---

[1] St. Matt. XXII. 30.
[2] Sura LV. 44-58 ; LVT. 17-36; LXXVI. 12-22.

shall be gardens beneath which the rivers flow, and
in which they shall abide for aye, and wives of stain-
less purity, and acceptance with God, for God regard-
eth His servants.

'They who say, O our Lord, we have indeed believed, pardon our sins, and keep us from the torment
of the fire.

'The patient are they, and the truthful, the lowly,
and the charitable, and they who ask for pardon as
each day breaks.' [1]

Surely here, as elsewhere, and increasingly so as
the Prophet drew near his end, it is the presence of
God, the knowledge of Him, the eternal Salaam or
Peace with which they shall salute one another, the
purity of love, and not its sensuality, which are the
most prominent ideas.

Heaven and Hell, indeed, were realities to the
Mohammedan mind in a sense in which they have
hardly ever been to any other nation.   With a more
than Dantesque realism, Mohammed saw the tortures
of the lost no less than the bliss of the faithful.

'They shall dwell,' he says, ' amidst burning winds
and in scalding water, under the shade of a black
smoke which is no shade, neither cool nor grateful,
. . . . . and they shall surely eat of the fruit
of the tree Ez-Zakkoum, and shall fill their bellies

[1] Sura XIII. 12-15.

therewith, and they shall drink thereon boiling water, even as a thirsty camel drinketh.'[1]

And again he says :

'They shall have garments of fire fitted unto them, their bowels shall be dissolved thereby, and also their skins, and they shall be beaten with maces of iron.'[2]

And once more, in one of his very early Suras, which, if it is memorable for nothing else, is memorable for its superb audacity, when we recollect that as yet Mohammed's prophetic claims were treated only with contemptuous indifference, and he himself was a mere outcast :

'Woe be,' he says, 'on that day to those who accused the prophets of imposture !

'It shall be said unto them, Go ye into that which ye denied as a falsehood.

'Go ye into the shadow of the smoke of hell, which, though it ascend in three columns,

'Shall not shade you from the heat, neither shall it be of service against the flames ;

'But it shall cast forth sparks as big as towers,

'And their colour shall be like unto that of red camels.

'Woe be on that day unto those who accuse the prophets of imposture !'[3]

[1] Sura LVI. 41-56.   [2] Sura XXII. 2c-21.
[3] Sura LXXVII. 29 to end.   The 'Woe be,' &c. is a refrain which recurs ten times in the Sura.

'What shall be our reward,' asked his earliest
followers of Mohammed, 'if we fall in battle?'
'Paradise,' said the Prophet, without the slightest
hesitation.   In the war of Tabuk his men demurred to
marching because it was harvest time. 'Your harvest
it lasts for a day,' said Mohammed; 'what will come
of your harvest through all eternity?' They com-
plained of the burning sun.   'Hell is hotter,' said the
Prophet, and on they went.[1]

That it was desirable to dwell with so much per-
sistence upon the enormous issues involved as regards the future life, in every act and thought of this,
I am far from asserting; since self-interest, however enlightened, and however refined, however even
spiritualised it may be, is self-interest still.   But at all
events it was stern reality to Mohammed and to his
followers.   The future was all as real and as instant
to him as it was to the Apostles when, expecting, as
they did, from the interpretation they put upon
Christ's words, to see Him in their own lifetime
coming in the clouds of heaven, they drove home their
warnings by bidding men flee from 'the wrath to come.'
In every successive crisis of the Christian Church, it
has been the belief of Christians that the darkest hour

---

[1] Carlyle's 'Heroes,' p. 239; and Sura IX. 82, &c.   In this
expedition water was so scarce that the fainting troops were obliged to
kill the camels and drink the water out of their stomachs.

is that before the dawn, and it has been used, however mistakenly, yet with effect and with sincerity, to comfort the depressed, to awaken the sleeping, and to arouse the dead. '*Finem suum mundus jam non nunciat solum, sed ostendit,*' says St. Gregory amidst the devastations of the Lombards. '*Appropinquante jam mundi termino,*' is the heading of even legal documents amidst the deeper depression of the tenth century caused by the ravages of the Hungarians by land and the Norsemen by sea. This is the burden of St. Bernard's hymns, of Savonarola's preachings, of Bunyan's allegories. Truly, if Mohammed sinned at all in this respect, he sinned in good company.

But the future world, ever present though it was to the minds of the early Mohammedans, did not supply the motive by which they were really inspired. Not such the motive which, at the present day, impels the Wahhabi missionary to brave social and religious ostracism in India, or the Negro Musalman to face the Great Desert, or the terrors of cannibalism and of human sacrifice, with the hope of winning new converts to their faith ; still less is it a sufficient, or, as I think, even a partial explanation of their astonishing success. A selfish hope of Heaven, and a slavish fear of Hell, may act as a 'negative stimulus '—may possibly teach passive resistance to temptation—but it does not nerve the arm to strike, or quicken the eye to see.

Perhaps, indeed, the highest heroism of all, that which consists in absolute conscious self-sacrifice or self-annihilation for the good of others—the heroism of the ideal just man in the second book of Plato's *Republic*; the heroism of Moses when he prayed to be blotted out of the Book that God had written ; the heroism of a greater than Moses when He died upon the cross—is impossible to those who believe firmly in a future life, the happiness or misery of which is to be exactly determined by the life here. But there may be true heroism even short of the truest ; and all true heroism, even if it cannot deny or forget its reward, is stimulated not so much by the reward as by the difficulty of obtaining it. The reward, to use an Aristotelian phrase, is an *ἐπιγιγνόμενόν τι τέλος*, something thrown in, an after-thought and accessory merely ; and this is what a future life was to the primitive warriors of the Crescent.

Nor is it true, in any sense of the word, if we appeal to its primal documents and not to the lives of its more unworthy professors, that Mohammed's is an easy or sensual religion. With its frequent fasts, its five prayers a day, its solitudes, its almsgivings, its pilgrimages, even in the tortures of Indian fakirs and the howlings of Mecca dervishes, which are the abuse, and not the use, of the religion—it certainly does not

appeal much to the laziness, or the sensuality, or the
selfishness of mankind.

In his capacity even of temporal ruler, Mohammed
rarely gave material rewards to his followers. Abu
Bakr, Ali, Omar, Hamza, when in his early days they
ranged themselves as friends round the then friendless
enthusiast, sacrificed, as it must have appeared to
them, all their worldly hopes ; they little thought that
they were enrolling themselves in that most select
band of heroes who may be said to have made
History. On one occasion, late in his life, Mohammed did give some material rewards to recent and
perhaps half-hearted converts ; but the exception only
proved the rule, and that in the most memorable
manner. The Helpers of Medina were naturally dissatisfied, but Mohammed recalled them to their allegiance by words which went straight from his heart
to theirs : that he had given things of the world to
those who cared for such things, but to them he had
given himself. Others returned home with sheep
and camels, the Helpers with the Prophet of God.
Verily, if all the men of the earth went one way, and
the Helpers of Medina another, he would go the way
of the Helpers of Medina.[1] The Helpers burst into
tears, and exclaimed that they were more than

---

[1] Alluded to in Sura LIX. 8 and 9, and VIII. 42. See Muir,
IV. 151–154.

satisfied with what he had given them. And, just
before his death, Mohammed commended these same
Helpers of Medina to the protection of the exiles who
had accompanied him from Mecca. ' Hold in honour,'
said he, ' the Helpers of Medina : the number of believers may increase, but that of the Helpers never
can.[1] They were my family, and with them I found
a home ; do good to those who do good to them, and
break friendship with those who are hostile to them.'

Perhaps there is no remark one has heard more
often about Mohammedanism than that it was so successful because it was so sensual ; but there is none more
destitute of truth, as if any religion could owe its permanent success to its bad morality ! I do not say that its
morality is perfect, or equal to the Christian morality.
Mohammed did not make the manners of Arabia, and
he was too wise to think that he could either unmake
or remake them all at once. Solon remarked of his
own legislation that his laws were not the best that he
could devise ; but that they were the best the
Athenians could receive ; and his defence has generally
been accepted as a sound one. Moses took the
institutions of a primitive society as he found them—

---

[1] Cf. Herodotus iii. 119. ὦ βασιλεῦ, ἀνὴρ μέν μοι ἂν ἄλλος γένοιτο, εἰ
δαίμων ἐθέλοι, καὶ τέκνα ἄλλα, εἰ ταῦτα ἀποβάλοιμι· πατρὸς δὲ καὶ μητρὸς
οὐκ ἔτι μευ ζωόντων ἀδελφεὸς ἂν ἄλλος οὐδενὶ τρόπῳ γένοιτο. Cf. also
Soph. *Antigone*, 909–912.

the patriarchal power, internecine war, blood feuds,
the right of asylum, polygamy and slavery—and did
not abolish any one of them ; he only mitigated their
worst evils, and so unconsciously prepared the way in
some cases for their greater permanence, in others for
their eventual extinction.

In like manner the religion of Christ did not sweep
into oblivion any national or political institutions.
He contented Himself with planting principles in the
hearts of His followers which would, when the time
was ripe for it, work out their abolition. Willing to
sow if others could reap, to labour if others could enter
into His labours, He cast into the ground the grain of
mustard seed, and was content, with the eye of faith
alone, to see it grow into the mighty tree whose
branches should overspread the world, and whose
leaves should be for the healing of the nations. With
sublime self-restraint and self-sacrifice, governed by
His thought for the boundless possibilities of the
future of His Church, rather than by the impulse of
the moment, He forbore to denounce in so many words
the inveterate evils of the Roman Empire, which must
have gone to His soul's soul—foreign conquest, tyranny,
the amphitheatre, slavery. He even used words which
have been wrongly construed to mean that at all times
passive obedience is a duty, and that the people have
nothing to do with the laws but to obey them. Nor

has the Christian Church—sections of which have for
strange and various, but intelligible, reasons, canonised
a Constantine and a Vladimir, a Cyril and a Charles
the Great, a Dunstan and a Becket—ever attached the
name of Saint to some who, in the fulness of time, have
carried out far more fully and in spirit Christ's work,
albeit in seeming contradiction to the letter of the law
which inculcated submission to existing powers and institutions—to a Telemachus or a Theodoric, to an
Alfred or a Wilberforce.   And yet no Christian will
deny that the monk Telemachus, who threw himself
between the swords of the gladiators, and, braving the
fury of the spectators athirst for blood, accomplished
by his death what his life could never have won, did
a deed which all the 'Acta Sanctorum' could be
searched to parallel.

Now Mohammed was a legislator and a statesman,
as well as the founder of a religion ; and why is the
defence which we allow to Solon, and the praise we
bestow upon the limited scope of the Mosaic legislation, denied to Islam ?

Polygamy is, indeed, next to caste, the most
blighting institution to which a nation, which has
passed through the early stages of its growth, can
remain a prey.   It tends to degrade love into an
animal passion, and so to unspiritualise all the relations
between the sexes.   It pollutes society at the fountain-

head, for the family is the source of all political and of all social virtues. Mohammed would have more than doubled the debt of gratitude the Eastern world owes to him had he swept it away, but I cannot think that he could have done so, even if he had fully seen its evils.

Polygamy is an institution which springs from causes far too deep down among the roots of society for any reformer, however great, to abolish it by the word of his mouth or the stroke of his pen. In abolishing idolatry, Mohammed found among the Arabs, as I have shown in my last Lecture, an historical groundwork of belief in the unity of the Godhead, and even an existing religious sentiment in his favour, and he was not backward to avail himself of its help. But in forbidding polygamy he would have found no such extraneous support : there does not seem among the higher spirits of Arabia to have been even so much as a floating sentiment in favour of monogamy, and the women themselves were as contented with this part of their condition as were their masters.

As a true Arab, Mohammed recognised polygamy as an existing institution ; as a reforming legislator, he made many regulations for lessening its evils ; but it is hardly more fair on these grounds to say that Mohammedanism is responsible for polygamy, than it is to say that Christianity is responsible for slavery.

The New Testament contains, it is true, no direct condemnation of slavery; on the contrary, it recognises it as an existing institution ; and St. Paul is at least as precise upon the duties of servants—whom, by the way, he calls by the downright name of slaves, a term hardly used in the Koran—to their masters, as he is upon the duties of masters to them ; but no Christian will grant, on this score, that his religion has either sanctioned slavery, or is responsible for it, for he will have no difficulty in showing that the humanity everywhere inculcated in it is inconsistent with the prolonged maintenance of slavery, and would of itself suffice, first in the case of individual Christians, and afterwards of Christian nations, to secure, as now, at last, it has secured, its abolition. Slavery, therefore, has simply co-existed with Christianity without being mixed with it, even as the muddy Arve and the clear Rhone keep their currents distinct long after they have been united in one river-bed. Perhaps it is strange that they ever could have co-existed, even for a day ; but we have to deal with facts as they are ; and it is a fact that slavery has co-existed with Christianity, nay, has professed to justify itself by Christianity, even till this nineteenth century. As a code, indeed, of law and morals, it is of course fairer to compare Islam with Judaism than, as I have just been doing, with Christianity ; for in manners and in civilisation, as in race, the Arabs of Mohammed's time resembled the Israelites far more nearly than they did any of those nations upon whom Christianity was destined to take real hold. Now the Mosaic law, so far from prohibiting polygamy, did not even put any limitation on it. The Patriarchs indulged in poly gamy ; so did the Judges ; so did the Kings ; and not least so the more elevated and the more spiritually-minded amongst them. The man after God's own heart, and the king whose wisdom and magnificence still form the folk-lore of so many Eastern countries, can hardly be surpassed in this particular even by those Musalman princes who break the laws of the Koran, and strain the traditions almost to bursting, that they may gratify their love of display, or their brutal appetites.

Mohammed could not have made a *tabula rasa* of Eastern society, but what he could do he did. He at least put some limitations on the unbounded license of Eastern polygamy,[1] and the absolute reck-lessness of Eastern divorce.[2] If the two social touch-stones of a religion are the way in which, relatively to the time, it deals with the weaker sex, and the way in which it regards the poor and the oppressed, Mo-hammed's religion can stand the test.[3] The laws of

[1] Sura IV. 3, &c.
[2] Sura IV. 39 and 127, XXXIII. 48, 52, &c.
[3] Among many other illustrations of this see (*a*) the oath taken

the Prophet in these particulars, as in others, were
greatly ahead of the pagan, and in some respects also
of the Hebrew practice.

The Arabs of the Ignorance, for instance, allowed
any number of wives; the Koran limits the number
of lawful wives to four.[1]   Among the Arabs of the
Ignorance divorce was a matter of the merest
caprice, and the divorced wife lost her dowry as well
as all conjugal rights.   The Koran orders the dowry
in all cases to be given back; and to ensure delibe-
ration, or to prevent mere caprice, in carrying out or
in recalling what, unlike his countrymen, the Prophet
considered so momentous and so objectionable a re-
solve, he ordained that a man who had once pronounced the formula of divorce should not be at
liberty to take his wife back till he had done some

---

early in his life with other Kuraish, 'to defend the oppressed so long as
a drop of water remained in the ocean,' an act the remembrance of
which Mohammed said 'he would not exchange for the choicest camel
in Arabia;' (*b*) the account given by Djafar to the Nagashy of Abyssinia of the change wrought by Mohammed among his followers;
perhaps the noblest and truest summary we have of the moral teaching
of the Prophet; (*c*) the pledge of Acaba, A.D. 621, taken by his first
converts from Medina; (*d*) Sura II. 172: 'There is no piety in turning
your faces towards the East or the West, but he is pious who believeth
in God . . . . who for the love of God distributeth his wealth to his
kindred, and to the orphans, and the needy, and the wayfarer.'

[1] It was a remark of Napoleon's that Mohammed was the only
Eastern legislator who ever attempted to impose any restraint on
polygamy; a fact which should be borne in mind.   See Lane's
'Modern Egyptians,' I. 121–128 for an analysis of the laws of Islam
relating to women and slaves.

penance for his thoughtless cruelty by setting a slave free.[1]

-The Arabs of the Ignorance allowed a woman no part of her husband's or father's property, on the ground that none should inherit property who could not bear arms. The Koran says women are entitled to a share of the inheritance : a daughter, for instance, should have half as much as a son.[2] The Arabs of the Ignorance treated the wife of a deceased husband as part of the inheritance of his heir-at-law, who would often be her own step-son. Mohammed condemned all such marriages, which were not uncommon before his time, as infamous. The Arabs of the Ignorance buried alive their female children ; for as the Arab proverb expressed it, ' To send women before to the other world is a benefit. The best son-in-law is the grave ;' and the wish offered to newly-married couples, ' With concord and permanence, with sons and no daughters,' implied similar ideas.[3] Mohammed

---

[1] See Sale's ' Preliminary Discourse,' VI. 95. If a man had pronounced the formula twice at different times, he was not to have the right to claim her again at all, until she had fulfilled the condition which, to the pride and jealousy of an Arab, Mohammed knew would be insupportable, of being married previously to another person. A third divorce was to be absolutely irrevocable.

[2] Sura IV. 12 ; and Sale's Preliminary Discourse, VI. 98.

[3] 'Women of the Arabs,' by the Rev. Henry Jessup, American Missionary in Syria, p. 2. The first two chapters give a forcible description of the degradation of women in the East now, among both Musalmans and Christians ; but in a summary, to which I am much

sternly forbade the cruel practice, and said that at the last great day the girl who had been buried alive would demand for what crime she had been slain. The Arabs of the Ignorance who believed in any form of future life denied all share in it to woman, and Mohammed has been thought by many to have done the same ; but the Koran says, ' Whoso doeth good works and is a true believer, whether male or female, shall be admitted into Paradise.' An old woman once came to the Prophet begging him to intercede with God that she might be admitted into Paradise. ' No old woman finds admittance there,' replied Mohammed. She burst into tears, when Mohammed smiled, and with the kindly humour which was characteristic of him, said, ' No old woman, for all will there be young again.' [1]

It has been said that ' husbands love your wives ' is a precept of the Bible, and not of the Koran.[2] Hear, however, the farewell address of Mohammed to the pilgrims assembled on Mount Arafat in the year before his death. ' Ye people, ye have rights over your wives, and your wives have rights over you. Treat your wives with kindness : verily ye havé taken

indebted, do full justice to the improvement in their condition effected, or at least aimed at, by Mohammed.

[1] Sale, ' Preliminary Discourse,' p. 73.

[2] By Dr. Jessup, *loc. cit.*

them on the security of God, and have made them lawful unto you by the words of God.'

The Prophet's personal view of the prevalent practice of divorce is well expressed in the beautiful saying attributed to him in the Traditions, 'God has created nothing which He likes better than the emancipation of slaves, and nothing which He hates more than divorce,' and it must be admitted that his example, in this respect at all events, was as good as his precept. It is difficult in this or in any other of his sayings [1] to find aught to justify the epithet used by the most recent writer on the Life of Christ when he speaks of the 'cynical sanction' given by Mohammed to polygamy or despotism ; [2] and it is to be regretted that in his treatment of the religion of One who said that 'those who were not against Him were for Him,' there is not a single passage which refers to the great kindred creed of Islam, which does justice either to its founder or to his reforms. Nor do the provisions I have mentioned above constitute the whole of what Mohammed did for the female sex, for besides imposing restrictions on polygamy, by his severe laws at first,

---

[1] Cf. Sura IV. 126–128, 175; and LXV., entitled 'Divorce,' throughout.

[2] Farrar's 'Life of Christ,' I. 269. The passage in Sura IV. 32, 'God desireth to make your burden light, for man hath been created weak,' is, surely, not 'cynical,' but the reverse, and may be compared with the 'hardness of their hearts' allowed as a sufficient reason for divorce under the Mosaic law by Christ himself. Matt. XIX. 8.

and by the strong moral sentiment aroused by these laws afterwards, he has succeeded, down to this very day, and to a greater extent than has ever been the case elsewhere, in freeing Mohammedan countries from those professional outcasts who live · by their own misery, and, by their existence as a recognised class, are a standing reproach to every member of the society of which they form a part.

I do not forget, on the other hand, that Mohammed authorised the corporal punishment of the wife by the husband in extreme cases, provided it was done with moderation ; that he allowed or enjoined the seclusion of women ; that he relaxed in his own behalf the restriction with regard to polygamy which he imposed on others, and that he allowed concubinage with captives taken in war;[1] and I fully admit that his followers have been far more ready to imitate and to obey him in these, the defective parts of his teaching and example, than in the more elevated ones ; but I say confidently that compared with Paganism, and even with Judaism, Mohammed gave women a

---

[1] Sale maintains, and he is supported by many Muslim doctors, and, to all appearance, by the words of the Koran (Sura IV. 3), that under no circumstances is a man allowed to take his slaves as concubines if he have the maximum number of four wives allowed him by the law. Mr. Lane maintains the contrary, and supports his argument by the authority of other Muslim doctors, and by the practice of some of the Companions of the Prophet ; but it is surely dangerous to lay stress on this. No Musalman will contend that the Companions are examples to be followed.

great advance on their previous position, and so has
deserved well of them. It must be remembered also,
what we are apt to forget, that it required not the
sublime moral precepts of Christianity alone, but the
influence of codes of Roman law, and the innate
respect felt by Teutonic nations for the female sex,
and centuries of civilisation also, to raise woman to
her proper position in European countries ; and can
we be surprised that the unprogressive East is some
centuries behind us in this as in other respects? I
think also that consistent and enlightened followers
of the Prophet, such as are Syed Ahmed and Syed
Ameer Ali in India, and Mir Aulad Ali, Professor
of Oriental Languages at Trinity College, Dublin,
have a right to say that Musalmans now would be
best carrying out the spirit of the Prophet, as shadowed
forth in many precepts of the Koran, in pronouncing
polygamy to be out of date, and therefore unlawful.

And how was it with Slavery? Here, too, the
advance is incontestable, and much more decisive
than in his legislation for women. Mohammed did
not abolish slavery altogether, for in that condition of
society it would have been neither possible nor desirable to do so ; but he encouraged the emancipation
of slaves ; he laid down the principle that the captive
who embraced Islam should be *ipso facto* free, and,
what is more important, he took care that no stigma

should attach to the emancipated slave in consequence of his honest and honourable life of labour. As to those who continued slaves, he prescribed kindness and consideration in dealing with them.[1] 'See,' he said, in his parting address at Mina, the year before his death, 'see that ye feed them with such food as ye eat yourselves, and clothe them with the stuff ye yourselves wear; for they are the servants of the Lord, and are not to be tormented.'

A slave thus protected by the law and by the highest sanctions of religion was not a slave in the modern sense of the word at all. It is significant, as I have remarked above, that the word itself hardly occurs in the Koran. The phrase that is used, 'those whom your right hand possesses,' means only those who have been taken prisoners in lawful warfare, and have lost their freedom. Such captives, if they became Musalmans, were set free; if they retained their own faith, they were, as Mohammed told his followers, none the less their brethren. The master who treated them kindly would be acceptable to God; he who abused his power would be shut out of Paradise. 'How many times,' asked a follower of Mohammed, 'ought I to forgive a slave who displeases me?' 'Seventy times a day,' replied the Prophet.

Concubinage, indeed, with his female captives,

[1] Sura XXIV. 34, 57.

Mohammed, like the chiefs of every other semi-civilised state that has ever existed, allowed to their captor, but she who bore her master a child was never to be severed from it. She could never again be sold, and at her master's death she received her freedom. These humane provisions are, as might be expected, in the same plane as those of the Mosaic law, but they are an advance, in many respects, upon it ; and they are such as no European or American slave-trading power ever enrolled in its code of laws till the wave of total abolition swept over Christendom. For example, when the Hebrew who had become a slave had served his time, he might go free ; but the wife his master had given him, and the children she had borne to him, were to be severed from him and to remain slaves.[1] The Musalman master who chastised his slave without cause was bound to set him free ; the Hebrew, on the other hand, who chastised his slave so severely as to cause his death at once, was liable to a certain penalty, but if he survived for a day or two, he got off scot free ; for, as the English version of the Bible expresses it with terrible bluntness, 'he is his money.'[2] In the Slave States of America, again, a slave had no legal rights : if a master treated his female slaves well, it was because he happened to be humane, not because, as in Islam

---

[1] Exodus XXI. 4.   [2] Exodus XXI. 21.

in its best days, the courts were open to compel him
to be so. The equality of all men before God was
a principle which Mohammed everywhere maintained,
and which, taking, as it did, all caste feeling from
slavery, took away also its chief sting. To Mohammed's mind labour could never be degrading; and the
domestic slavery of the Arabs, under which, thanks
to him, parents were never to be separated from their
children, nor indeed relations from each other at all,
though always to be condemned in the abstract,
became, under the Prophet's hands, a bond closer
and more lasting, and hardly more liable to abuse,
than domestic service elsewhere.

Mohammedanism, in fact, preaches equality almost as explicitly as does Christianity. 'No more
pride in ancestry,' said Mohammed to the assembled
Musalmans, the haughty Kuraish themselves among
them: 'ye Musalmans are all brothers, all equal;'
and it must be admitted that Mohammedans have,
from whatever causes, acted up to their creed in
this respect more fully than have Christians.[1] In

---

[1] See Wood's 'Oxus,' p. 194. 'Nowhere is the difference between
European and Mohammedan society more strongly marked than in the
lower walks of life. The broad line that separates the rich and poor
in civilised society is as yet but faintly drawn in Central Asia. Here
unreserved intercourse with their superiors has polished the manners of
the lower classes, and instead of this familiarity breeding contempt, it
begets self-respect in the dependent. . . . indeed all the inferior
classes possess an innate self-respect and a natural gravity of deport-

India, for instance, Mohammedans make converts by hundreds from among the Hindus, while Christians with difficulty make ten, and this partly at least because they receive their converts on terms of entire social equality, while Europeans, in spite of all the efforts of missionaries to the contrary, seem either unwilling or unable to treat their converts as other than inferiors. The Hindu who becomes a Christian loses, therefore, his own cherished caste without being admitted into that of his rulers. The Hindu who turns Mohammedan loses his narrow caste, but he becomes a member of the wide brotherhood of Islam. In Africa there is, happily, no caste system analogous to that of India, but like causes have, even there, produced like effects or like contrasts. The 'Negro' convert to Islam is received at once as an equal by the Arab, or the Moorish, or the Mandingo missionary who has brought him his message ; he is enrolled in a fraternity which has influenced half the world, and in which Negroes themselves have played no inconsiderable part. A literature and a language are thrown open to him which, if they are not his own, are yet a classical literature and language, and one which he may well claim as, in some sense, his, in view of what they have already done for his race.

ment which differs as far from the suppleness of a Hindustani as from the awkward rusticity of an English clown.'

He thus acquires a sense of independence, of dignity, and of brotherhood, to which he was before a stranger. The Christian Negro, on the other hand, with few exceptions, still feels at an immeasurable distance from those Europeans to whom, indeed, he owes the message of love that he has received, but who, as a race, for centuries past, have enslaved and sold him, and, alien as they are to him in all respects, still debar him from the possession of his own coasts that they may enrich themselves with his merchandise, or flood his country with those ardent spirits which are the curse of their own. He sets to work to imitate, as best he may, the dress and the habits, the virtues and the vices, of those who have so little in common with him ; and the result is that with which we are all familiar.[1] Christianity is not to blame for this, but Christian nations are. As to his religion, while nothing can quite deprive him of the sense of equality before God, and of the bright hopes beyond the grave which the self-sacrificing missionary preaches to him, in spite of all the caste prejudices and that most fatal of obstacles to missionary work, the example of the Europeans themselves, he naturally takes

[1] See on this subject a very remarkable article in Fraser's Magazine for November 1875, by a Negro, the Rev. Edward Blyden, headed 'Mohammedanism and the Negro Race.' The author speaks in great measure from his own experience, and treats the subject with originality, with earnestness, and with deep pathos.

hold of that side of Christianity which any religion that is of such universal applicability must certainly contain ; the side, I mean, which dwells upon the helplessness of man to help himself, his dependence upon merits not his own, the sense that even his best efforts and aspirations have something in them of the nature of sin. These notions have much truth in them, but they are only one side of the truth, and they require to be balanced and held in check by that other side of Christianity which inculcates self-reliance and self-respect, the active and the heroic, as well as the passive and the saintly virtues. Races which are more energetic, more fortunate, or more highly-gifted, are, in some imperfect sense, better able to lay hold of this other side of Christianity, and the result, such as it is, is seen in the progressive nations of the West. Christianity has done much for Europe, but Europe has done much also for Christians. Down-trodden and unfortunate nations like the African, which have been brought into contact with more powerful races only to be oppressed by them, and have, by their mere geographical peculiarities, been unduly weighted throughout their history in the struggle for existence, naturally lay hold, with few exceptions, of that side of Christianity which comes most home to them, and which appeals most to their depressed condition. The same general causes which,

with or without reason, make the Turk despise the
Armenian, the Druse despise the Maronite, and the
Copt the Abyssinian, are at work in Central Africa
also ; and in spite of the ineffable superiority of
Christianity in its purity, serve to point the contrast
between the dependence and the servility of the
average Christian, and the dignity and the self-reliance of the average Musalman, Negro.

'La carrière ouverte aux talens' has thus been
throughout the history of Islam something of a reality.
No considerations of birth, or race, or colour, or
money, have prevented a man rising to the post for
which it had been recognised that he was best fitted.
Zeid, the Prophet's freedman, led his armies in war.
Bilal, a blind Negro, became the first Muezzin ; and,
as Deutsch remarks, even Alexander the Great is at
this day an unknown personage in Asia compared to
him. A dynasty of Circassian slaves ruled Egypt
for a century before its conquest by the Ottoman
Turks, and it is said that Christians from the Caucasus
were glad to be carried off as slaves to Egypt because
each one felt that he might rise to be sultan.[1]   In
Islam the emancipated slave is actually, as well as
potentially, equal to a free-born citizen, and throughout the Turkish Empire at all periods of its history,

---

[1] Mohammed's Religion, by J. J. Döllinger, p. 32.

slaves have risen repeatedly to the highest offices, and
have never been ashamed of their origin.[1]

The orphan was not less than the slave the object
of the Prophet's peculiar care, for he had been an
orphan himself; and what God had done for him, he
was anxious, as far as might be, to do for others.[2]
The poor were always present with him, and their
condition never absent from his mind. In one of his
early Suras, 'the steep,' as he calls it—that is to say,
the strait and narrow way, is said to be to release
the captive, to give food to the poor that lieth in the
dust, and to stir up one another to stedfastness and
compassion.[3] And in another Sura Jews and Arabs
are alike warned in their exclusive pride in their
common progenitor, Abraham, that verily the nearest
of kin to Abraham are they who follow him in his
works.[4]

And how, as a matter of history, has Islam dealt
with these classes of society, which more even than

---

[1] Captain Burton mentions ('Pilgrimage,' I. p. 89) that the pacha
of the Syrian caravan with which he travelled to Damascus had been
the slave of a slave. Sebuktegin, the father of the magnificent Mahmud, and founder of the Ghaznevide dynasty, was a slave; so was
Kutb-ud-din, the conqueror and first king of Delhi, and the true
founder, therefore, of the Mohammedan Empire in India. (See
Elphinstone's 'India,' p. 320, and 363, and 370.) The dynasty of
the Egyptian Mamelukes derived their name from an Arabic word
meaning slave.

[2] Sura VIII. 42, and XCIII. 6 to end.

[3] Sura XC. 12, 15, and *passim*.   [4] Sura III. 61.

the ordinary poor, need the help of those who are richer, stronger, more fortunate than they? It is the glory of Christianity to have created that enthusiasm of humanity which, from the earliest times, has made the care of the sick and the relief of the distressed to be not only the first of duties, but of happinesses. The Emperor Julian, an unwilling and therefore a trustworthy witness, remarked with reference to the 'splendid outpouring,' even in his own day, of charity among the Christians whom he despised, that it was a scandal that the Galileans should support the destitute not only of their own religion, but of his. Following Christ's example, and believing what He taught, that in finding out the afflicted and in tending the leper and the outcast, Christ Himself may in some 'sense be found and tended, Christians have everywhere erected orphanages for the bereaved, refuges for the aged, penitentiaries for the fallen, hospitals for the sick, and asylums for the insane. These institutions are the result not of any positive external law among Christian nations, but of that glowing impulse of love which Christ has breathed into His true disciples, and which, under their influence, has become a second nature to numbers who do not acknowledge either its origin or its sanction. They have grown with the growth of Christianity, and in their number, in their size, and their efficiency,

those of the present day throw into the shade the
efforts of all other religions and of all previous ages.

But no Christian need be sorry to learn, or be
backward to acknowledge, that, contrary to what is
usually supposed,[1] two of those noble institutions which
flourish now most in Christian countries, and are
assuredly most characteristic of Christianity, owe their
origin and their early spread not to his own religion, but
to the great heart of humanity which beats in two
other of the grandest religions of the world. Hospitals are the direct outcome of Buddhism, and from
the time of the charitable edicts of King Asoka for
the establishment of medical dispensaries both for
men and animals, three hundred years before Christ,
began to overspread the Buddhist East.[2] To

---

[1] ' Amid all the boasted civilisation of antiquity there existed no
hospitals, no penitentiaries, no asylums.' Farrar's 'Life of Christ,' I.
334.

[2] For the Buddhist origin of hospitals see some facts collected by
the Rev. J. Hoare, of Killiskey, Dublin, in an interesting and able
sermon on hospitals ; and for the origin of lunatic asylums, and some
of the facts here mentioned, see Mr. Lecky's 'History of European
Morals,' II. 94. Mr. T. Wheeler in his ' History of India' (III.
257) quotes from Fa-hian, a Buddhist pilgrim from China to India
about A.D. 400, a vivid description of the hospitals at Patali-putra or
Patna, the former capital of King Asoka, which were open gratuitously
to the poor and the diseased of all countries. A hospital for the
relief of animal suffering on an extensive scale existed at Surat down to
the beginning of this century. It doubtless owed its origin to Buddhist influences, flourished throughout the period of the Musalman
rule under the special guardianship of the Jains, and has only fallen
into decay in very recent times.

Mohammedanism, it would seem, Christendom is indebted for the foundation of lunatic asylums, and for the comparatively humane treatment of the insane. .The lunatic asylum at Cairo was founded in A.D. 1304, and it was not till more than a century afterwards that we hear of any institutions of the kind in Europe, and then only in that part of it which was most open to Mohammedan influences—I mean in Spain. It was from Spain that they gradually spread over Europe ; and it was to the Spaniards, strange to say, that Rome itself, the capital of Christendom, owed in the year 1548 the foundation of its earliest asylum. In the fifteenth century Leo Africanus found that portions of several hospitals at Fez, in the interior of Morocco, were dedicated to the care of the insane ; and the Mosque itself, so far from being exclusively dedicated, as Europeans commonly suppose, to those services which alone we are apt to call religious, is in most Musalman countries immediately connected with schools for the young or hospitals for the sick and the insane ; and its guardians, in the belief that those serve God best who most benefit their fellow-creatures, have generally devoted a part of the funds of the foundation to these most truly sacred purposes. Instead of the harsh treatment which, till lately in the West, has been thought to be the only possible one, lunatics have in the Mohammedan East been treated generally not only with humanity, but with respect. They are regarded in Egypt now, Mr. Lane tells us, as men who, their minds being in heaven, are not responsible for what their bodies do on earth : their souls being absorbed in devotion, it is thought only natural that their passions should be without control.[1]

Nor does Mohammed omit to lay stress on what I venture to think is as crucial a test of a moral code, and even of a religion, as is the treatment of the poor and the weak—I mean the duties we owe to what we call the lower animals. There is no religion which has taken a higher view in its authoritative documents of animal life, and none wherein the precept has been so much honoured by its practical observance. ' There is no beast on earth,' says the Koran,[2] ' nor bird which flieth with its wings, but the same is a people like unto you—unto the Lord shall they return ; ' and it is the current belief that animals will share with men the general resurrection, and be judged according to their works. At the slaughter of an animal, the Prophet ordered that the name of God should always be named, but the words ' the Compassionate, the Merciful,' were to be omitted ; for on the one hand such an expression seemed a mockery to the sufferer, and, on the other, he could not bring

[1] Lane's ' Modern Egyptians,' p. 288.
[2] Sura VI. 38, and Sale's note *ad loc.*

himself to believe that the destruction of any life, however necessary, could be altogether pleasing to the All Merciful. 'In the name of God,' says a pious Musalman before he strikes the fatal blow; 'God is most great; God give thee patience to endure the affliction which He hath allotted thee!'[1] In the East there has been no moralist like Bentham to insist in noble words on the extension of the sphere of morality to all sentient beings, and to be ridiculed for it by people who call themselves religious ; there has been no naturalist like Darwin, to demonstrate by his marvellous powers of observation how large a part of the mental and moral faculties which we usually claim for ourselves alone we share with other beings; there has been no Oriental 'Society for the Prevention of Cruelty to Animals ;' but one reason of this is not far to seek. What the legislation of the last few years has at length attempted to do, and, from the mere fact that it is legislation, must do ineffectually, has been long effected in the East by the moral and religious sentiment which, like almost everything that is good in that part of the world, can be traced back, in part at least, to the great Prophet of Arabia.[2] In the East, so far

[1] Lane's 'Modern Egyptians,' I., 119.

[2] The sympathy of the Prophet for his domestic animals is well known. There is a great variety of traditions respecting his horses, his mules, his milch and riding camels, and his goats. It would be easy to write a complete biography of his favourite she-camel, Al

as it has not been hardened by the West, there is a real sympathy between man and the domestic animals ; they understand one another, and the cruelties which the most humane of our countrymen unconsciously inflict in the habitual use, for instance, of the muzzle or the bearing-rein on the most docile, the most patient, the most faithful, and the most intelligent of their companions, are impossible in the East. An Arab *cannot* ill-treat his horse ; and Mr. Lane bears emphatic testimony to the fact that in his long residence in Egypt he never saw an ass or a dog (though the latter is there looked upon as an unclean animal) treated with cruelty, except in those cities which were overrun by Europeans.[1]

Mohammed was not slow to forbid the practices nearest to the Arab heart if he saw them clearly to be wrong ; a strong reason surely for putting the most charitable interpretation possible upon his retention of polygamy. All hostilities and plundering excursions

Kaswa. Her eccentricities and perversities exercised an influence on some critical occasions in the Prophet's life—*e. g.* on his entrance to Medina, and at Kodeiba. Among the phenomena attending Mohammed's fits, it is recorded that if one came on him while riding, his camel itself became first wildly excited, and then fixed and rigid ! And I have little doubt that the story arose from the almost electric sympathy that exists between an intelligent animal that is kindly treated and its master.

[1] Lane, I., 359–361. Many mosques in Egypt and in other parts of the Mohammedan East have funds belonging to them which are specially appropriated to the relief or support of animals.

between neighbouring tribes that had become Musalman he forbade on pain of death ; and this among those who had hitherto lived by plunder or by war, and who he knew might be deterred by such prohibition from joining him. 'Let us make one more expedition against the Temim,' said a tribe that was almost, but not altogether, persuaded to embrace the faith, 'and then we will become Musalmans.'[1]   Usury and divination, drunkenness and gaming, were, as I have shown in my Second Lecture, among the darling practices of the Arabs : how did the Prophet deal with them ? 'O true believers, surely wine, and lots, and images, and divining arrows are an abomination of the work of Satan : therefore avoid them, that ye may prosper.   Satan seeketh to sow dissension and hatred among you, by means of wine and lots, and to divert you from remembering God and from prayer : will ye not therefore abstain from them ?'[2]

By thus absolutely prohibiting gambling and intoxicating liquors, Mohammed did much to abolish, once and for all, over the vast regions that own his sway, two of the worst and most irremediable evils of European society ; evils to the intensity of which the Christian Governments of the nineteenth century are hardly yet beginning to awake.

[1] Quoted by Dr. Cazenove, 'Christian Remembrancer,' January 1855, p. 71, from Caussin de Perceval.
[2] Sura V. 92.

Can anyone then who recollects what the Arabian Prophet did for woman, and the slave and the orphan, for the poor and the sick, and the lower animals, and who knows also how much he has done to restrain throughout the East certain vices which are still rampant in Christendom, deny what I have already hinted above, that, looking at him merely as a moral reformer, and apart from his great religious revolution, Mohammed was really doing Christ's work, even if he had reverenced Christ less than in fact he did ?

And this brings me to the most important question that I shall touch upon at present ; and one, but for which, in its various bearings, I do not know that I should have written these Lectures: I mean the attitude that Christianity ought to bear to Mohammedanism now. To say that in spite of the theoretic intolerance of Mohammedanism, it ought, unless its theory is put into practice, itself to be tolerated, is happily now a mere truism. But it ought not to be treated with a merely contemptuous or distant recognition, or to be inserted *tanquam infamiæ causâ*— 'Jews, Turks, Infidels, and Heretics'—in a collect, once a year, upon that day of all others upon which the universality of Christ's self-sacrifice is brought before us. When the draft of a treaty was brought to the General of the armies of revolutionary France, the first clause of which contained a formal recognition by the Emperor Francis of Austria—the representative of legitimacy, absolutism, and divine right—of the existence of the French Republic, 'Strike that clause out,' said Napoleon; 'the French Republic needs no recognition from him—it is as clear as the sun at noonday.' Mohammedanism needs no formal recognition of its existence by a faith with which it has so much in common. The immemorial quarrel between Mohammedanism and Christianity is, after all, a quarrel between near relations ; and, like most immemorial quarrels, is based chiefly on mutual misunderstandings. Without any appearance of extraordinary condescension, we should recognise the fact which Mohammedans themselves might at present certainly be inclined to deny, that Islam is the nearest approach to Christianity, I would almost call it, remembering Mohammed's intense reverence for Christ, the only form of Christianity, which has proved itself suited to the nations of the East. John Cantacuzene, the Greek Emperor of Constantinople, who calls himself in the title of his book ' the most pious and Christ-loving ' king, and who was often compelled to sharpen his sword, as well as his pen, against the Turkish foes who were then closing in around his capital, yet treats them throughout as sectaries only, and not pagans.[1]

---

[1] The title of the book is suggestive : τοῦ εὐσεβεστάτου καὶ φιλο-χρίστου βασιλέως 'Ιωάννου τοῦ Καντακοῦ (ἤνου . . . . κατὰ τῆς Σαρακηνων

Dante himself placed Mohammed in the 'Inferno,' not as a heathen, but as a heretic ; and is there any reason why our notion of Christianity should be less comprehensive than that of the patriot Greek Emperor or of the Christian poet ?

Mohammedanism is the one religion in the world, besides our own and the Jewish, which is strictly and avowedly Monotheistic. 'Dispute not,' said Mohammed to his followers, 'against those who have received the Scriptures, that is Jews and Christians, except with gentleness ; but say unto them we believe in the revelation which hath been sent down to us, and also in that which hath been sent down to you ; and our God and your God is one.' [1] And again he says in another place, 'Verily the Believers, and those who are Jews, those who are Christians and Sabeans, whoever believeth in God, and the last day, and doeth that which is right, they shall have their reward with their Lord, there shall come no fear upon them, neither shall they be grieved.' [2] And in a still more striking passage we find it written : 'Unto every one have we given a law and a way. Now if God had pleased, He would surely have made you one people, but He hath made you to differ that He might try

αἱρετικῶς ἀπολόγηται Δ. He married his daughter to a Turk. See Ibn Batuta's Travels, p. 79–85, for an interesting account of a similar occurrence.

[1] Sura V. 73.　　　　　　　　　　[2] Sura II. 59.

you in that which He hath given to each, therefore strive to excel each other in good works. Unto God shall ye all return, and He will tell you that concerning which ye have disagreed.'[1]

The three Creeds are branches from the same parent stock, not different stocks; and they all alike look back to the majestic character of Abraham as the first teacher of the unity of God. Mohammed says, again and again, that the belief he inculcates is no new belief—it is the original creed of Khalil Allah, the Friend of God. The heroes of the Old Testament history, Isaac and Jacob, Joseph and Joshua, David and Solomon, are heroes of the Mohammedan religion as well as of the Jewish and Christian.

I remarked in my Second Lecture that Mohammed may have thought himself justified in breaking the moral law he himself imposed, because a somewhat similar concession had been made to Moses. This is not a mere conjecture on my part, for it is certain that Mohammed had, for one who was so careless of facts, acquired somehow a full and fairly accurate knowledge of the history of the great Lawgiver. He relates it at length,[2] and recurs to it with a passionate fondness

---

[1] Sura V. 52, 53. Cf. Acts x. 35. These are passages on which the comparative mythologist the Musalman reformer, and the Christian missionary would alike do well to dwell. It is noteworthy also that the fifth Sura, from which two of them come, is placed by Rodwell and others last in the chronological order.

[2] See especially Suras VII. XVIII. XXVII. XXVIII. LV.

from an early period in his career, evidently dwelling mentally on the striking parallels between himself and Moses, the shepherd life, the call to the Prophet's office, the rejection by their own countrymen, no less than—be it always remembered to Mohammed's credit that he does not disguise it—the main point of difference, the prodigality of miracles performed by the one, and the inability to work them in the other. One most sacred spot actually connects the two Prophets together. There is a tradition, to some extent authenticated, that Mohammed drove the camels of Khadijah to the very place where Moses had tended the flocks of Jethro. Moses and Mohammed may have reposed on the same rock, watered their cattle at the same springs, looked upon the same weird mountains.[1] And it is a redeeming point, perhaps the only redeeming point, in the melancholy history of St. Catherine's Monastery, that from age to age within the convent walls, Mosque and Church have stood side by side, and Muslims and Christians have knelt together worshipping the same God ; and there, if only there in the world, venerating with a kindred, if not with an equal reverence, the same prophets, Moses and Mohammed, and One who is infinitely greater than them both.[2]

[1] Sura II. 57, VII. 160.
[2] See the account of St. Catherine's and its degradation in 'The Desert of the Exodus,' by E. H. Palmer ; and in Stanley's 'Sinai and

Again, Mohammedanism is in a true sense of the word a spiritual religion. As instituted by Mohammed it had 'no priest and no sacrifice;'[1] in other words, no caste of sacrificing priests were ever to be allowed to come between the human soul and God: forbidding the representation of all living things alike, whether as objects of use or of admiration, of veneration or of worship, Mohammedanism is more opposed to idolatry even than we are ourselves. Mohammed hated images more sternly even than the Iconoclasts of Constantinople or the soldiers of Cromwell. Every mosque in the world of Islam bears witness to this. Statuary and pictures being forbidden, variegated marbles, and festoons of lamps, and geometric shapes and tortuous inscriptions from the Koran, have to supply their place as best they can, and form that peculiar species of ornamentation, strictly confined to the inanimate world, which we call Arabesque, and

Palestine,' p. 53-54. Dean Stanley draws my attention to the fact that there is a large mosque in the principal street of St. Petersburg; and it is said that at Nijni Novgorod the same phenomenon, mosque and church as near and not unfriendly neighbours, may be observed ; but there no doubt it is commerce rather than religious sympathy which we have to thank for it.

[1] The Sacrifice at the Annual Pilgrimage is a mere relic of the Pagan practice ; it has little religious significance, and does not imply priestcraft ; it indicates only the belief that sin deserves death. At the feast of Beiram a victim is offered, but only in commemoration of the ram accepted by God in the place of Isaac, or rather, as the Musalmans represent it, in the place of Ishmael. Each worshipper, moreover, offers the victim for himself, without the intervention of any official.

which is still to be traced in the architecture of so many churches and so many mosques along the frontier line of four thousand miles which divides the realm of the Crescent from that of the Cross.[1]

This hatred of idolatry has been found even among the most uncivilised followers of the Prophet. The gorgeous ritual, the gaudy pictures, and the pious frauds which play so large a part in the conversion of the Sclavonian nations to Christianity seem only to have alienated these semi-barbarians. Mahmud the Ghaznevide, the son of a slave and the conqueror of Hindustan, was offered a sum of ten millions sterling if only he would spare the famous idol in the pagoda of Somnat. Avarice is said to have been his besetting fault, but he replied in the memorable words, ' Never shall Mahmud be a merchant of idols ; ' and broke it into pieces.[2]

In this horror of all objective symbols, in the simplicity of its liturgical forms,[3] in the absence of a

---

[1] Cf. Stanley's ' Lectures on the Eastern Church,' p. 273. Without discussing the general question at length, I may remark here that Gothic architecture, though it is not very ready to acknowledge the debt, owes much to Moorish architecture—in particular the Horse-shoe or Crescent Arch. The pointed arch itself is to be found in many early mosques, and some of the most famous Venetian buildings, St. Mark's among them, owe much to Saracenic architecture.

[2] Ferishta's ' History of Mohammedan Power in India ' (Briggs's translation), I. p. 72 ; and Elphinstone's ' History of India,' p. 336.

[3] See the forms of prayer, &c., given by Garçin de Tassy, ' L'Islamisme,' p. 207–285. Most of them are of course an after-growth.

priestly caste, and therefore of all belief in such
doctrines as those of apostolical succession, inherent
sanctity, indissoluble vows, the duty of confession or
powers of absolution, Islam stands alone among the
religions of the world. Yet without compromising
seriously this its essential character, it was able
originally, and it is able still, in Africa and in
Hindustan, in Central Asia and the East Indian
islands, to win over, and that often by pure conviction, Pagans from the most debasing and materialistic forms of idolatry, and this to an extent which is
quite unequalled in modern times by any form of
Christianity, or by any other proselytising creed. In a
Protestant country in which the missionary spirit is
still strong, but in some portions of which a florid
ritual and an exotic æstheticism seem to be the order
of the day, it is well to draw pointed attention to
what another creed can do without any such accom-
paniments, and to the stumbling-block which these
would inevitably place in the way of a Musalman
who might otherwise be disposed to listen to the
Christian message.[1]

Finally, Mohammedanism, in spite of centuries

[1] One of the forms of idolatry which Mohammed found among the
Pagans of Arabia, and which he overthrew, was the worship of bread.
A tribe called the Hanifa used to pay Divine honours to a shapeless
lump of dough ; which, however, with characteristic levity, they were
not unwilling to eat when pressed by want of food.

of wars and misunderstandings, looks back upon the Founder of our religion with reverence only less than that with which the most devout Christians regard Him.

So far from its being true, as is commonly supposed, that Mohammedans regard Christ as Christians have too often regarded Mohammed, with hatred and with contempt; Sir William Muir remarks that devout Musalmans never mention the name of Seyyedna Eesa, or Our Lord Jesus, without adding the words 'on whom be peace.' The highest honour that a Musalman can conceive is given to Christ in the grave reserved for Him by the side of the Prophet himself in the great Mosque at Medina. Mohammedans expect that He will one day return to earth, and having slain Antichrist, will establish perfect peace among men. And Dr. Hunter[1] tells us that the Indian Shiahs avowedly look forward to his reappearance simultaneously with that of the last of their twelve Imams, and to an amalgamation of the two creeds; of Islam as the followers of Ali hold it, and of Christianity, not as it is, but as they believe it was taught by Christ Himself.[2] A Christian indeed is not received by Mohammedans with quite the open

---

[1] 'Our Indian Mussulmans,' p. 120, by W. W. Hunter.

[2] For a curious discussion on the return of the Messiah to earth held at Timbuctu, see Barth's 'Travels in Central Africa,' V., p. 4.

arms of hospitality with which they welcome a brother
Mohammedan ; but a traveller who was the first to
explore the source of the Oxus, and the adjacent
countries in Central Asia, tells us, as the result of his
own wide experience, that a Christian may count
upon a courteous, if not upon a cordial, reception
from them, and that he is always treated with kindness and respect.[1]   A Mohammedan, he goes on to
say, looks upon Christians in the light indeed of
benighted and misguided men, but yet, as the Prophet
himself so often called them, as 'people of the Book,'
who, though not heirs to the high destinies of Mohammed's followers, are nevertheless, from the sacred
character of Seyyedna Eesa, entitled to the commi-
seration and sympathy of the faithful.   The fact is
that though, since the first spread of Islam, comparatively few Christians have ever become Musalmans, a
Musalman is still disposed to look upon a Christian
as, potentially at least, a brother Musalman.   It was
a saying of the Prophet himself, that 'everyone is
born a Musalman:' Abraham was one, so was Jesus,
in that he was resigned to God's will and had unbounded faith in Him.   The two systems of belief,
therefore, were, in the Prophet's view, in no way con-
tradictory to each other.   Islam was, as he taught
at one stage of his life, a religion co-ordinate with

---

[1] Wood's 'Oxus,' p. 93, 94.

Christianity; at another a development, but not more than a development of it. To revile Jesus has therefore always been looked upon by the Prophet's consistent followers as no less an offence than to revile Mohammed. In the time of Mohammed IV. a convert to Islam at Constantinople, in order to prove, as he thought, the sincerity of his conversion, or to ingratiate himself with those who were now his co-religionists, began to blaspheme Christ. He was dragged off by the Musalmans who heard him to the Divan, and was ordered out for instant execution.

If it be asked, why then did Mohammed not accept Christianity, I apprehend that the reasons are threefold; and that it appears from the chronological order lately assigned to the Suras of the Koran, that at one period, that of the Fatrah, Mohammed did consider whether first Judaism, and secondly Christianity, as he knew it, contained the message he had to give.

I. The first explanation I would suggest is, that the Christ known to him was the Christ, not of the Bible, but of tradition; the Christ, not of the Canonical, but of the Apocryphal Gospels, and even these only from general tradition. The wonder is, Mohammed's information being confined to the incoherent rhapsodies and the miraculous inanities of the Gospels of the Infancy, the Acta Pilati and the

'Descensus ad Inferos,' not that he reverenced Christ so little, but so much. In the whole of the Koran there are only three passages which look like any direct acquaintance with the Evangelists; and one of these, the well-known passage about the Paraclete, he misunderstands himself, and accuses Christians of intentionally perverting from its proper meaning, a prediction of the coming of the Periclyte, the Greek form of Mohammed, the Illustrious, or the Praised.[1]

II. Secondly, the worship of saints and images, and the shape which certain floating ideas had taken when they were stereotyped in the formulas of the Christian Church, seemed to Mohammed to conflict with his fundamental doctrine of the unity of God. The mysteries of the Trinity were to be appraised and handled by every one who called himself a Christian, not merely as a test, but as the test of his Christianity. Mohammed accuses even the Jews of having lost sight of their primary truth, which was also his, in calling Ezra the Son of God,[2] and what wonder if he rejected a religion the essence of which he understood, and too many Christians of his time understood to be, not a holy life, but, as it is still represented in the Athanasian Creed, an elaborate and unthinkable mode of thinking of the Trinity? It is doubtful indeed whether a people that has once become mono-

[1] Sura LXI. 6.   [2] Sura IX. 30.

theistic in any other form than the Christian, can ever
be brought to accept, I do not say Christianity
altogether, but the doctrines that are often supposed
to be of its very essence. Among such a people the
missionary invariably finds that the doctrine of the
Trinity, however explained, involves Tritheism, and
their ears are at once closed to his teaching. To a
Pagan who accepts Christianity the change no doubt
is one from Polytheism to Monotheism, but to the
Jew or Mohammedan, except in very rare instances,
it is the opposite.

Let us hear on these points, however, Mohammed
himself, remembering all the while how slight was his
knowledge of the doctrine which he travestied, and
how dim the outline of the majestic character which
yet filled his imagination :—

'They surely are infidels who say God is the third
of three, for there is no God but one God.' [1]

'Say not three; forbear, it will be better for thee;
God is only one God.' [2]

Christ was with Mohammed the greatest of
Prophets.[3] He had the power of working miracles;
He spoke in his cradle; He made a bird out of clay.[4]
He could give sight to the blind, and even raise the

[1] Sura V. 77.   [2] Sura IV. 6.   [3] Sura II. 254.
[4] Incidents drawn from the Gospels of the Infancy or of St.
Thomas.

dead to life.[1] He is the Word proceeding from God ;
His name is the Messiah. Illustrious in this world
and in the next, and one of those who have near
access to God.[2] 'He is strengthened by the Holy
Spirit,' for so Mohammed, in more than one passage,
calls the Angel Gabriel.[3] Mohammed all but believes in the Immaculate Conception of the Virgin,[4]
and certainly in the miraculous nature of the birth of
Christ, to which he recurs repeatedly.[5] But that
Jesus ever claimed, as is affirmed by the writers of
the New Testament, and as we know He did, to be
the Son of God, still less that He ever claimed to be
equal with God, Mohammed could not bring himself
to believe.

'It becometh not a man that God should give him
the Scriptures, and the Wisdom, and the spirit of
Prophecy, and that then he should say to his followers
Be ye worshippers of me as well as of God, but rather
Be ye perfect in things pertaining to God, since ye
know the Scriptures, and have studied them.'[6]

And again, 'For the Messiah himself said, Oh
children of Israel, worship God, my Lord and
yours.'[7]

---

[1] Sura III. 41-43.   [2] Sura III. 40.   [3] Sura II. 81.
[4] Sura III. 30. There was a well-known sect of Christians called
Collyridians in Arabia who paid the Virgin divine honours, and offered
her a twisted cake (κόλλυρις). Thence, no doubt, came Mohammed's
idea that the Virgin was one of the Persons of the Trinity.
[5] Sura XIX. 20.   [6] Sura III. 73.   [7] Sura V. 76.

And once more, 'Those who say that Jesus, the Son of Mary, is the Son of God, are infidels, for who could stop the arm of God if He were to destroy the Messiah and His mother, and all who are in the earth together?'[1]

Neither can Mohammed ever believe that Jesus could have been crucified. 'It is so long ago, let us hope that it is not true,' said an old Cheshire woman when she heard for the first time in her life the story of the Crucifixion. 'If I and my brave Franks had been there, we would have avenged His injuries,' was the exclamation of the fierce barbarian Clovis when he received his first lesson in the Christian life. The Dreamer of the Desert sympathised rather with the first of these. As Stesichorus[2] believed that the Greeks and Trojans fought for the phantom of Helen, and not for Helen herself; as the Docetists held that the phantom of Jesus and not Jesus Himself had been crucified; so Mohammed rebels at the thought that God can ever have allowed such a tragedy to take place. Some one else, he curiously supposes, who deserved such a death—perhaps it was Judas himself—may have been substituted for Christ; and Christ being taken up to heaven, must have felt that the deception thus practised on the Jews was a kind of punishment to Himself for not having taken

[1] Sura V. 19.   [2] Plato, 'Republic,' IX. 86.

T

greater pains to prevent men calling Him the Son of God.[1] And at the resurrection Jesus will Himself testify against both Jews and Christians ; the Jews for not having received Him as a prophet, the Christians for having received Him as God.

There is a short chapter in the Koran which Muslims look upon as equal to a third of the whole in value :

> 'Say there is one God alone—
> God the Eternal ;
> He begetteth not, and He is not begotten,
> And there is none like unto Him.'[2]

And once more, 'They say the Merciful hath gotten offspring. Now have ye done a monstrous thing ; almost might the very heavens rend thereat, and the earth rend asunder, and the mountains fall down in fragments, that they ascribe a son to the Merciful, when it becometh not the Merciful to beget a son. Verily there is nobody in the heavens nor in the earth that shall approach the Merciful but as a servant.'[3]

It is certain that the notions conveyed to Mohammed's mind by the words he so often uses, 'begetting and begotten,' and which called forth this torrent of indignant invective, were such as might well do so ; and such also as he might, under the circumstances,

---

[1] Sura III. 49, IV. 156.   [2] Sura CXII.   [3] Sura XIX. 91-94.

not unnaturally attribute to Christians. A learned critic to whom I am much indebted, Dr. G. P. Badger, points out that the word 'Walada' used by Mohammed throughout the Sura quoted just now, does necessarily involve notions of sex and of physical paternity ; and it was doubtless against these that Mohammed hurled his anathemas. On the other hand, Dr. Badger remarks that the equivalent of this word is never used in the New Testament to express the Christian doctrine of the Divine Sonship; and that the term 'Word of God' is applied to Christ as much by Mohammed and the Koran as by St. John in his Gospel. If this can be made evident to Musalmans, it is clear that one great cause of misconception will be lessened or removed ; and, even if it cannot, it is still fair to remember that for centuries the battle of Ecclesiastical warfare in the East had been raging round the words which should be used to express the idea of a relationship which, it is admitted, human language cannot adequately convey nor human thought conceive. The followers of the party which had triumphed at the councils of Ephesus and Chalcedon, which had made the word Theotokos, for the time, to be the watchword of mitres and of thrones ; and had driven the Nestorians, with their rival watchword, Christotokos, into exile in the remote East, were not likely to steer clear of the physical questions which

might be involved in the controversy ; and no impartial
enquirer will be surprised to hear that in Arabia the
Christian doctrine of the Trinity was believed to be a
Trinity of a Father, a Mother, and a Son ; or that the
Almighty is represented in the Koran as enquiring of
Jesus, the son of Mary, 'hast thou indeed said unto
men, Take me and my mother for two Gods besides
God ?' The honours indeed paid to the ' Mother of
God ' by the party which had triumphed, were little
less than divine ; and Mohammed may therefore be
excused for believing that in rejecting Christianity as
he knew it, he ·was rejecting Saint-worship and Polytheism, as well as the adoration of pictures and of
images.

I have dwelt thus at length upon Mohammed's
views of Christ, partly because of the intrinsic interest and importance attaching to the views held by
one so great of One so infinitely greater ; partly
because they show how little Mohammed, and indeed how little Christians themselves, understood
the real nature of Christianity ; partly also because
the strictures of Mohammed, however exaggerated
and however mistaken, seem to me to suggest a
caution necessary for us all. Christ came to reveal
God, not to hide Him ; to bring Him down to earth,
not to shroud Him in an immeasurable distance ; to
tell us that God is not primarily Justice, or Truth,

or Power, but Love. Do Christians always remem-·
ber this? Are our views of Justification, of Original Sin, of a Future Life, when drawn out in the
forensic and almost legal language in which some
Churches foolishly delight to clothe them, always
consistent with it? Do our prayers always pre-
suppose a God who, in His own intrinsic nature, is
anxious to receive them? Are we not apt to forget
the unity of God, while we dogmatise on the Trinity?
Do we not sometimes place Christ as it were in front
of God, thinking so much of the Son who sacrificed
Himself, that we ignore the Father who ' spared Him
not ;' forgetting the Giver in the very magnitude of
the gift?

III. And the third reason, and perhaps the
most important of all, for Mohammed's rejection of
Christianity is the fact that Christianity as he knew
it had been tried and had failed. It had been known
for three hundred years in Arabia, and had not been
able to overthrow, or even weaken, the idolatry of
the inhabitants.

It is strange, with this fact and the whole course
of history before him, with which evidently few are
more familiar, that a great writer can conclude a
review of Mohammedanism, which is otherwise fair
and able, by endorsing the charge made against it,
that it has kept back the East by hindering the spread

of Christianity. The charge has been often made before,[1] but it rests on so slender a basis that I should not have thought it necessary to discuss it here, had I not found at the last moment that one who is apparently so high an authority has lent the weight of his name to it. That I may do him no injustice, I quote his own words :—

'Mohammed in his own age and country was the greatest of reformers—a reformer alike religious, moral, and political. . . . . . But when his system passed the borders of the land in which it was so great a reform, it became the greatest of curses to mankind. The main cause which has made the religion of Mohammed exercise so blighting an influence on every land where it has been preached, is because it is an imperfect system standing in the way of one more perfect. Islam has in it just enough of good to hinder the reception of greater good. . . . . . . Because Islam comes nearer to Christianity than any other false system, because it comes nearer than any other to satisfying the wants of man's spiritual nature, for that very reason it is, above all other false systems, pre-eminently anti-Christian. It is, as it were, the personal enemy and rival of the Faith, disputing on equal terms for the same prize !'[2]

---

[1] As, for instance, by Sir W. Muir, IV. 321.
[2] *British Quarterly Review*, Jan. 1872, p. 132–134.

This indictment is so well drawn, at first sight it
so carries conviction with it, and yet, if true, it is so
fatal to any favourable or any fair judgment of
Mohammedanism, that I am compelled, while I gladly
acknowledge the author's fair and sympathetic treatment of the subject in every page that precedes and
follows those I have quoted, to contest, from my
point of view, as strongly as I can, upon this question,
alike his facts and his inferences.

Upon what single fact then, either before or after
Mohammed's time, does the writer ground this charge ?
If the purest Christianity of all, preached by Christ
and His Apostles, did not make way in the Eastern
world ; if the few Christian Churches which did exist
among the half Roman or Hellenic inhabitants of
Syria and of Africa had sunk to the condition in which
we know they were when Mohammedanism swept
them away, what reason have we, either *à priori* or *à
posteriori*, for supposing that the Christianity of any
later time would have been more successful ? Have
Christian nations been so energetic or so successful in
converting any of those African or Asiatic nations
which Mohammedanism has never reached, as to entitle us to turn round upon the religion which has re-
moulded so large a portion of the human race, and tell
it that it is a curse to humanity because, forsooth, while
we admit it was in its time a grand forward movement

and has been a higher life to untold millions since, we
wish that Fetish worship should have lasted on perhaps
till now, that Christianity may now have the chance of
doing the work somewhat better? If this is Christianity, I only say most certainly it is not of Christ.
It is not of the Spirit of Him who said that those who
were not against Him were with Him; and rejoiced
that good was done by others, even if it seemed an
infringement of His own Divine commission. Christ
was not like the Prætorian prefect of Tacitus, '*Consilii,
quamvis egregii, quod non ipse afferret inimicus,*'
though some Christians would have it that He was.
The only monopoly of good that Christianity, if it is
of the spirit of its Founder, may claim, is the monopoly
not of doing good, but of rejoicing at it whenever it
is done, and whoever does it; of showing, if it carries
out its Founder's intentions, that it is wide enough to
recognise as its own and to embrace within its ample
bosom all honest 'seekers after God,' and all true
benefactors of humanity. The most 'anti-Christian'
religion is not that which comes nearest to Christianity,
but that which is furthest removed from it; and the
religion which after Christianity comes nearest to
'satisfying the wants of man's spiritual nature' is
really not its most deadly enemy, but its best ally.
To say otherwise, liberal and tolerant as the author
unquestionably is, is to encourage weaker men under

the shadow of his name,[1] not merely to indulge in the *odium theologicum*, but to assert that the *odium theologicum* itself is Christian.

> ' Non tali auxilio nec defensoribus istis
> Tempus eget.'

Can it be forgotten that the churches planted by the great Apostle were, without exception, to the west of Palestine—that star-worship and fire-worship were unaffected by Christianity then, even as Brahminism and Buddhism are unaffected by it now? Can we point to a single Oriental nation which has been able to accept and to retain Christianity in its pure form, or to a single religion to be named with Mohammedanism in point of purity and sublimity, which has ever been able to overthrow any national Oriental faith? And, if we cannot, what right have we to say that it is Islam, and not Nature, that has hitherto stood in the way of Christianity in Arabia and Persia, in Africa and India? The triumphs of the Cross have indeed been far purer, far wider, far sublimer than those of the Crescent; but they have been hitherto confined to the higher races of the world. Uncivilised nations of

---

[1] This has actually been the case, for the passage I have quoted was the only one in an otherwise most temperate essay upon which religious periodicals pounced, and, by quoting apart from its context, fanned the flame of misconception and prejudice which, even when read with everything which tends the other way, it would, in my judgment, be likely to kindle.

the higher stock, Ostrogoths and Visigoths, Vandals
and Lombards, Franks and Northmen, the Celt, the
Teuton, and the Sclavonian, invaded Christianity only
to be conquered by it. But upon the Oriental barbarians of a lower race who invaded Europe, with
the one exception of the Magyars, whose case is
special,[1] Huns and Avars, Turks and Tartars, it has
had no influence. Shall Christians, then, complain
of Mohammedans for having succeeded in some
measure in doing for the East what they have failed
to do ; or would Christ have rejected what good
service Mohammed did because his credentials were
not precisely those of the Apostles ? What superficial appearance of truth there is in the charge is this
—that no Mohammedan nation has hitherto accepted
Christianity, while some nations that were nominally
Christians have accepted Mohammedanism. But to

---

[1] The Magyars, whatever their original home—and it seems that
they were of the Finnish stock—are probably the most mixed race on
the Continent of Europe, and were so even before they settled within
the limits of the present Hungary. In their march towards Europe
they were joined by hosts of Chazars, Bulgarians, and Sclavonians.
During their ravages, which lasted for some fifty years, and spread
from the Oural Mountains to the Pyrenees, they transported women
and children wholesale from the countries they overran to their head-
quarters on the Danube ; and it is probable that at the time of their
avowed conversion by Adalbert, about A. D. 1000, they had almost as
much German and Italian as they had Tartar blood in their veins. St.
Piligrinus (quoted by Gibbon, VII. 172), the first missionary who
entered Hungary, says that he found the 'majority of the population
to be Christians,' *qui ex omni parte mundi illuc tracti sunt captivi.*

establish the charge, it would, of course, be necessary to show that the East, if it had not accepted Mohammedanism, would have accepted a real Christianity, or any religion so much like Christianity as Mohammedanism unquestionably is ; and to do this we must read history backwards.

Now Mohammed offered to the Arabs an idea of God less sympathetic and less loveable, indeed, but as sublime as the Christian, and perhaps still more intense, and one, as it turned out, which they could receive. Christianity was compelled to leave its birth-place—the inhabitants and subsequent history of which it has scarcely affected, except indirectly—to find its proper home in the Western world, among the inhabitants and progressive civilisation of Greece and Rome. The lot of Mohammedanism has been different ; ' it is the religion of the shepherd and the nomad, of the burning desert and the boundless steppe.' So admirably suited was it to the region in which it was born, that it needed no foreign air or change of circumstances to develope it.[1]

---

[1] Compare throughout this paragraph, M. Barth. St. Hilaire, p. 230 seq. Sir Emerson Tennent, in his 'Christianity in Ceylon,' after pointing out (p. 272–273) that education must precede direct missionary efforts, remarks that ' neither history nor more recent experience can furnish any example of the long retention of pure Christianity by a people themselves rude and unenlightened. In all the nations of Europe Christianity has taken the hue and complexion of the social state with which it was incorporated, presenting itself un-

In its simple grandeur it has been able, without tampering with that which is its Alpha and Omega—the belief in one God, who reveals Himself by His prophets—to leave the most essential elements of national life to the various nations which made up the Arabian empire ; and to adapt itself to every peculiarity, mental and moral, of the inhabitants of Central and Western Asia. The rapid intuition and the wild flights of imagination ; the vivid mental play around the Antinomies of the reason, and the craving for the supernatural in the utmost particularity of detail ; the fervid asceticism of the Dervish, and the mystic Pantheism of the Sufi, have each found in Islam something to meet their wants.

But, on the other hand, Mohammedanism has never passed into countries of a wholly different nature, and held them permanently. Spain is not a case in point, though it was never so well governed as under the Mohammedans ; for the Spaniards themselves never to any great extent became Mohammedan, and the Moorish settlement there was only

sullied, contaminated, or corrupted in sympathy with the enlightenment, or ignorance, or debasement of those by whom it has been originally embraced. The rapid and universal degeneracy of the early Asiatic Churches is associated with the decline of education, and the intellectual decay of the communities among whom they were established.' Apply these remarks, *mutatis mutandis*, to Islam, and how many of the charges made against it fall at once to the ground, or fail to hit their mark !

like a Greek ἐπιτείχισμα or a Roman colonia—an out-
post in the heart of the enemy's country.   Much the
same may be said of Turkey, where the majority of
the subject population has always remained Christian.
I cannot, therefore, '*pace tanti nominis*,' follow Gibbon
in his picture of the probable consequences to European civilisation had Charles Martel been conquered
at Tours ; of Musalman preachers demonstrating to a
circumcised audience, in the mosques of Paris and of
Oxford, the truth of the religion of Mohammed !
The wave of conquest might have spread over Europe ;
but it would have been but a wave, and few traces
would have been left when it had swept on.   In
Africa the case was different ; the Greek colonists
and Roman conquerors—the higher races, in fact—
were driven out by the Saracens, and, 'in their climate
and habits, the wandering Moors who remained behind
already resembled the Bedouins of the Desert.'[1]
Mohammedanism is the only form in which the knowledge of the true God has ever made way with the
native races of Africa ; and the form of Christianity
which it supplanted in the North—the Christianity
of the Donatists and of the Nitrian monks ; of Cyril,
strangely called a saint ; and of the infamous George
of Cappadocia, still more strangely transformed into
St. George of England, the patron of chivalry and of

[1] Gibbon, VI. LI. p. 473.

the Garter—was infinitely inferior to Mohammedanism itself.

I fully admit that Mohammedanism, if indeed it
had succeeded in conquering the most civilised races
of the world and the Christianity of the West,
as it succeeded in conquering the Eastern nations
and their various forms of belief, would have conquered something that was potentially better than
itself, and then it would have been what Christian
writers are so fond of calling it—a curse to the world
rather than a blessing. It would have stepped beyond
what I conceive to have been its proper mission ; but I
maintain that it stopped short of this, and that it destroyed nothing that was not far inferior to itself.

I should hesitate to say that even its conquest of
Spain was not, while it lasted, a blessing to Spain itself, and through Spain to the whole of Europe. Has
Spain exhibited more order, more toleration, more
industry, better faith, more material prosperity, under
her most Christian Kings, or under her Ommiade
Khalifs ? The names of the three Abdul Rahmans,
and of Almamun, suggest all that is most glorious in
Spanish history, and much that has conferred benefit
on the rest of Europe in the darkest period of her an-
nals—religious zeal without religious intolerance, philosophy and literature, science and art, hospitals, and
libraries, and universities.

Nearly three centuries have elapsed since the fatuous decree of Philip III. banished from Spain and from Europe the most enlightened and industrious portion of his subjects; yet even now the traveller in Spain feels as he approaches Andalusia that he is breathing a clearer atmosphere, that he is brought into contact with a finer literature, and is contemplating a far nobler architecture, than any which the more northern parts of the Peninsula can boast. Moorish, not Catholic, is every thing that appeals to his imagination and to his finer feelings; Moorish are the legends and the ballads of the country; Moorish are the Alcazar and the Giralda of Seville; Moorish everything that is not discordant in the once matchless Mosque, now the interpolated Cathedral of Cordova;[1] Moorish all the glories of the Alhambra. And as the traveller passes the hill which is still called, with such deep pathos, 'the last sigh of the Moor,' he feels that the day which saw the fall of Granada is a day over which every Spaniard may well sigh for what it cost Spain, and every European for what it cost humanity at large.

Sicily again was conquered by the Arabs and held

---

[1] When Charles V. saw the havoc that had been wrought by those who had converted the Mosque into a cathedral, he reproached the bishop and chapter, saying, 'You have built here what you might have built anywhere else, but you have destroyed what was unique in the world.'

by them for two hundred years; and it was their rule that gave to the island the only period of prosperity and good government which it has enjoyed from the time of the first Punic war till now; and when at last the rule of the Fatimite Khalifs was overthrown by the crusading chieftains of the house of Tancred of Hauteville, the comparative prosperity which still smiled on Sicily was due to those Norman princes who adopted the customs and the manners of the people they had overthrown; and some of whom, like William the Good, are said to have been at least as much Musalman as Christian.[1]

In spite, however, of what I maintain it has done under exceptional circumstances even for European countries, it follows from what I have equally freely admitted above that Mohammedanism is not a world-wide religion. The sphere of its influence is vast, but not boundless; in catholicity of application it is as much below the purest Christianity as the Semitic and Turanian nations which have embraced it are below the Western Indo-Germanic. I say the Western Indo-Germanic races, for among the Eastern branches of that great family, the inhabitants of Persia and of Hindustan, Mohammedanism did establish itself.

The Persians are of a race and genius widely different from the Arabs; but the surroundings and the

---

[1] See Deutsch, 'Literary Remains,' p. 457–465.

general mode of life are the same in each, and the exception, so far as it is an exception, to the rule I have laid down, tends rather, in its results, to prove its general truth, for the hold of Mohammedanism on them has been much modified by the difference of race. The religion which proclaimed the absolute supremacy of God was no doubt an infinite advance upon the ' chilling equipoise ' of good and evil to which the creed of Zoroaster had at that time sunk.[1] Nor was the national existence of Persia stamped out, as has been often said, by the Khalifs; for the Persian province of Khorasan was itself strong enough to place the Abbasside Khalifs on the throne of Bagdad; the Persian dynasties of the Samanides and Dilemites gave to the nation a new lease of life, and a wholly new national literature; and it is to a Mohammedan Sultan of the Turkish race that Persia owes her greatest literary glory, her national epic, the ' Shahnameh ' of Firdausi. Still it cannot be said that the religion proved itself altogether suited to the people. In other countries the scymitar had no sooner been drawn from its scabbard than it was sheathed again. But in Persia the scymitar had not only to clear the way, but for some time afterwards to maintain the new religion.[2] The Persians corrupted its

---

[1] See Elphinstone's ' India,' V. I. 313.
[2] See Sir John Malcolm's ' History of Persia,' I. VIII. p. 277, &c.

simplicity with fables and with miracles ; they actually imported into it something of saint-worship, and something of sacerdotalism ; and, consequently, in no nation in the Mohammedan world has the religion less hold on the people as a restraining power.   The most stringent principles of the Koran are set at nought ; beng and opium are common ; the Ketman, or religious equivocation, is held to be as allowable as it has been by the Casuists or the Jesuits; and the nation which Herodotus tells us devoted a third of its whole educational curriculum to learning to speak the truth, now contains hardly an individual who will speak the truth unless he has something to gain by it.

In Hindustan, amidst the other branch of the great Aryan race which did not move westward, Mohammedanism has obtained finally a very strong footing ; but it was slow in winning its way ; and the forty millions of Musalmans over whom we rule—and a tremendous and but half-recognised responsibility it is [1]—devout as they are, have become so by long lapse of time, by social influences, and by intermixture with conquering Arabs, Ghaznevides, and Afghans, rather than by the

---

[1] Since this was written, the grievances of Mohammedans in India, so ably and temperately stated by Mr. Hunter, have been in part alleviated by the adoption of some of the remedies he suggests, at least as far as regards education.

sudden fervour of religious enthusiasm.[1] The reverence paid to saints and their tombs, which has, in defiance of the letter of the Koran and the traditions, crept into so many parts of the Musalman world, is, as was to be expected, more noticeable in Persia and in India than elsewhere. The festival of the Moharram, commemorating the martyrdom of Hassan and Hosein, sons of Ali, and observed in Persia with such passionate indications of grief, is celebrated with hardly less solemnity in India also, and resembles in many particulars the Mysteries and the Miracle-Plays of the Middle Ages. Islam has in the course of centuries and by long contact with Hindu idolatry naturally made many compromises with it. Some of the Musalman saints are reverenced by the Hindus as well as by the Musalmans ; and these last have in their turn accommodated the accessories of their Pilgrimages, of their Fasts, and their Feasts, to the tastes of the Hindus ; to a religion, that is, which speaks more to the senses than to the reason, to the imagination than to the soul.[2]

---

[1] Elphinstone, V. I. 314, and Cap. III. on the Reign of the Sultan Mahmud.

[2] See the interesting memoir appended by M. Garçin de Tassy to his 'Islamisme,' on the peculiarities of the Musalman religion in India, p. 289 –403, especially p. 296. I am indebted to the courtesy of the Rev. T. P. Hughes, missionary at Peshawur, for some valuable 'Notes on Mohammedanism,' in which he describes the ceremonies and the formalities which unhappily now form so large a part of the religion in India and else-

Those who have followed me thus far will perceive that my main object in writing these Lectures has been, if possible, to render some measure of that justice to Mohammed and to his religion which has been all too long, and is still all too generally, denied to them. I have naturally, therefore, been led to dwell rather on the points in which Mohammedanism resembles Christianity than on the points in which it differs, and I have been led, also, to some extent, to compare the persons of their respective Founders. It is not possible to avoid this. Of the Founder of Christianity I have necessarily spoken only under that aspect of His character which Muslim as well as Christian, friend as well as foe, will perforce allow Him ; and in which alone, by the nature of the case, He can be compared with any other Founder at all. In like manner, in comparing the two Creeds, I have insisted mainly on the points in which they approximate to each other ; and to do this is more necessary, more just, and, I venture to think, more Christian, than to do the opposite.

But if, in order to prevent misconception, the two

where, and throws some light on the nature of the Wahhabi revival—an obscure subject, on which he has been able to obtain information from very original sources. It is worth remarking that in India the schism between Sunnis and Shiahs is not nearly so marked as in other parts of the Mohammedan world. They both join, for instance, in the Moharram.

Creeds must necessarily be contrasted rather than compared, nothing that I have said, or am going to say, will prevent my admitting fully—what, indeed, is apparent upon the face of it—that the contrasts are at least as striking as the resemblances.

The religion of Christ contains whole fields of morality and whole realms of thought which are all but outside the religion of Mohammed. It opens humility, purity of heart, forgiveness of injuries, sacrifice of self to man's moral nature ; it gives scope for toleration, development, boundless progress to his mind ; its motive power is stronger, even as a friend is better than a king, and love higher than obedience. Its realised ideals in the various paths of human greatness have been more commanding, more many-sided, more holy, as Averroes is below Newton, Harun below Alfred, and Ali below St. Paul. Finally, the ideal life of all is far more elevating, far more majestic, far more inspiring, even as the life of the founder of Mohammedanism is below the life of the Founder of Christianity.

And when I speak of the ideal life of Mohammedanism I must not be misunderstood. There is in Mohammedanism no ideal life in the true sense of the word, for Mohammed's character was admitted by himself to be a weak and erring one. It was disfigured by at least one huge moral blemish ;

and exactly in so far as his life has, in spite of his earnest and reiterated protestations, been made an example to be followed, has that vice been perpetuated. But in Christianity the case is different. The words, 'Which of you convinceth me of sin?' forced from the mouth of Him who was meek and lowly of heart, by the wickedness of those who, priding themselves on being Abraham's children, never did the works of Abraham, are a definite challenge to the world. That challenge has been for nineteen centuries before the eyes of unfriendly, as well as of believing, readers, and it has never yet been fairly met ; and at this moment, by the confession of friend and foe alike, the character of Jesus of Nazareth stands alone in its spotless purity and its unapproachable majesty. We have each of us probably at some period of our lives tried hard to penetrate to the inmost meaning of some one of Christ's short and weighty utterances—

> ⸱ 'Those jewels, five words long.
> Which on the stretched forefinger of all time
> Sparkle for ever.'

But is there one of us who can say there is no more behind? Is there one thoughtful person among us who has ever studied the character of Christ, and has not, in spite of ever-recurring difficulties and doubts, once and again, burst into the centurion's exclamation, 'Truly this was the Son of God'?

Nor are the methods of drawing near to God the same in the two religions. The Musalman gains a knowledge of God—he can hardly be said to approach Him—by listening to the lofty message of God's Prophet. The Christian believes that he approaches God by a process which, however difficult it may be to define, yet has had a real meaning to Christ's servants, and has embodied itself in countless types of Christian character—that mysterious something which St. Paul calls a 'union with Christ.' 'Ye are dead, and your life is hid with Christ in God.'

But this unmistakeable superiority does not shake my position that Mohammedanism is, after all, an approach to Christianity, and perhaps the nearest approach to it which the unprogressive part of humanity can ever attain in masses; and yet how large a part of the whole human race are unprogressive! Whatever we may wish, and however current conversation and literature may assert the contrary, progress is the exception, and not the rule, with mankind. The whole Eastern world, with very few exceptions, has been hitherto, and is still, stationary, not progressive. What Oriental society is now, it was in the time of Solomon—I might say, in the time of Abraham. Even those nations which, like the

Chinese, have considerable powers of invention and mechanical skill, reach a certain height rapidly, and then stop short.[1]

Accepting, then, the non-progressiveness of a large part of the human race, when left to themselves, as a fact, cannot we estimate other religions, not by our conception of what we want, but by their bearing on the life of those whom they affect, ennobling them so far as the other conditions of their existence may render possible?

We are apt to forget that there are two factors to be considered in testing the value of a religion in any given case, the Creed itself and the people who receive it. There are of course good and bad men, and these of every degree of goodness and badness, to be found professing every Creed, but the average morality of the followers of an imperfect Creed may, in this very imperfect world, be better than the average morality of those who profess a higher one, and of course *vice versâ*. πάντων μέτρον ἄνθρωπος. Judged, then, by

---

[1] I specify China; for I cannot accept the changes relied upon by Dr. Bridges, in his very able essay on China, in 'International Policy,' as being evidence of continuous and progressive change, which is the real point at issue. Of course this in no way affects the more important questions treated of in the essay, the moral elevation of which seems to me almost unequalled in the writings even of those who, like the contributors to the volume referred to, and the followers of Auguste Comte generally, have laboured most earnestly to treat all political questions from a moral standpoint.

this relative standard—which is, as I conceive, the
only true one—Mohammedanism has nothing to lose,
and much to gain, by the keenest criticism.[1] I grant
to the full everything that can be said by travellers
such as Burckhardt, and Burton, and Palgrave, upon
the degradation of the mass of the Bedouins and the
Turks, and the want of all vital religion, sometimes
of the very elements of religion, among them. And
no one will deny there is much indeed in the present
state of the whole Mohammedan world to make every
thoughtful person, Musalman as well as Christian, ask

---

[1] Abyssinia is a case in point for those who think that a religion,
because it is better and purer in itself, is necessarily better than all
other religions, wherever and whenever and in whatever degree of
purity it may be found. Abyssinia has been nominally Christian since
very early times, and yet it would puzzle the greatest enemy of Islam
to name a single particular in which the inhabitants are superior to
their Musalman neighbours. In the matter, for instance, of marriage
and divorce see the following quotation from Bruce's ‘Abyssinia,’ IV.
p. 487:—‘There is no such thing as marriage in Abyssinia, unless that
is to be called so which is contracted by mutual consent without other
form, and subsists only till dissolved by the dissent of one or other, to
be renewed, however, or repeated as often as it is agreeable to both
parties; for when they please, they live together again as man and wife,
after having been divorced, had children by others, or whether they
have had children by others or not. I remember once to have been at
Koscam in presence of the Itighè (or Queen), when in the circle
there was a woman of great quality, and seven men, who had all been
her husbands, but none of whom was the happy spouse at that time.’
See also a vigorous description of the barbarism and superstitions of the
Abyssinian Church in Dean Stanley's ‘Eastern Church,’ p. 10-12.
Spain may suggest thoughts similar to those suggested by Abyssinia,
and equally applicable to the question in hand, which is indeed one of
the main questions of my Lectures.

himself with the prophet of old, whether what seem to be dry bones can live.

As regards the faith itself, schisms more numerous even than the seventy-three which the Prophet himself predicted, have sprung up from a very early period in Islam ; and, while they have doubtless contributed to keep up a spirit of free enquiry and of intellectual energy, which the simplicity of a creed that ' can be written on a finger-nail ' has often been supposed to suppress, they have turned chiefly upon questions which have been still more unintelligible or devoid of practical results, and have been fought out with passions even fiercer than those which have prevailed in Christendom. Questions as to the proper successor of the Prophet, resulting first in the great Shiah schism, and afterwards in the belief among many Persian sects in the incarnation of God in Ali, and the Imams ; questions as to the precise nature of the Divine attributes, the upshot of which has now been something resembling the dualism of the ancient fire-worshippers, now the mystic pantheism of the Sufis, and now again the strange amalgam of doctrines which is to be found among the Druses, the Rosheinias or the Yezidis. The predestinarian expressions of Mo-hammed, harmonising, as they did, better than his equally strong assertion of free-will, with the natural quietism of the East, have degenerated into a fatalism

which tends to sap the springs of human energy in
those countries where energy is now most required,
and have made men look upon a famine, a pestilence,
or a tyrant, as an inevitable dispensation of destiny,
to be patiently submitted to, not to be grappled with
and overcome.

The few stains which, making every allowance
for his manifold temptations and for the times in which
he lived, a Christian must yet always consider to be
stains on the grand character of the Prophet, have
been fatally improved on by the Eastern dynasties
which own his sway. The assassinations at which the
Prophet once or twice connived, and the indulgence
which he claimed in the observance of the Harem
laws which he had himself made, have been prominent
features in the history of those who have called themselves his successors in the Khalifate, and of less conspicuous Musalman rulers. The murder of the
nearest relations by a sovereign on his accession to
the throne, as the best means of securing his title to
it, has been a common occurrence; and, though the
Ottoman Sultans might justly have retorted upon
Lord Bacon, who points one of his most brilliant
apophthegms by an allusion to it, that they were only
imitating the example of many of the Christian Cæsars
who had preceded them, there is no doubt that the
horrible practice has been raised by them in times

past almost to the dignity of a maxim of Imperial policy. The human body and human life itself have rarely in the East been invested with that sanctity with which Christianity alone of Eastern-born religions regards them. With the example before them of One who was solicitous for the happiness and the lives of all around Him, and prodigal only of His own —with the belief, too, that the human body is not the prison but the temple of the soul, and of something holier even than the soul, shame indeed would it be to Christians if the respect for human life were not greater, the average standard of personal purity far higher, and the enthusiasm of humanity more deep and lasting, than in the average of the followers of other Creeds. Unfortunately it has not been always so ; and the dealings of the Holy Father and the Holy Office with suspected heretics, of the Spaniards with the Indians of America, of the Portuguese and the Dutch with the East Indian islanders, of the French with the Arabs of Algeria, of the English, under the rule of the East India Company, with the Hindus, and of all the Christian nations, who in bygone times have had the chance, with the downtrodden Negroes of Africa, will hold their own in the hideous race of cruelty and oppression with the worst deeds of Orientals ; but in the absolute recklessness of human life which has marked Eastern wars, and

in the barbarous nature of the punishments inflicted
by Eastern rulers, it cannot be said that Musalman nations have fallen far behind the Tartars
or the Chinese.[1] Again, the death-bed commands
of Musalman princes have rarely breathed forgiveness
of their enemies; they have resembled the last in-
junctions of the aged David to his son Solomon—
surely one of the darkest pages in his history—or the
reckless revenge of the younger Marius when he saw
that his fate was sealed, rather than the ' Father, forgive them,' of the Founder of Christianity ; that
prayer which has done something to temper the
violence and sheath the swords of so many semi-
Christian conquerors or rulers, and has filled the souls
of so many Christian saints and martyrs.

Women, again, in spite of the beneficent legislation
of the Prophet—the nature of which it has been one
of my objects as clearly as possible to bring out—
have rarely exercised in the East the humanising, the
elevating, the spiritualising influence on husbands,

---

[1] Vambéry (' Central Asia,' p. 139), after describing a horrible execution of prisoners by the Khan of Khiva, remarks, ' Such treatment is
indeed horrible, but it is not to be regarded as an exceptional case. In
Khiva, as well as in the whole of Central Asia, wanton cruelty is
unknown ; the whole proceeding is regarded as perfectly natural, and
usage, law, and religion, all accord in sanctioning it.' The word
' religion ' can only be understood here in a sense which excludes the
Koran and the Traditions—all the documents, in fact, on which the
Religion rests.

fathers, or sons, which it is their glory to have exercised again and again in Christendom, and that even
through its darkest ages. The life of the Harem, so
far as its influence has extended, is not a life in which
any of the finer qualities of the human soul, still less
love itself in any sense of the word which entitles it
to be so called, naturally thrive. Triviality, selfishness, heart-burnings, deadly hatreds, if nothing worse,
are the weeds which must, in the nature of things, as
soon as society has passed beyond its earlier stages,
find in it a congenial soil.

The professed teachers of the people, again,
whether theologians or legists—Muftis and Mullas,
Kadis and Imams—have sometimes, on the one hand,
claimed powers which Islam itself never gave them ;
and on the other, have all too often been without those
fundamental qualities of zeal for learning, of justice,
and of humanity, which should alone entitle them to
the offices they hold.[1] As to the practical religion of
the masses in the towns—more especially those towns
which have received a whitewash of European civilisation—it is not so much what its Founder intended it
to be, a brotherly affection, at all events, within the
ranks of the faithful, the relief of the orphan and the
oppressed, the practice of sobriety, truthfulness, and
hospitality, but, as has so often been the case in the

---

[1] Cf. the anticipation of the Prophet himself, quoted below, p. 314.

history of Christendom, a frigid round of traditional observances, fastings for fasting's sake, and prayers consisting of a mechanical enumeration of the Divine attributes many times repeated, and accompanied by a childish ceremonial.[1] An Arab will often say the Bismillah when he is meditating an atrocious crime ; just as 'the Most Christian king' would be most particular in his religious observances when he was perpetrating his worst deeds ; the whole resulting, very often, in as complete a separation between religion and morality as was the case in Christendom, for instance, in the age of Leo X. at Rome, of Charles II. in England, or of Louis XV. in France.

Nor, at first sight, is the prospect more bright politically than it is in its social and its strictly religious aspects. 'When the prophets prophesy falsely, and the kings bear rule by their means,' what wonder that the Khalifate of the faithful Abu Bekr, the intrepid Omar, the saintly Ali, has degenerated into the self-seeking and short-sighted rule of the Sultan or the Shah? It has been said, not without exaggeration, but still not without some truth, that most of the countries ruled by Musalman princes are deserts, or tend to become so. Towns have dwindled into villages, and whole villages have often disappeared. Fields lying untilled and mines unworked, justice

[1] See Hughes, Notes, p. 63-75.

polluted at its source, excessive taxation and arbitrary
punishments—such are some of the features which
belong to the decadence of a once Imperial race, and
which we are apt to attribute to the decadence of
a religion.   Meanwhile Christian nations, propelled
partly by ambition, partly by a blundering philanthropy, partly by the mere pressure of events, are
threatening to absorb large portions of the Musalman
world, and are putting the bit and bridle for the first
time in their history on the wildest and most fanatical
of the followers of the Prophet who have roamed for
ages over the barren steppes of Central Asia, Kirghis
and Khivese, Uzbeks and Turkomans.   The Caucasus, again, has since the lamentable Circassian Exodus, ceased to be Mohammedan, and become Christian, if, indeed, a solitude can ever be so called.   Al-
giers belongs, by military occupation at least, to
France ; and Cairo under the rule of the Khedive is
rapidly becoming, for good or evil, a second Paris,
and is taking kindly to all the vices of the West.

How, then, it may be asked again, can these dry
bones live ? why busy ourselves about a dead creed,
or trouble about that against which, as it may seem,
has already gone forth the sentence of God and of
the big battalions ?

But look once more a little closer and see if this
is really so ; or if all the facts correspond to the super-

ficial appearances. I alluded in my First Lecture to the claims which the marvellous history of Islam, its achievements in centuries and on continents other than ours, the intimate relations in which we must stand to it now, the proselytising enthusiasm it still exhibits, and the unmeasured influence it may yet exert on the virgin soil of Africa [1] or among the teeming millions of India, have at once upon our attention, our sympathy, and our respect ; but it may be well— now that I have, in order to prevent misconstruction, set forth, in spite of myself, the worst that can be said with any approach to fairness of Musalman countries at the present day—to call renewed attention to those claims, and thereby at once to appraise the evils mentioned at their proper value, and to point out the grounds of hope for the future.

And, first, it should be remembered that to say that a religion is stationary, and presents an obstacle to the progress and the innovations and the restless struggles which are the life of the West, is no reproach at all in the eyes of a people that is itself stationary and unprogressive. It is precisely this that has enabled it to take such deep hold of all the nations that have accepted it, and to intertwine itself with all

---

[1] 'In Cairo and Constantinople Islam may appear to be decaying, but in the heart of Africa it is young, vigorous, victorious as in the early days.'—Winwood Reade's 'African Sketch-book,' p. 315.

their thoughts and feelings. 'A Musalman first and a Turk, an Afghan or an Arab afterwards,' is no mere formula or figure of speech with that vast assemblage of peoples and of tongues to whom the Prophet of Arabia, by teaching them to worship the one true God, has given a bond of union stronger than any tie of blood or nation; and that, by means which were nobler and with objects that were higher than those with which Papal Rome is striving, in these latter days, to implant a similar feeling in the Catholic. Sublime and Eternal and Unchangeable as its God, Islam appears to its votaries a religion worthy at once of the worshipper and of the Being that he worships; and is it for us to say that it is not so?

Secondly, it must be borne in mind that Musalman countries and Musalmans themselves, whether stationary or progressive, whether elevated or degraded, are not Islam itself, any more than Christendom and Christians are Christianity. The Faith is something infinitely greater than even its greatest and worthiest votaries; else it would not be a living Faith at all. The best cure for the evils of Christendom is Christianity; and the cure for many, at least, of the evils in Musalman countries now, which, if not ideally the best, is yet the most natural, the most ready to hand, and the most likely to be efficacious, is not, perhaps, Islam itself, yet something so nearly akin to Islam that it can confidently appeal to its most authoritative documents in its support.

Thirdly, as to the desolation of countries which were once flourishing, the question has never, so far as I know, been fairly raised how much of it is, even at this distance of time, the direct consequence of the wholesale havoc and destruction wrought by the successive inroads of the Mongols and Tartars who followed Chenghis, or Octai, or Kublai Khan.[1] Whatever the answer to such an enquiry might be, Asia would not be the only part of the globe in which devastations far less than theirs would seem in very truth to have sown the land with salt and to have rendered it incapable of revivification. Has Sicily, in spite of all its changes of rulers, and its incomparable advantages of air and soil, ever recovered from the havoc wrought in it by the first Punic War?

Fourth and lastly, the same travellers who give

---

[1] For the devastations of Chenghis Khan see Ibn Batuta, p. 87 seq.:—'He came with the Tartars into the countries of Islam, and destroyed them.' 'He left the country quite desolate, destroying the cities, and slaughtering the inhabitants.' 'In Irak alone 24,000 learned men were put to the sword' (p. 89). Balkh still lay in ruins, 'not having been rebuilt since its destruction by the cursed Chenghis Khan' (p. 93). Cf. also the terrible illustrations collected by Col. Yule, in his edition of Marco Polo, I. 256-257. Marshman ('History of India,' I. 49) says: 'From the Caspian to the Indus, more than 1000 miles in extent, the whole country was laid waste with fire and sword by the ruthless barbarians who followed Chenghis Khan. It was the greatest calamity which had befallen the human race since the Deluge, and five centuries have been barely sufficient to repair that desolation.'

us so gloomy a picture of the condition of the Ottoman Empire are careful to point out that that condition is, in great part, the result of the misgovernment
and the corruption of a clique ; of elements, in fact,
which in great measure have intruded into Islam and
are not of it, and is in no respect the result of the
religion.[1]   On the contrary, it is that religion which
alone gives stability to the tottering fabric, and is the
one principle of life amidst all the jarring elements of
destruction.   It is the religion which merges all
colours, ranks, and races in the consciousness of a
common brotherhood.[2]   It is the religion which

[1] See 'Quarterly Review' for October, 1874 :   Art. 'Provincial
Turkey;' Admiral Slade's 'Turkey, Greece, and Malta,' I. 298 seq.,
318 seq.; Urquhart's 'Spirit of the East;' and Palgrave's 'Eastern
Essays,' *passim*.   Admiral Slade says : 'If people were only to take
the trouble to enquire into the state of the Mosque, their voices would
be hushed ; for they would see in the Mosque the healer of the sores
caused by the worst of governments ; they would find libraries, and
schools, and hospitals for the insane on the foundation of the Mosque ;
they would see well-cultivated estates belonging to it, and would learn
that through its agency a man may secure a provision for his wife or
daughter after his death. . . . Not one of the reasons ordinarily urged
against a Church establishment—tithe, ministers of religion chosen from
particular classes, monastic seclusion, celibacy—is applicable to the
Mosque.'   So, too, Mouradgia d'Ohson, a high authority, quoted in
'East and West,' p. 185, says : 'Tous les maux politiques qui affligent
les peuples Mussulmans devinrent de leurs préjugés, de leurs fausses
opinions, les vices de gouvernement, mais non des vraies principes de
la religion et de la loi.'

[2] Among Mohammedans there is much kindly feeling ; their
religion knits them as it were into a general fraternity, in which every
member, rich or poor, is, though a stranger, affectionately received.
Much of this charitable disposition is no doubt to be traced to those

elevates the mind by drawing it from the Transitory
to the Eternal, and which gives to the half-starved
or ill-used peasant that courage in calamity, that calm
amidst confusion, and that ineffable dignity in distress,
which is found nowhere but in Islam. Without a
Khalif, without a hierarchy, without good schools or
teachers, the peasants of Asia Minor still cling to
their creed as firmly as ever, and, what is more important, to the practical duties enjoined by it. Nowhere in the world—so I heard it stated at a meeting
in London the other day for the relief of the Turkish
famine, by traveller after traveller who knew the
country well—is there more hospitality to strangers,
greater self-respect, more personal cleanliness, greater
temperance, freer toleration, than amongst them. The
one building well cared for everywhere, well built,
well white-washed, well swept, is the village Mosque.
The houses of the peasantry may be mere hovels
falling into decay for lack of the means to build
them up, but each possesses the niche which points
towards the holy place, and five times a day does
each peasant, at the summons of the village Muezzin,
pour forth his heart to God, not so much in petitions

-causes which make the inhabitants of thinly-peopled districts so
generally hospitable: more, however, is attributable to the precepts of
the Koran, nor are the followers of Mohammed exclusive in their
benevolence, for all strangers share their charities.'—Wood's 'Oxus,'
p. 93.

for relief of his pressing temporal necessities—for this, be it remembered, is not the characteristic of Musalman prayer[1]—but rather in a meditation on the power and the majesty, the wisdom and the mercy of God.

Does all this look much like decadence in their religion? And even if every item of the accusation detailed above be true, and no account be taken of the considerations which, as I have endeavoured to indicate in the enumeration itself, may be urged in explanation or extenuation of many of them, I still ask whether the state of the Mohammedan world, as

[1] The notion of the duty of submission to God's will, whatever it may be, is perhaps stronger among Muslims than among Christians; on the other hand, the idea of a filial relation on the part of the worshipper to the Being whom he worships, which enables a man to lay all his wants before God as before a father, is almost wanting in Islam; and hence the distinguishing characteristics of Musalman and Christian prayer. The ordinary form of prayer among the Muslims is as follows:—

> Holiness to Thee, O God!
> And praise be to Thee!
> Great is Thy Name!
> Great is Thy greatness!
> There is no God but Thee!

Then comes the Fatihah, or first chapter of the Koran:

> Praise be to God, Lord of all the worlds!
> The compassionate, the merciful,
> King on the day of reckoning!
> Thee only do we worship, and to Thee do we cry for help.
> Guide Thou us in the straight path;   .
> The path of those to whom Thou hast been gracious;
> With whom Thou art not angry,   .
> And who go not astray.   Amen.

a whole, is worse, in proportion to its light, than has been that of Christendom in many stages of its history, and which it has yet passed safely through? Is it half as bad, for instance, as the age when Brunehaut and Fredegonde ruled the Franks; as the age when Theodora and Marosia dispensed the patronage of the Church from the Vatican; or as the age when, at length, the cup of iniquity of Papal Rome was full, and a Luther was born? To take an instance nearer home, has religion less hold upon the Arabs than it had upon the English throughout the last century, till the evangelical revival of Wesley and Whitefield roused it from its sleep? Has it less hold even upon the 'Frenchmen of the East,' as the Persians have been called—liars, drunkards, profligate though they are—than it has at this moment upon the Frenchmen of the West? What account do travellers in Russia give us of the state of religion among the masses there? And what judgment must pious Mohammedans form of Christianity, if their knowledge of it is confined to the average lives of Europeans who profess it?

To say that gross abuses have crept into Mohammedanism—that the lives of many, or even of the majority, who profess it are a disgrace to their name— is only to say that it is not exempt from the common conditions of humanity.

Take one instance drawn from the history of the Christian Church.   Christianity was in its origin and in its essence a creed entirely spiritual; but Christians, forming, as they did, a new human society, were allowed by their Founder to symbolise this close union, and to bring it home more vividly to themselves and to the world, by two external rites.   The mere fact that they were external, in a religion which was otherwise a matter of the heart, ought to have put men on their guard, lest they should assume in time a too prominent place ; lest what was accidental, and secondary, and relative, should dominate over what was absolute, and primary, and eternal.   Baptism was of considerable importance in the infancy of the Church, for it was a pledge of fidelity consciously and voluntarily given by a new recruit, in the face of the enemy, to a cause whose victories were yet in the future.   It was, as it were, the uniform assumed by the small army which at its Master's bidding went forth against the world.   The Love-feast also was of special importance among the earliest Christians, as a constant reminder that those who had taken upon themselves the commission of the Cross, that crowning act of love, were bound to one another by the same enthusiasm of love which bound them to their common Master.   Both did good service then, and in the history of the Christian Church have done good service since, in so far as they have acted upon the heart, and thence upon the conduct, through the medium of a very powerful appeal to the religious imagination. But in so far as any mysterious or supernatural efficacy has been attached to the form of either, they have sapped the root of Christianity. They have done for Christianity what of good, no doubt, Mohammed thought, and, half rightly, half wrongly, thought, that pilgrimages to the holy places might do for Mohammedanism. Both were so far concessions to human weakness that they introduced formal, or even material, conceptions into a spiritual religion ; both, in fact, were capable of being used to advantage ; and experience has proved that they were both alike liable to the same kind of abuse.

Every human institution, therefore—religion itself, so far as man can affect it—is exposed to inevitable decay; and the purer the religion, the more inevitable the degradation which contact with the world, which is not of it, must bring.[1] Accordingly, a religion which is not waiting for a revival is waiting only till it be swept away.

But, on the other hand, we must not judge of a religion by its perversions or corruptions ; and it is as fair to take Turkish despots, and maniac dervishes, and Persian libertines, as types of the Mohammedan

[1] Max Müller, ‘Chips,’ Preface, p. 23.

life, as it would be to take Anabaptists, or Pillar Saints,
or Shakers, as types of the Christian life. Most of
the well-known vices of our Mohammedan fellow-
subjects in India are Indian vices, and not Mohammedan. Professor Max Müller has remarked with
truth, that without constant reformation—that is to
say, without a constant return to the fountain head—
every religion, however pure, must gradually degen-
erate. Christianity has always reformed itself, and
will to the end of time continue to reform itself, by
going back to the words and to the life of Christ. It
is a maxim of the Buddhists that 'what has been
said by Buddha, that alone is well said;'[1] and
it is currently believed that Mohammedanism is dying
out because it has no such power of revival. But the
very reverse of this is, rather, true. The Prophet himself must have foreseen the need there would be for a
reformer when he so sorrowfully remarked to Abu
Taleb, 'The time is near in which nothing will remain
of Islam but its name, and of the Koran but its mere
appearance; and the mosques of Musalmans will be
destitute of knowledge and worship, and the learned
men will be the worst people under the heavens, and
contentions and strife will issue from them, and it will
return upon themselves;' but he also confidently hoped
that when the time was ripe for it, a reformer would be

---

[1] Quoted by Max Müller, loc. cit. p. 23.

found. 'Certainly,' he said to Abu Hurairah, 'certainly, God will send my sect at the expiration of every hundred years a person who will renew my religion.'[1] Probably no religion has produced, in the various parts of its vast empire, a more continuous succession of reformers whose aim has been to bring it back, by fair means if possible, and if not by force, to its original simplicity and purity.[2] Such was one object, however wildly they set about it, of the Carmathians in the ninth century; and, to select one amongst many individual reformers, such was the career of Abdul Wahhab, the son of a petty Arabian sheik, a hundred and fifty years ago. The facts I take almost *verbatim* from an interesting and able essay on 'Our Indian Mussulmans,' by Dr. Hunter.[3]

Commencing by a moral attack upon the profligacy of the Turkish pilgrims and the mummeries which profaned the holy cities, Abdul Wahhab gradually elaborated a theological system which is substantially identical with the original creed of Mohammed. He taught, first, absolute reliance on one God, and the rejection of all mediators between man and God, whether saints or Mohammed himself; second, the

---

[1] 'Mishkat-ul-Masabih,' II., III., 68, and II. II., 62.

[2] See Döllinger, p. 42-49, for an enumeration of attempted reformers throughout the history of Islam. He hardly does justice to some of them.

[3] See Hunter, p. 55-60; and for a further account of the Arab movement, see Burckhardt's 'Notes on the Bedouins and Wahhabis.'

right of private interpretation of the Koran and of the
Traditions ; third, the prohibition of all forms and
ceremonies with which the pure faith has been over-
laid in the lapse of centuries ; finally—and this is the
only part to be regretted in the movement—he reasserted the obligation to wage war upon the infidel.
In 1803 Wahhab's successors took the holy cities, and
desecrated the sacred mosque at Mecca and the
Prophet's tomb at Medina, to save them from the
greater desecration, as it seemed to those Puritans of
the Desert, involved in the almost Divine honours
lavished on them by ignorant or profligate pilgrims.

Here was an act upon the significance of which
we may well dwell for a moment, and endeavour, by
comparing it with somewhat parallel and better-
known cases, to realise what it must have seemed like
then, and what it proves about Mohammedanism
now. Imagine the feelings of pious Jews when their
most religious king broke into pieces the relic of
relics, the memorial of the Divine deliverance and of
their desert life, and stigmatised it as a bit of brass !
Imagine, if you can, the feelings of the Apostles when
it dawned upon them that one of their number, even
then, was a traitor in his heart ! Imagine, to take a
parallel case suggested by Dr. Hunter,[1] Mediæval
Christendom, when the news spread that Bourbon's

---

[1] Hunter, p. 59.

cut-throats were installed in the Vatican, and that the head of the Christian Church had been taken captive by a revolted subject of the Church's eldest son! Imagine Luther, when in the fervour of youthful enthusiasm he visited the Rome of the Martyrs and of the Apostles, and found it to be the Rome of the Papacy, the Rome of impostures and indulgences, of the Borgias and the Medici! And we can then picture to ourselves the thrill of horror that must have passed through the orthodox Musalman world when they heard that a sect of reformers, whose one idea of reform was a return to the life and doctrine of the Prophet, had rifled the mosque whose immemorial sanctity the Prophet had himself increased by making it the Kiblah of the world, and had even violated the Prophet's tomb. Imagine, on the other hand, what it must have cost the Wahhabis to have, like Luther, the courage of their convictions, to appear to stultify themselves, to dishonour their Prophet, and all that they might make their religion the spiritual religion that it had once been! And then say if you can, that Mohammedanism has no power of self-reform, and is dying gradually of inanition!

Beaten down at last by the strong arm of Mohammed Ali, Pasha of Egypt in 1812, helped, I regret to say, by Englishmen, the Wahhabis disappeared temporarily from Arabia,[1] only to reappear in 1821 in India, under the leadership of the prophet Syed Ahmed ; and the despised sect of Wahhabis are now, perhaps, the real ruling spirit of Musalman politics in India, and enjoy the singular honour of having, as much, no doubt, by their gloomy fanaticism as by their moral lives and their missionary zeal, attracted to themselves considerable attention even from their English rulers at home.   Puritans of the Puritans of Islam, they are despised and hated by the so-called orthodox Musalmans, as the Lutherans were hated by Leo, and the Covenanters by Claverhouse.

And it must be remembered that Wahhabiism, while it denounces, as I have shown, all the existing forms of Islam, and, in its turn, is denounced by them, has yet done much outside of the sphere of its im- mediate influence to purify the Faith, and to reform abuses throughout the Musalman world.   The Refor- mation, it has often been observed, did as much good for Europe by the reforms which it drove the nations who rejected it, for very shame, to introduce for them- selves, as by what it did directly for those German

---

[1] For a graphic and not very favourable account of the Wahhabi Empire as it exists now in Arabia, and its seat of Government at Riad, see Palgrave's 'Arabia,' Chap. IX.-XIII.   There are one or two passages in this account—*e. g.*, Vol. I. 365-373, 427-437—in which I cannot but think, with all my admiration for Mr. Palgrave's varied powers, that he has not been, even on his own showing elsewhere, altogether fair to Islam as a system.

peoples who threw off for ever the yoke of Rome. Even so has Wahhabiism compelled many who are anything but Wahhabis to reform the most crying abuses, and so to make the discrepancy between their practice and their creed less glaring than it was before.

The extraordinary phenomena attending the great religious movement called Bâbyism now going on in Persia, the ecstatic martyrdoms and the prodigality of tortures submitted to amidst songs of triumph by women and children, the followers of the ' Bâb,' are well worth the study of all who are interested in the history of religion ; and, however we explain the facts, much that I have said of Wahhabiism may, *mutatis mutandis*, be said of it ; and at all events its existence is a standing proof that Persian Mohammedanism possesses so much of vitality as is necessary to adapt an old creed to a new belief.[1]

When I first wrote the above paragraphs on the power of revival which I conceive to be inherent in Islam, I did not know that my words were at that very time being illustrated in the most striking way, not only in India and Persia and Arabia upon which I then dwelt, but also throughout the Asiatic dominions of the Ottoman Sultans. Since then Mr. Palgrave's most interesting ' Essays on Eastern Questions '

[1] See Gobineau, 'Les Religions et les Philosophies dans l'Asie Centrale,' p. 141-215.

have come into my hands ; and I find in them both evidence to show that there is such a revival, and a graphic account of its leading symptoms.

Secular and denominational schools are everywhere giving place to schools of the most strictly Musalman type. Mosques which were deserted are now crowded with worshippers ; mosques which were in ruins are rebuilt. There is a general reaction, not perhaps to be wondered at, against the employment in public offices of the European and the Christian. Wine and spirit shops are closed, for their trade is gone except among the Levantine residents. Even opium and tobacco are becoming luxuries which are not forbidden only, but forsaken.

Add to this, what Mr. Palgrave has also shown, that a new nation is as it were growing up under our eyes in Eastern Anatolia, rich with all the elements of a vigorous national and religious life ; and we shall then have reason to believe that though the Ottoman supremacy may pass away, as Khalifs and Sultans, Attabeks and Khans, Padishahs and Moguls, have passed away before them, yet Islam itself is a thing of indestructible vitality, and may thrive the more when rid of the magnificent corruptions and the illusory prestige of the Stambul successors of the Prophet. In truth, Islam has existed for centuries in spite of Othmanli rule, and not because of it ; and this the ambassadors lately sent to the Porte from the most distant parts of the Musalman world—from Bokhara and Khokand, from the Sultan of Achin and the Sultan of the Panthays—must have learnt to their cost, when they found that the so-called Commander of the Faithful was sufficiently employed nearer home, and had neither the power nor the will to give them the help or even the advice they asked.

Mohammedanism, therefore, can still renew its youth, and it is possible that the present generation, in face of the advance of semi-barbarous Russia, may see a revival of the old Crusading spirit—an outburst of stern fanaticism, which, armed with the courage of despair, obliterating, as it did among the tribes of the Caucasus in the Circassian war,[1] even the immemorial schism of Sunni and Shiah, may hurl once more in simple self-defence the united strength of the Crescent

[1] See Baron Von Haxthausen's 'Tribes of the Caucasus;' especially his interesting account of the rise of Muridism, and the heroic struggle of Shamil, his personal influence, and his genius for military and political organisation. Truly while Mohammedanism can throw off geniuses like Shamil, it may well be able to dispense with such governments as that of the Turks. The Baron's prophecies of a general collapse of Mohammedanism are being signally falsified. The union of Sunnis and Shiahs was one principle of Muridism as taught by Mulla Mohammed, and after him by Shamil. Elijah Mansur, the great Circassian hero towards the close of the last century, appears to have been far superior even to Shamil in ability. Like him, he united the characters of warrior, priest, and prophet, and there is a belief among the natives that he is to reappear at the end of a hundred years and drive back the Muscovite from his native country.

upon the vanguard of advancing Christendom. It is a
prospect formidable to every Christian Power—formidable above all to those who for good or for evil
rule forty millions of Musalmans in India. Then if
anywhen, and there if anywhere, will be the Arma-
geddon of Islam.

It may be that nothing—not even a holy war
waged in self-defence—can arrest the onward march
of the Colossus which, gaunt and grim and inex-
orable, like one of the primeval forces of Nature,
is pressing, or is being pressed on, towards the East
and South ; and is, in the nineteenth century,
turning back, in some sense, itself upon itself, that
tide of Tartar aggression which, in by-gone times,
carried now an Attila from the wall of China to the
Catalaunian fields, and now a Tamerlane from Kara-
korum to the Vistula or the Danube. Licking up
Khanates and kingdoms like the grass of the field in
its gradual but irresistible advance, it is threatening
at once the national existence of Turks and Persians,
and is exciting the uneasy apprehensions alike of
those who rule at Calcutta, and of those who rule at
Pekin. Doubtless it is well that something like
order should be introduced into the wildest and most
lawless people in the world, the nomade hordes of
Turkistan ; but it is at least open to question whether
this could not be as well done by the religious en-

thusiasm of some new Commander of the Faithful, of
some heroic Elijah Mansur or Shamil or Abdel Kader
on a vaster scale, as by the dull, heavy tread of military despotism beneath the shadow of the Czars of
All the Russias. The rule of General Kaufmann is
not likely to do more for Central Asia [1] than is already
in the way of being done for it by Yakub Beg; and
surely those who imagine that the Russian arms of
precision are carrying any form of Christianity with
them which will get hold of the native mind and
character, are indulging in the wildest of chimæras.
Injustice has doubtless often been done by travellers
who know them but superficially to the sterling
qualities which are to be found on a closer investigation in some of the scattered Christian communities
of the East. They have expected to find in them
energies which can only be the offspring of freedom ;
and one who knows them intimately avers that credit
has not been given to the Christians of the East for
the industry, the enterprise, and the social morality,
which are to be found amongst them in spite of all the
drawbacks of their political position. But Dr. Badger
himself would probably admit that the isolation of
these communities is too great, their superstitious

---

[1] The attack on the Yomud Turkomans in the recent Khiva cam-
paign was as murderous, as purposeless, and as cruel as any of which
the wildest Asiatics were ever guilty.

practices and their mutual misconceptions too numerous, and the want of a missionary spirit amongst
them too marked, to enable them, under any circumstances, to do more than hold their own in the East ;
and as to the religion of the 'orthodox' Greek Church,
which is the form of Christianity, if any, which will
accompany the Russian arms, who can find in its
history of a thousand years any germ of progress,
any spark of missionary enthusiasm, any sublimer
idea of God, or any nobler conception of man's duty
to Him and to his brother man, than is to be found
in the authentic documents of Islam?

And here, perhaps, will be the place to make
a few remarks upon a subject which cannot have
failed to attract the attention of the more thoughtful
among us in recent years—I mean the attempt made
to introduce Western manners and customs into
Eastern countries.

We live in days when we hear of Khans and
Khedives, Shahs and Sultans, giving up their immemorial passivity and seclusion, and even coming to
Europe with the avowed intention of carrying back to
Asia or Africa what they can of Western science and
civilisation. I should be slow indeed to complain of
any steps taken by the Western Powers to do away
with any institutions which, like the Suttee, the festivals
of Juggernaut, the East African slave trade, or the
traffic in opium, are a curse to our common humanity,

or are not grounded on any fundamental peculiarity of the Eastern world. But to attempt by force, or even by influence brought to bear upon Eastern rulers, to do away with any domestic or national institutions, such as the form of government, or patriarchal slavery, or even polygamy, can do no good.

Eastern despotism is not what Western despotism is, nor is Oriental slavery like American. Nor is even polygamy in the East so intolerable an evil as it would be in the social freedom of the West. For example, an Eastern sovereign has all the power over his subjects that a father had in the most primitive times, and had even in Rome, over his children. His power is liable to the same abuses; but it has also some of its safeguards and redeeming points. To introduce into his government, as the Shah has been supposed to wish, a system of Boards and Parliaments, of checks and counter-checks, such as works fairly well in this country because it has grown with our growth and is suitable to our instinct of compromise in everything, would be to make many tyrants instead of one, and to cripple the power and lessen the responsibility of the only man in Persia whose interest it is, whether he sees it or not, to let no one commit injustice but himself. Asia, till its whole nature be changed, can probably never be better governed than it was by the early Khalifs; and if an Abu Bakr or an Omar, or even a Harun or a Mahmud, a Baber or an Akbar, do not come twice in a century, it is probable that Nature has endowed Asiatics with precisely those qualities of patience, docility, and inertness which harmonise better with the evils of such a government than with those of any other.

Polygamy is a more difficult question, and it is impossible, for obvious reasons, to discuss it adequately here. It is a gigantic evil, worse even than slavery ; for with its attendant mischiefs, so far as it extends, it does away with all real sympathy and companionship between man and woman ; it is unnatural, in the fullest sense of the word, in a highly civilised nation, for Nature, by making the number of men and women equal, has declared decisively for monogamy. But, in a barbarous people, polygamy has this one redeeming point, that it is less likely that any woman will be left without a natural protector ; and, as a matter of fact, it is almost universal in primitive stages of civilisation.[1]   In the

---

[1] In an uncivilised nation, split up, as Arabia was before Mohammed, into a number of hostile tribes, or overrun by its more powerful neighbours, as was Palestine in the time of the Judges, the number of births of men and women is no doubt, as in more civilised nations, about equal ; but the adult male population being reduced by war to half its proper number, the preponderance of women in such a state of society renders Polygamy possible, and the insecurity renders it from that one point of view allowable.   Sir Samuel Baker, in his 'Albert Nyanza,' Introduction, p. 25, remarks that ' In all tropical countries Polygamy is the prevailing evil.'   He might have gone on to say much the same of slavery ; but then what would become of the charge he so often makes against Islam—that it is responsible for polygamy and slavery ?

East it is the almost inevitable result of that fundamental institution of Eastern, as well as of Muslim
society, the absolute seclusion of women. There is
an impervious bar to all social intercourse between the
sexes before marriage. The husband's knowledge of
his future wife is at second hand only, and rests on
the report of a Khatibeh,[1] or professional match-maker.
Such a marriage is more than a lottery ; there can be
no affection to begin with, and, except on rare occasions, it is not likely that it will turn out to be really
happy. If it be thoroughly uncongenial, a man tries
his luck once more in the same miserable lottery, and
for his own happiness, and probably also for that of all
concerned, annuls the previous bond. Hence polygamy implies freedom of divorce, and both together
are the inevitable result of the seclusion of the female
sex. But to abolish by law the two former without
dealing with the far more fundamental institution
which is its root, would be to carry on a war with symptoms only, and to introduce evils worse than those it
is wished to prevent. The only way of going to the
root of the matter would be, if it were possible, to allow
a freer intercourse between the sexes at all times ; and
Sir William Muir admits that this could not be done
at all with the present freedom of divorce.[2] It is a
melancholy fact, but a fact still, that the strict checks

---

[1] Lane's 'Modern Egyptians,' I. 199.
[2] Muir, III. 234, and note.

imposed by Mohammed on married women, degrading
though they are,[1] are essential to prevent what is still
worse, and, be it remembered, what was far worse,
before the reforms and limitations which Mohammed
himself imposed.   It is a complete dead-lock ; and
the greatest reformers, Moses no less than Mohammed,
have been unable to. deal with the root of the evil.
It is to be remembered, on the other hand, that both
Moses and Mohammed did what they could to restrain
and modify its abuses ; and at present neither polygamy nor divorce is so common as is often supposed.
The humanity of human nature has asserted itself ;
and Lane, the most accurate of observers, says that
polygamy is in Egypt at all events very rare among
the higher classes, and not common even among the
lower.[2]

Much the same may be said of slavery.   The
slavery of the East is a patriarchal institution, coeval

[1] Sura XXXIII. 6 and 56.   Also Sura XXIV. 32.

[2] Lane, I. 231 : ' Not more than one husband in twenty has two
wives at the same time.'   But divorce is very common.   If it were not
for Lane's proverbial accuracy, one would be inclined to suspect that
in the passage referred to in the text he had either accidentally trans-
posed the words higher and lower, or had for once made a mistake on
a matter of fact.   It appears, however, that he is strictly accurate; and
the dropping of Polygamy in Egypt by the higher classes is a clear
indication that its continuance there is only a question of time.   Certainly in other parts of the Mohammedan world polygamy is, for
obvious reasons, much more common among the rich than among the
poor.   But the current of opinion, like the general conditions of
society, seems to be everywhere setting against it, especially in India.

with the very dawn of history. It is an institution allowed and modified by Moses, even as it was allowed and modified by Mohammed, for people in that stage of civilisation which required it. In neither nation has it anything in common with slavery as it was in America, or indeed with slavery at all as practised by civilised nations. It has been remarked with truth that the cruel treatment of domesticated slaves is the shameful and exclusive prerogative of civilisation. To do away with domestic slavery by force, as has been the case in Khiva, though we naturally rejoice at it, will probably do little permanent good. It will revive in another, and probably a worse, shape. Perhaps we have hit upon the one means of gradually getting rid of it in Arabia by making it as difficult as possible to recruit slavery from without by means of the slave trade. Much will have to be done henceforward by free labour in Arabia, in Persia, and in Egypt, which has hitherto been done by slaves; and we need not fear but that the result will be so good, that even in a stolid Oriental people the gradual movement will be one in the direction of abolition.

The horrors of the Slave Trade in East Africa have recently been most graphically described by Dr. Livingstone, by Dr. Schweinfurth, and by Sir Samuel Baker; and all that they have written falls probably far short of the terrible and overwhelming reality.

'May Heaven's rich blessing,' says Dr. Livingstone, and in accents that are all the more touching, and it is to be hoped may be all the more effectual, because they come to us from his grave, 'may Heaven's rich blessing descend on every one, American, English, or Turk, who will help to heal the open sore of the world!' Every true friend of humanity will echo his prayer, and will rejoice to know that every one, whether he be Jew or Christian, Hindu, Musalman, or Buddhist, who joins in healing that open sore will be acting not against but in accordance with the precepts and the spirit of his religion. The Slave Trade, in fact, rests for its support on no religion at all, but only on that which is cruel and selfish and licentious in human nature. It is a common mistake, but a mistake still, to suppose that the Slave Trade ever received any sanction either from Moses or from Mohammed. Moses ordered the man-stealer and the man-seller to be put to death.[1] Mohammed is reported by the Sunna to have said, 'the worst of men is the seller of men.' It is no more fair, then, to tax Islam itself, as is often done, with the horrors of the East African Slave Trade, than it would have been in the last century to blame Christianity for the still greater horrors of the West African traffic and its *sequelæ* in America.

[1] Exod. XXI. 6.

It is well therefore, in furtherance of my object in writing these Lectures, to remind once more those who, like the great travellers I have mentioned, have been led to condemn in the most sweeping terms Islam itself, because it happens now that Arabs and Egyptians are the chief slave traders, that the Slave Trade is not Islam, but is opposed to it.[1] It is condemned by the whole spirit of the Koran, condemned by the Traditions, condemned by the doctors of the Mohammedan law. If so-called Musalmans are now the chief slave-traders, it is not long since so-called Christians were the same; and some of them, the Portuguese for example, are not clean-handed even yet. The spread of Islam over the African continent from the North and West, so far from extending the Slave-Trade, tends, in one important particular, to suppress it, by limiting more and more the area from which slaves are drawn ; for even the most degraded Musalmans have that notion of brotherhood amongst themselves which forbids them to enslave one another. Dr. Schweinfurth himself admits in one passage, what he unfortunately forgets in a score of others, that the

---

[1] I should be as sorry to think that the doings of the Arab slave-hunters described in such forcible language by Sir Samuel Baker were characteristic of Islam in its sacred book, and in its true spirit, as I should be sorry to think that some of the doings of Sir Samuel, as described by himself in ' Ismailia ' (see especially his dealings with the Baris), were in any way characteristic of Christianity.

Arabs in Eastern and in part of Central Africa 'have suppressed the true doctrines of their Prophet which would have enfranchised the very people whom they oppress, and would have raised them to a condition of brotherhood and equality.'[1]   And if this be true, as it undoubtedly is, would it not be well for Christian missionaries to attempt to carry their message of love to African Musalmans by telling them that the Slave-Trade is inhuman in itself, and should be doubly hated by those whose Creed in its authentic documents condemns it, rather than by telling them that their whole Creed is worthless and detestable because many amongst them are untrue to it?   Which course is likely to be the most successful, which is the truest, which the most Christian?

The question indeed is answered by being asked. Yet authoritative Missionary periodicals,[2] and there-

---

[1] The Arab slave-trader does not preach Islam in Eastern Africa for two reasons : first, because he cares not for his Creed himself ; and secondly, because to do so would lessen his hunting-ground, and cut off the supplies of his nefarious traffic.

[2] See 'Church Missionary Intelligencer' for July 1872, August 1874, March 1875, April 1875, &c. &c.   In the number for August 1874, one excellent missionary, the Rev. H. Townsend, who, it is said, has been a missionary in Africa for forty years, makes the astounding assertion that 'even the religious creed of Muhammadans is further removed from the truth than is that of the heathen ; ' in other words, Polytheism is better than Monotheism, and idolatry than a sublime spiritualism.   After this we need not be surprised at being told by the same writer that the morality of Islam 'makes its Negro Proselyte twofold more a child of Hell than before ! '

fore it is to be feared Missionaries themselves, have all too often adopted the latter course. They have treated Islam as the deadliest foe instead of a potential friend of Christianity, and then they wonder at their want of success in dealing with it.

Western science, with its railways, its canals, and its printing-presses, may, no doubt, do something for the material prosperity of Eastern countries, but by itself it will do little for their moral welfare ; and a thin varnish of Western civilisation introduced by rulers who have been forced to admire the material power of the West, and have lost their own self-respect in the process, is earnestly to be deprecated. Those Orientals who have been most influenced by the Franco-mania of Stambul are, beyond all comparison, the most degraded and profligate of their race, and no earnest observer can wish to see imported into other parts of the Mohammedan world that indescribable combination of all that is contemptible in human nature conveyed by the word Levantine.

The heroic and unselfish lives of a few such men as Livingstone are the only legitimate means of introducing into semi-civilised countries such benefits as we think we have to bestow. A life and character like Livingstone's has done more to regenerate the African races than any amount of direct preaching, or any number of European settlements, with the miserable and immoral wars that so often follow in their train. Such men are the true pioneers of civilisation and Christianity—of the only species of civilisation and the only form of Christianity which we have any reason to expect will be a real benefit to the East.

But does it follow, from what I have said of the immobility of the East, that it is impossible for Islam to make any advance at all ; that it is impossible for it to yield anything to the progressive civilisation of Christianity and of the West ?

How Christianity and civilisation should deal with Mohammedanism I have partly indicated already, and shall have a very few more words to say upon the subject presently. But, first, what can Islam do on its part ? Where religion and law are indissolubly bound up together, as they are in the Koran, each loses, and each gains, something. What they gain in stability, they more than lose in flexibility. And yet it may be safely said that there is nothing more extraordinary in the whole history of Islam than the way in which the theory of the verbal inspiration of the Koran, and the consequent stereotyped and unalterable nature of its precepts, have, by ingenuity, by legal fictions, by the 'Sunna,' or traditional sayings of Mohammed, and by *responsa prudentum*, been accommodated to the changing circumstances and the various degrees of civilisation of the nations which profess it. When the Kadi fails to find in the law laid down for the nomad Arabs a rule precisely applicable to the more complex requirements of Smyrna or of Delhi, he places the sacred volume upon his head, and so renders homage to human reason and to the law of progress. He does what Puritans and Churchmen would alike do well to remember, when each professes to find in the varying or convertible expressions of the writers of the New Testament a divinely ordered and unalterable model of Church government. It is not, therefore, quite so true as is commonly supposed, that Islam is reconcileable with one narrow form of government or society only; and it is quite possible that where so much has been done already, more may be done in future, and means may be found for reconciling, for instance, the laws against taking interest for money with the requirements of modern society. Already within the ranks of Indian Musalmans is to be found a party of social and religious reformers, who, without a suspicion of heresy, so far as I know, having been breathed against them by their co-religionists, can yet maintain that the passages of the Koran which legalise Polygamy and Slavery have done their work, that they are out of date, and that the spirit and purpose of the great Arabian can now be best attained by abolishing them

altogether.[1]   In other Musalman countries the intolerant principles of the Koran have long since been
reconciled, except where there is a passing outburst of fanaticism, with the utmost practical toleration ; and the standard of the 'Jihad,' or holy war,
will probably never henceforward be raised on an
extensive scale, except in a war of self-defence, and
unless the lives and liberties of Mohammedans, as
well as their religion, are at stake.

And, what is infinitely more important, it seems
to me that while Mohammedans cling as strongly as
ever to their rigid Monotheism, and to their unfaltering
belief in the Divine mission of their Prophet—and
what serious person could wish them to do otherwise ?
—to give up those beliefs which have made them
what they are, which have given them a glorious
history, and which have influenced half a world ; to
give up—

> '. . . Those first affections,
>   Those shadowy recollections,
>   Which, be they what they may,
> Are yet the fountain-light of all their day,
> Are yet a master-light of all their seeing;
>   Uphold them—cherish—and have power to make
> Their noisy years seem moments in the being
> Of the eternal silence : truths that wake
>   To perish never ! '—

---

[1] See on this subject some interesting details in M. Garçin de
Tassy's 'Annual Lectures on the Hindustani Language and
Literature.'

while they cling, I say, to these, as strongly, yes, more strongly than ever, they may yet be brought to see that there is a distinction between what Mohammed said himself, and what others have said for him ; and that there is a still broader distinction between what he said as a legislator and a conqueror, and what he said as a simple prophet. There are some among them who see now, and there will be more who will soon see, that there may be an appeal to the Mohammed of Mecca from the Mohammed of Medina ; that there may be an idolatry of a book, as well as of a picture, or a sta-tue, or a shapeless mass of stone ; and that the Prophet, who always in other matters asserted his fallibility, was never more fallible, though certainly never more sincere, than when he claimed an equal infallibility for the whole Koran alike. Finally, with the growth of knowledge of the real character of our faith, Moham-medans must recognise that the Christ of the Gospel was something ineffably above the Christ of those Christians from whom alone Mohammed drew his notions of Him ; that He was a perfect mirror of that one primary attribute of the Eternal of which Moham-med could catch only a far-off glance, and which, had it been shown to him as it really was, must needs have taken possession of his soul.

All this may or may not be in our own time ; but in a sympathetic study even of Mohammedanism as

z

it is, Christians have not a little to gain. There is the protest against Polytheism in all its shapes; there is the absolute equality of man before God; there is the sense of the dignity of human nature; there is the simplicity of life, the vivid belief in God's providence, the entire submission to His will; and last, not least, there is the courage of their convictions, the fearless avowal before men of their belief in God, and their pride in its possession as the one thing needful. There is in the lives of average Mohammedans, from whatever causes, less of self-indulgence, less of the mad race for wealth, less of servility, than is to be found in the lives of average Christians. Truly we may think that these things ought not so to be; and if Christians generally were as ready to confess Christ, and to be proud of being His servants, as Mohammedans are of being followers of Mohammed, one chief obstacle to the spread of Christianity would be removed. And the two great religions which started from kindred soil, the one from Mecca, the other from Jerusalem, might work on in their respective spheres—the one the religion of progress, the other of stability; the one of a complex, the other of a simple life; the one dwelling more upon the inherent weakness of human nature, the other on its inherent dignity; [1] the one the

---

[1] Perhaps the two views are, after all, only different aspects of the same truth.

religion of the best parts of Asia and Africa, the other of Europe and America—each rejoicing in the success of the other, each supplying the other's wants in a generous rivalry for the common good of humanity.

A few words more about Mohammed himself, and I have done. The world, in its wisdom or unwisdom, has never thought proper to distinguish Mohammed from the millions of Mohammeds named after him, by calling him 'the Great.' Perhaps he was too great for such an external distinction. People call the conqueror of Constantinople, eight centuries later, Mohammed the Second. But I do not think they ever speak of the Prophet as Mohammed the First; and perhaps the unconscious homage thus rendered to him by a world which ostensibly, and till very lately, has done him such scant justice, is the highest tribute that can be given to his greatness. The Greeks paid the highest compliment they could to the surpassing splendour of the King of Persia when, consciously or unconsciously, they dropped the article before his name, and so put him on a level, grammatical and moral, with the sun, the moon, and the earth, which could by no possibility need any such distinguishing mark. Compare Mohammed with the long roll of men whom the world by common consent has called 'Great;' while I admit that there is no one point in his character in which he is not surpassed by one or other, take him all in all, what he was, and what he did, and what those inspired by him have done, he seems to me to stand alone, above and beyond them all. A distinguished writer on the Holy Roman Empire has remarked of Charles the Great that, 'like all the foremost men of our race, he was all great things in one.'[1] But though Mr. Bryce does not illustrate the truth of his remark by Mohammed—nay, by not including him among the foremost men of the world whom he goes on to enumerate, he seems designedly to exclude him—I venture to think that of no one of them all is the remark more strictly true.

Mohammed did not, indeed, himself conquer a world like Alexander, or Cæsar, or Napoleon. He did not himself weld together into a homogeneous whole a vast system of states like Charles the Great. He was not a philosophic king like Marcus Aurelius ; nor a philosopher like Aristotle or like Bacon, ruling by pure reason the world of thought for centuries with a more than kingly power ; he was not a legislator for all mankind, nor even the highest part of it, like Justinian ; nor did he cheaply earn the title of 'the Great' by being the first among rulers to turn, like Constantine, from the setting to the rising

[1] Bryce's 'Holy Roman Empire,' p. 73.

sun. He was not a universal philanthropist, like the greatest of the Stoics,

'Non sibi sed toti genitum se credere mundo ;'

nor was he the apostle of the highest form of religion and civilisation combined, like Gregory or Boniface, like Leo or Alfred the Great. He was less, indeed, than most of these in one or two of the elements that go to make up human greatness, but he was also greater. Half Christian and half Pagan, half civilised and half barbarian, it was given to him in a marvellous degree to unite the peculiar excellences of the one with the peculiar excellences of the other. ' I have seen,' said the ambassador sent by the triumphant Kuraish to the despised exile at Medina; ' I have seen the Persian Chosroes and the Greek Heraclius sitting upon their thrones, but never did I see a man ruling his equals as does Mohammed.'

Head of the State as well as of the Church, he was Cæsar and Pope in one ; but he was Pope without the Pope's pretensions, and Cæsar without the legions of Cæsar. Without a standing army, without a bodyguard, without a palace, without a fixed revenue, if ever any man had the right to say that he ruled by a right Divine, it was Mohammed ; for he had all the power without its instruments and without its supports. He rose superior to the titles and ceremonies, the solemn trifling, and the proud humility of court etiquette. To hereditary kings, to princes born in the purple, these things are, naturally enough, as the breath of life ; but those who ought to have known better, even self-made rulers, and those the foremost in the files of time—a Cæsar, a Cromwell, a Napoleon—have been unable to resist their tinsel attractions. Mohammed was content with the reality, he cared not for the dressings, of power.[1] The simplicity of his private life was in keeping with his public life. 'God,' says Al Bokhari, 'offered him the keys of the treasures of the earth, but he would not accept them.'

Hagiology is not history ; but the contemporaries of Mohammed, his enemies who rejected his mission, with one voice extol his piety, his justice, his veracity, his clemency, his humility, and that at a time before any imaginary sanctity could have enveloped him. A Christian even, as is remarked by a great writer whom I have quoted above, with his more perfect code of morality before him, must admit that Mohammed, with very rare exceptions, practised all the moral virtues but one ; and in that one, as I have shown, he was in advance of his time and nation.

Assuredly, if Christian missionaries are ever to win over Mohammedans to Christianity, they must alter their tactics. It will not be by discrediting the great

[1] See 'British Quarterly Review,' Jan. 1872, p. 128.

Arabian Prophet, nor by throwing doubts upon his mission, but by paying him that homage which is his due; by pointing out, not how Mohammedanism differs from Christianity, but how it resembles it; by dwelling less on the dogmas of Christianity, and more on its morality; by showing how perfectly that Christ, whom Mohammed with his half-knowledge so reverenced, came up to the ideal which prophets and kings desired to see, and had not seen, and which Mohammed himself, Prophet and King in one, could only half realise. In this way, and in this alone, is it likely that Christianity can ever act upon Mohammedanism; not by sweeping it into oblivion—for what of truth there is in it, and there is very much truth, can never die—but by gradually, and perhaps unconsciously, breathing into its vast and still vigorous frame a newer, a purer, and a diviner life.

By a fortune absolutely unique in history, Mohammed is a threefold founder—'of a nation, of an empire, and of a religion.' Illiterate himself, scarcely able to read or write, he was yet the author of a book which is a poem, a code of laws, a Book of Common Prayer, and a Bible in one, and is reverenced to this day by a sixth of the whole human race as a miracle of purity of style, of wisdom, and of truth. It was the one miracle claimed by Mohammed—his 'standing miracle' he called it; and a miracle indeed it is. But looking at the circumstances of the time, at the unbounded reverence of his followers, and comparing him with the Fathers of the Church or with mediæval saints, to my mind the most miraculous thing about Mohammed is, that he never claimed the power of working miracles. Whatever he had said he could do, his disciples would straightway have seen him do. They could not help attributing to him miraculous acts which he never did, and which he always denied he could do. What more crowning proof of his sincerity is needed? Mohammed to the end of his life claimed for himself that title only with which he had begun, and which the highest philosophy and the truest Christianity will one day, I venture to believe, agree in yielding to him—that of a Prophet, a very Prophet of God.

The religion, indeed, that he taught is below the purest form of our own as the central figure of the Mohammedan religion is below the central figure of the Christian—a difference vast and incommensurable ; but, in my opinion, he comes next to Him in the long roll of the great teachers and benefactors of the human race ; next to Him, *longo intervallo* certainly, but still next. He had faults, and great ones, which he was always the first himself, according to his light, to confess and to deplore ; and the best homage we can render to the noble sincerity of his character is to state them,

as I hope I have tried to do, exactly as they were.
' It was the fashion of old,' to quote once more the words
of our greatest novelist and greatest psychologist—
and so to conclude this course of Lectures, of the
manifold imperfections and shortcomings of which
no one of those who have so kindly listened to me
week after week can be half so conscious as myself
—'It was the fashion of old, when an ox was
led out for sacrifice to Jupiter, to chalk the dark
spots, and give the offering a false show of un-
blemished whiteness. Let us fling away the chalk,
and boldly say—the victim *is* spotted, but it is
not therefore in vain that his mighty heart is laid on
the altar of men's highest hopes.'

APPENDICES.

APPENDIX TO LECTURE I.

SIR BARTLE FRERE, in an interesting and able and catholic essay in 'The Church and the Age' on Indian Missions, takes a hopeful view of the future of India, as influenced by Western civilisation and Christianity. He begins (p. 318) by showing, rightly enough, that almost everything we do in India tends to break up old beliefs, and so to prepare the way for a new one, and is, therefore, more or less Missionary work; 'not only railways and printing-presses, education, commerce, and the electric telegraph; our impartial codes and uniform system of administration; but our misfortunes and our mistakes, our wars, our famines, and our mutinies.' He then gives (p. 334-337) elaborate statistics of the Missionary agencies at work in 1865 in Western India; they have enormously increased in the last 30 years, and he estimates the number of Missionaries at work at about 105, and the number of converts at somewhere about 2,200; and this, multiplied by six or seven, would probably, he thinks, give a general idea of the direct results of Missionary work during that period throughout all India (I would remark here that an official statement published in 1873 gives a much more favourable account, estimating the number of communicants at 78,494); but when Sir Bartle Frere comes to deal with Mohammedanism (p. 354–356) he gives no statistics on the point we most desiderate—the number of converts, if it be at all appreciable, from Islam to Christianity; the general remarks, indeed, he does make, seem to me to go exactly contrary to the conclusions he draws from them—*e.g.*, Mohammedans study portions of the Bible more than they did formerly; but these portions unfortunately seem to be the prophetical writings, especially those of Daniel; and they find therein the denunciations of Christianity which Christians find in it against other creeds; they are humiliated by the fact that Mohammedanism is no longer the Imperial creed of India; but the upshot of their depression is not Christianity, but Wahhabiism, *i.e.*, a return to Islam in its simplest and sternest shape. Brahmoism, which is really Brahmanism as modified by Christianity, Brahmanism *minus* caste and *minus* idolatry of every kind, seems to be in some respects the beginning of a national movement, and, judging from the authoritative sermon (p. 346–352) delivered in Calcutta on the 39th anniversary of the Brahma Samaj, and entitled 'The Future Church,' seems to me to give real hope for the future, and to be very suggestive as to the way in which Missionaries should go to work. 'The answer,' says the preacher, 'of Jesus the immortal Son of God, Thou shalt love the Lord thy God with all thy heart, and with all thy mind, and with all thy soul, and with all thy strength, and thy neighbour as thyself, is the essence of true religion simply and exhaustively expounded.' 'The composite faith of the future Church is to combine in perfect harmony the profound devotion of the Hindu and the heroic enthusiasm of the Musalman ;' but, unfortunately, the simplicity and intelligibility of the Mohammedan creed render it incapable at present of actually coalescing with the eclectic spirit of Brahmoism. It is strange at first sight that Mohammedanism, originally the most eclectic of religions, should, in India at all events, prove itself to be the least capable of settling down on terms of equality with other creeds, or of combining with them. No doubt the fact that Mohammedanism has been the Imperial creed and is so no longer, and the proud memories of Mahmud and Akbar, of Baber and of Aurungzebe, are a formidable, though it is to be hoped a passing, difficulty. If the Mohammedan revival now going on in India under the influence of the Wahhabis, the Firazees, and the followers of Dudu Miyan, can only be accompanied by a great moral reformation, such as Sprenger himself does not seem to despair of (I., p. 459, 'the Arabs only want another Luther'), the result, partially at least, of Christian influences, the simplicity of Islam will no doubt in its turn give it a great advantage over the Brahma Samaj in the struggle to fill the void created by the crumbling fabric of Hinduism. It has another great advantage in being already to some extent in possession of the ground. I observe that one of the speakers at the recent Allahabad Missionary Conference says that thirty millions, the estimated number of Musalmans in India, is much below the mark.

The unfavourable opinion expressed by Dr. Livingstone on the effects of Mohammedanism in Africa (Expedition to the Zambesi, p. 513–516, and 602–603) appears opposed to the general view I have taken in the Lecture; and of course, so far as his personal experience goes, is unimpeachable and conclusive. But it is clear that Dr. Livingstone drew his general conclusions almost entirely from his acquaintance with the Arab slave traders in the south and east of Africa, whom it was the main purpose of his noble and heroic life to put down. In the Lecture I have purposely not dwelt upon the extension of Islam along the coast to the south of the Equator, for the simple reason that the inhabitants are Mohammedans in nothing but the name. The Arabs there are of the most degraded type, and are engaged almost to a man in the brutalising slave trade, which by itself is a complete obstacle to every species of civilisation and religion. No doubt, as Dr. Livingstone remarks, the native African there contrasts favourably with the Mohammedan—as favourably, I would add, as he does even with the Portuguese; but that Dr. Livingstone judged of the whole of Mohammedan Africa by his experience of its worst part, is clear from his remark—opposed as it is to the unanimous testimony of travellers in Northern and Central Africa— 'that the only foundation for the statements respecting the spread of Islam in Africa is the fact that in a remote corner of North-West Africa, the Foulahs and Mandingoes, and some other tribes in Northern Africa, have made conquests of territory; but that even they care so little for the extension of their faith, that after conquest no pains whatever are taken to indoctrinate the adults of the tribe' (p. 513). Captain Burton asserts that 'Mohammedans alone make proselytes in Africa.' Dr. Livingstone says as explicitly 'in Africa the followers of Christ alone are anxious to propagate their faith.' Here is a direct contradiction; and it is obvious that in a country of such vast extent as Africa no such sweeping statement can be absolutely true. Perhaps Sierra Leone, to which Dr. Livingstone paid a visit for the purpose of testing the results of missionary enterprise, and to which he specially refers (p. 663), will furnish us with the best materials for pointing out how far the two statements are reconcileable with each other, and with substantial accuracy. In Sierra Leone there is a large negro community, the members of which having been brought for many years into contact not only with direct Christian preaching, but, what is more important, with Christian education, government, and example, are both excellent citizens and sincere Christians, and, as one would expect, contrast favourably in point of morality even with the best Mohammedans. This is unquestionably true; and of the self-denying efforts of the missionaries, especially the native ones, within certain limits, it is impossible to speak too highly. As to the exact number of Christians in the colony at this moment it is rather difficult to arrive at an accurate conclusion; but to take Dr. Livingstone's figures, he remarks (p. 605) that in the census of 1861 the whole population of Sierra Leone itself was 41,000 souls, 27,000 of them being Christian, and 1,774 Mohammedan, 'not a very large proportion,' he observes, 'for the only sect in Africa which makes proselytes. It is not a large proportion, but what is the number now? Sierra Leone now affords the most striking proof that can be given of the extent to which on the one hand Islam is spreading in that part of Africa by the efforts of unassisted missionaries, and on the other of the absence of any such propagation of the Christian faith among the tribes beyond the limits of the settlement. When Dr. Livingstone visited

Sierra Leone a few years ago, Islam was, as he says, hardly known there ; since then Mohammedan missionaries have come thither from the Foulahs and from the far interior, and with what result ? No one will say that it is the sword to which they owe their success, for the peace of Sierra Leone has been for years undisturbed. And now we have (Government Report of West African Colonies, 1873) the testimony of Mr. Johnson (p. 15), the able and excellent missionary whom I have quoted in my Lecture, endorsed as it would seem by the Bishop of the Diocese, that the Christian community at Sierra Leone, however flourishing itself, has exercised no influence on the large number of native Africans resorting annually to the town for the pur-pose of trade, and still less has it done anything to propagate itself by sending out missionaries among adjoining tribes. On the other hand, a few active and zealous Mohammedan missionaries have carried their peaceful war into the enemies' country, and have produced great results even among the Christian and native population of Sierra Leone itself ; insomuch that the religion of a large portion, the Governor says of the majority, of the Christians within the settlement has been actually changed by their preaching ! There may be, and it is to be hoped there is, exaggeration as to the numbers ; but there can be no doubt, looking to the *consensus* of testimony, that Islam is propagated in Western, Northern, and Central Africa ; that it is propagated by simple preaching and with marked success even where a Christian Government, and, what is better, Christianity itself, is to a great extent in possession of the ground. One wishes that Dr. Livingstone, the greatest and most single-minded of all the friends of Africa, had himself come into contact with a few of these simple and single-minded Mohammedan missionaries. They come so near in many respects to his own ideal of what a Christian missionary ought to be, that one feels sure he would have been led to modify his judgment as to the system which produces them, and to the great teacher whom he rarely mentions but as the 'false prophet.'

The remarks I have made in the Lecture as to the attitude which it seems to me that Christian Missionaries should adopt, wherever their efforts appear to have a chance of being successful—and surely there is too much evil in the world that is remediable, to allow of a great expenditure of labour or money where there is no such prospect—have been suggested to me mainly by way of contrast to what I have read in most books devoted to the cause of Missions. Even so noble, and self-sacrificing, and single-hearted a man as Henry Martyn appears to have gone out as a Missionary to India, nay to have argued with Mohammedans, without having first read a word of the Koran, even in its English dress (Memoir of Rev. Henry Martyn, by Rev. J. Sargent, p. 177 : cf. 225); and throughout his career he treats it as an 'imposture ;' 'the work of the devil.' He is sent to fight 'the four-faced devil of India,'—*i.e.* Hindus, Mohammedans, Papists, and Infidels (p. 259); and see a summary of his written arguments against Mohammedans (on p. 335), which are quite enough by themselves to account for his ill success. See also the account by another devoted missionary, the Rev. C. B. Leupolt, of his mission at Benares ('Recollections of an Indian Missionary'), who takes much the same position. 'The so-called Prophet of the Mohammedans ;' the Koran is an assemblage of facts and passages taken from the Bible mixed with a great number of gross and cunningly devised fables;' 'no Mohammedan who believes the whole Koran can have the notion of the true God;' 'the Koran is calculated to lead man daily further from God, and to unite him closer to the Prince of darkness;' 'Satan holds them enthralled by a false religion,' and so on. How not to deal with a different faith could hardly be better demonstrated than by the writings of two such admirable and devoted men. Surely the system has been to blame! There is an anecdote related of Aidan, first Bishop of Lindisfarne, which every one interested in missions, and most of all those who themselves attempt to bring over to their own faith the followers of another creed, and that one so sublime and so nearly connected with their own as is Islam, would do well to bear in mind. When a monk of Iona who had been sent at the request of King Oswald to preach the Gospel to the heathens of his Northumbrian kingdom, returned disheartened to his native country, and reported that success was impossible among a people so stubborn and so barbarous : 'Was it their stubbornness or your severity?' asked another monk, who was sitting by ; 'did you forget God's word to give them the milk first and then the meat?' The speaker was Aidan. He was begged, by all present, himself to take in hand the mission that had been abandoned. He settled as Bishop in the isle of Lindisfarne, and, influenced by his spirit and instinct with his charity and wisdom, missionaries went forth from there, who, in a generation or two, evangelised all the north of England.

Happily, as is shown from the general tone of the Allahabad Conference, and the explicit testimony of the Government of India in 1873, there has been a great advance in the right direction lately. Not to go beyond the limited circle of one's own acquaintance, such men as Bishop Cotton and the Rev. T. P. Hughes, in India ; the Rev. George and the Rev. Arthur Moule, in China ; and the Rev. James Johnson, native of Sierra Leone—though I would not venture to say that they would in any degree accept my point of view—yet in reality would have much in common with it ; and all would certainly admit the immense amount of good that is to be found in the creeds, which it is their duty to controvert. Alas, that those who knew Bishop Cotton well, and who therefore know what his catholic spirit might have done for India, can only now, when they think of him, repeat to themselves, consciously or unconsciously, the touching lament,

> ‘ But oh for a touch of the vanished hand,
> And a sound of the voice that is still ! ’

APPENDIX TO LECTURE III.

THAT the assertions I have made in the Third Lecture, as to the comparative ferocity of Christian and Musalman religious wars, are within the mark, it would be easy to bring abundance of proof. I will adduce here one illustration only, drawn from the chief battle-ground of the contending forces, the Holy Land. Jerusalem capitulated to Omar, the third Khalif, after a protracted blockade in the year 637. No property was destroyed except in the inevitable operations of the siege, and not a drop of blood was shed except on the field of battle. Omar entered the city with the Patriarch, conversing amicably about its history; at the hour of prayer he was invited by the Patriarch to worship in the Church of the Holy Sepulchre, but he refused to do so for fear that his descendants might claim a similar right, and so the freedom of religious worship, which he wished to secure to the inhabitants by the articles of capitulation, might be endangered. In the year 1099 the Holy City fell before the arms of the Crusaders after a much shorter siege. It was taken by storm, and for three days there was an indiscriminate slaughter of men, women, and children; 70,000 Musalmans were put to the sword, 10,000 of them in the mosque of Omar itself: '*in eodem templo decem millia decollata sunt;*

*pedites nostri usque ad bases cruore peremptorum tingebantur,
nec feminis nec parvulis pepercerunt.'* This comes not from
an enemy but from the monkish historian, an eyewitness and
a partaker of what he relates, Foulcher of Chartres. Ray-
mond of Agiles and Daimbert, Archbishop of Pisa, give similar details, and all with approval. The city itself was
pillaged; but the turn of the Saracens came once more in
the year 1187. The breach was already forced, when the
great Saladin retracted a hasty vow he had made to avenge
the innocent blood that had been shed when the city had
been sacked by the Crusaders, and took not Godfrey de
Bouillon but Omar for his model. No blood was shed, and
the captives were allowed to ransom themselves, the Frankish
Christians leaving the city, the Eastern Christians continuing
to reside there in peace.

As to humanity in war in general, the progress made has
not been so great as is commonly supposed, even among
those who pride themselves, and who to some extent
pride themselves with reason, on being the pioneers
of Christianity and civilisation. Take the case of Africa.
I am not aware that the Saracens in the full career of
conquest deliberately burnt a single city in the whole of the
North of Africa, whether as a precautionary measure, or to
support their prestige, or to glut their revenge. Can England
say the same? If we assume—a large assumption—that the
war on the Gold Coast in 1874 is wholly justifiable, if we
also assume that the burning of the enemy's capital was
indeed a necessity, it was a necessity for which a Christian
nation should go into mourning, and should contemplate not
with feelings of triumph, but with those of humiliation and
regret. Is there anything of the kind, or has one single

ruler either in Church or State—now that the elections are over, and the moral iniquity of the war has been condoned by its success—been heard to raise his voice in condemnation of it, as even Omar or Saladin might have done? It is difficult to see how the English nation, which has abolished the slave trade in the West of Africa, and is in its best portions profoundly philanthropic, can honestly believe that they are advancing the objects they have at heart when, in support of such a treaty as I have alluded to in the Lecture, they lead on a weaker barbarous nation, whom *pro hac vice* we designate as ' our allies,' against a more powerful one, and deliberately burn out of their homes a people who, barbarous and cruel as they were, have offended us not by their cruelty, or by their human sacrifices, but by their honest belief that we had come to Africa to bar them from access to their own coast. It seems not to have occurred to anyone that our 'prestige' would have been sufficiently vindicated, and our future security sufficiently provided for, if we had burned down the palace of the king, the chief offender. But our ' prestige ' serves as an ample excuse for committing what we should condemn as crimes in any other nation. It is an entity that has juggled us into the belief that to destroy what we cannot retain and cannot use is the prerogative, not of barbarism, but of civilisation and of Christianity. Had the war upon the Gold Coast been avowedly a war not for the spread of our influence, or for the security of a territory acquired by questionable means, but a moral crusade against human sacrifice, or for any purely unselfish object, the case would have been different. Truly this war will be a *damnosa hereditas* to posterity, alike whether we accept or disclaim the fearful responsibilities in which it has involved us.

There is an anecdote related of Mahmud the Ghaznevide, the great Turkish conqueror of Central Asia, which seems to me to be suggestive. Soon after the conquest of Persia, a caravan was cut off by robbers in one of its deserts, and the mother of one of the merchants who was killed went to Ghazni to complain. Mahmud urged the impossibility of keeping order in so remote a part of his territories, when the woman boldly answered : 'Why, then, do you take countries which you cannot govern, and for the protection of which you must answer in the Day of Judgment ?' Mahmud was struck with the reproach : whether it would have prevented all further conquests on his part we do not know, for he died soon afterwards; but he liberally rewarded the woman, and took immediate and effectual steps for the protection of the caravans.

INDEX.

LONDON : PRINTED BY
SPOTTISWOODE AND CO., NEW-STREET SQUARE
AND PARLIAMENT STREET

CPSIA information can be obtained
at www.ICGtesting.com
Printed in the USA
BVHW041335180819
556079BV00015B/22/P

9 780353 875173